C000067281

797,885 Books

are available to read at

www.ForgottenBooks.com

Forgotten Books' App
Available for mobile, tablet & eReader

ISBN 978-1-331-17584-1
PIBN 10154264

This book is a reproduction of an important historical work. Forgotten Books uses
state-of-the-art technology to digitally reconstruct the work, preserving the original format
whilst repairing imperfections present in the aged copy. In rare cases, an imperfection in
the original, such as a blemish or missing page, may be replicated in our edition. We do,
however, repair the vast majority of imperfections successfully; any imperfections that
remain are intentionally left to preserve the state of such historical works.

Forgotten Books is a registered trademark of FB &c Ltd.
Copyright © 2017 FB &c Ltd.
FB &c Ltd, Dalton House, 60 Windsor Avenue, London, SW19 2RR.
Company number 08720141. Registered in England and Wales.

For support please visit www.forgottenbooks.com

1 MONTH OF
FREE
READING

at

www.ForgottenBooks.com

By purchasing this book you are eligible for one month membership to ForgottenBooks.com, giving you unlimited access to our entire collection of over 700,000 titles via our web site and mobile apps.

To claim your free month visit:

www.forgottenbooks.com/free154264

* Offer is valid for 45 days from date of purchase. Terms and conditions apply.

English
Français
Deutsche
Italiano
Español
Português

www.forgottenbooks.com

Mythology Photography **Fiction**
Fishing Christianity **Art** Cooking
Essays Buddhism Freemasonry
Medicine **Biology** Music **Ancient
Egypt** Evolution Carpentry Physics
Dance Geology **Mathematics** Fitness
Shakespeare **Folklore** Yoga Marketing
Confidence Immortality Biographies
Poetry **Psychology** Witchcraft
Electronics Chemistry History **Law**
Accounting **Philosophy** Anthropology
Alchemy Drama Quantum Mechanics
Atheism Sexual Health **Ancient History**
Entrepreneurship Languages Sport
Paleontology Needlework Islam
Metaphysics Investment Archaeology
Parenting Statistics Criminology
Motivational

LIFE

OF

ALGERNON SIDNEY;

WITH

SKETCHES OF SOME OF HIS CONTEMPORARIES AND
EXTRACTS FROM HIS CORRESPONDENCE AND
POLITICAL WRITINGS.

BY

G. VAN SANTVOORD.

NEW YORK:

CHARLES SCRIBNER, 145 NASSAU STREET.

1851.

Entered according to Act of Congress, in the year 1851, by
CHARLES SCRIBNER,
In the Clerk's Office of the District Court of the United States for the Southern
District ot New York.

THE LIBRARY
OF CONGRESS
WASHINGTON

C. W. BENEDICT,
Stereotyper and Printer,
201 William st., N. Y.

CONTENTS.

CHAPTER I.

CHAPTER II.

CHAPTER VIII.

CHAPTER IX.

INTRODUCTORY CHAP...

THE history of England, whence our language, our literature, our common law, and some of our noblest elementary institutions are derived, is second, in interest, only to the history of our own country. It is, in one sense, a part of our own history. The ancestors of the men who achieved the American Revolution fought at Touton and at Bosworth field; they sat in the parliament of Henry VIII. and of Elizabeth. Between the period of the first settlement of the colonies and the era of American Independence, our own history is not only intimately blended with that of the mother country, but forms part of it. Separated by the waters of an ocean we were still one people, bound together by a community of interest as well as a common language, common laws, and a common lineage. To us, then, the history of the British empire, the changes in its government, the progress of its civilization, its political and social revolutions, and above all, the character and genius of the men who wrought these great changes and revolutions, must remain a subject not only of pleasing interest ... of the most instructive study.

No portion of the annals of England deserves a more close and discriminating perusal in a country where the principles of republicanism are established as the fundamental basis of government, than that which records the remarkable event commonly called the Revolution. It properly embraces a period of nearly half a century; commencing with the rupture between Charles I. and his parliament in the year 1640, and ending with the expulsion of James II., and the election of William and Mary to the throne, by the parliament, in the year 1688. The first twenty years of this preiod is, undoubtedly, to the republican reader, the most striking chapter of English history, comprising, as it does, the record of the downfall of the ancient monarchy—the solemn judgment of the people upon a king once almost absolute—the temporary triumph of free principles—the establishment of a republic, and its overthrow by a military usurper. It was a period rife with momentous events—fertile of remarkable men. The events of that period have been much misunderstood even on this side the Atlantic; the really great men—the republicans who sought to elevate the people by the establishment of civil and religious liberty, have been misrepresented, or what is, perhaps, equally unjust, have been passed over in contemptuous silence. It is true, the names of the illustrious commoners, PYM and HAMPDEN, stand out prominent upon the annals of that age;

and so do those of the victorious soldiers, CROMWELL, FAIRFAX, IRETON, and their associates, who headed the parliamentary army. The most zealous royalist has not been able to trace the history of those times, and follow the mighty events which the revolution developed, without assigning to each a place, a character, and a name. But the less prominent sphere of action of the statesmen and civilians, who established and sustained the Republic, has not been thought worthy the same particularity of narrative; and we have been left to estimate their characters, not so much from a faithful record of their lives and actions, as from the partial and unjust judgment pronounced upon them, unheard, by writers, who, like HUME, have shared the opinions, and drawn so largely from the narrative of that vengeful and bigoted royalist, LORD CLARENDON. Thus, some of the purest and noblest statesmen that England, or the world, has produced, have been neglected and forgotten, or, if remembered, and a place assigned them on the page of history, have been remembered only to have their characters misunderstood, and their opinion condemned or execrated. To many readers, even in our own country, scarcely anything more than the mere names are known of such men as Vane, Bradshaw, St. John, Scott, Marten, Ludlow, and Sidney; to the great majority of their own countrymen, for more than a century and a half, most of them have appeared merely as rebels, fanatics, and traitors! It is the peculiar province of biography to correct the errors, as well as the defects, of general history, in respect to the characters of eminent individuals, and to rescue from unmerited neglect and oblivion, the memory of great and good men, who have deserved well of their country and posperity. The present biography is undertaken with this view. It aims at no higher object than to rescue from obscurity and unmerited neglect, the name, the opinions, and the public acts of one of those noble Republican states-men whose memory deserves to be cherished forever by the lovers of liberty.

I design to sketch the main incidents in the life and public career of ALGERNON SIDNEY, so far as they are now known, or can be gathered from history, or contemporary annals. I shall present such extracts from his letters, (many of which have been pre-served,) and, also, from his other writings, as will serve to illustrate his character, his opinions, and his history; and, in order the more fully to appreciate his true position and character, I shall notice, inciden-tally, some of his republican contemporaries and asso-ciates, who labored with him in the same glorious cause. Sidney lived in the stirring period of which I have spoken; he was an actor in the drama of the Revolution; he commanded a regiment against the king, under the lead of Manchester and Cromwell; he was a member of that famous legislative assembly, known in history as the long parliament; he was appointed a member of the commission to try the king, and though he did not act in that capacity, yet he never disavowed the principle of the men who sat with John Bradshaw in that tribunal which condemned Charles Stuart to death ; he was the friend of Bradshaw, of Vane, of Milton, of the best and wisest men of the age : with them he resisted, in vain, the usurpation of Cromwell; when, upon the restoration of Charles II., liberty was proscribed from England, he chose banishment rather than submission to tyranny ; and when, after a period of seventeen years of voluntary exile, he returned to his native country, it was not to recant an opinion, or seek the favor of government by an abject confession of past error ; but to maintain, silently, the doctrines of his life, and, if necessary, to die rather than renounce them.

Sidney was a pure and enlightened republican statesman. Like Vane, he died on the scaffold, faithful among the faithless, and bearing witness in his death to the truth of the principles he maintained with inflexible constancy through life. Had he no other history than this, his name and memory should be cherished by the friends of free institutions. But he has a higher claim on the admiration of posterity. It is not merely in the silent teachings of his fortitude upon the scaffold, in his heroic constancy and truth to republican principles, that he has left a salutary impression upon the world. His precepts, even more than his example, have been eminently favorable to the progress of liberty and free institutions. The written words he left behind him—those philosophical reflections upon liberty and free institutions—that graceful and conclusive argument in favor of popular government which his elaborate "Discourses" contain, are a rich legacy, bequeathed by a master mind, to his countrymen and the world.

Not only was Sidney a Republican statesman and patriot, but he was a philosopher, scholar, and man of genius. His writings, so little appreciated, and, indeed, in our day so little known, were, at one time, extensively read and widely influential. The "Discourses on Government" was a political text-book with the fathers of our Republic, and the men who achieved the American Revolution. Their influence upon the minds of the first statesmen of that age is plainly apparent. Between the views of Sidney, and the political doctrines laid down in the Declaration of Independence, a striking resemblance can be traced; indeed, they are almost identical. A distinguished American statesman,* criticising the preamble to that Declaration, which he calls a "hypothetical truism," traces it directly, as an abstract proposition, to the writings of Sidney and Locke. So much for the influence which these writings have had upon the minds of our own statesmen, and incidentally upon the political character of our government It may be added, that their influence has extended even to other lands. At the dawn of the French

* The late John C. Calhoun. It is proper to add, however, that Mr. Calhoun's criticism is merely verbal. We do not understand him as dissenting from the general principle of political equality and rights laid down in the Declaration.

Revolution, when the principles of popular liberty were minutely investigated by the keenest intellects of the age, Sidney's Discourses were republished, and, with the writings of Rousseau, contributed to the awakening of the revolutionary mind of France.

These writings, once so highly prized as to be thought adequate to supply the loss of Cicero's six books *de Republica*, have, in our day, sunk into obscurity, if not oblivion. Perhaps they have fulfilled their mission, and, with the writings of Bacon, have become obsolete, and are passing away. It may be so; but their influence, like the thoughts of Bacon, will live for ages to come. Nor is the task an unpleasing one to remove the dust of three quarters of a century from these almost forgotten volumes, and to bring them anew before the public. If not a study of practical utility in an age like ours, so rich in lessons of political philosophy, and in the science of government so far in advance of the age in which Sidney wrote, still it cannot fail to be a matter of curiosity to note the bold speculations, as well as just conclusions, of a political writer, educated under an arbitrary government like that of Charles I.; and who, if not the very first, was amongst the foremost in modern Europe to assert and defend the fundamental doctrines of political liberty; and our curiosity is enhanced, and our interest increased, by the reflection that we are perusing the words which awakened the intellect, and confirmed the political faith, of the sages of our own Revolution. The ven-

erable John Adams, in his elaborate and now almost
forgotten treatise in defence of " the Constitutions of
Government of the United States of America," published in London in the year 1788, speaking of these
Discourses of Sidney, in connection with the writings
of Harrington, Milton, Locke, and other champions
of popular government, says, "Americans should
make collections of all these speculations, to be preserved as the most precious relics of antiquity, both
for curiosity and use.   There is one indispensable
rule to be observed in the perusal of all of them, and
that is to consider the period in which they were
written, the circumstances of the times, and the personal character as well as the political situation of the
writer."

Another reflection may here be properly made.   It
is one calculated still further to enhance the value of
this last legacy of Sidney to his countrymen.   He
literally proved a martyr, and died for the principles
advocated in these Discourses.   A portion of them,
or of similar works, found in manuscript in his closet,
was produced as evidence against him on his trial, as
we shall see when we come to speak more particularly
of that event.   Two witnesses were necessary, by the
law of England, in order to convict for treason.   Only
one was found against Sidney, and these manuscripts
were held equivalent to another!   To the modest
remonstrance that there was nothing treasonable in
the writings, the Chief Justice Jeffries, replied,
" There is not a line in it scarce, but what is trea-

son ;" and immediately added, " That is the worst part
of your case. When men become so riveted in their
opinions as to maintain that kings may be deposed,
that they are accountable to their people, and that a
general insurrection is no rebellion, and justify it, it
is high time, upon my word, to call them to account."

And, for holding opinions like these, but little
more than a century and a half ago in England,
Algernon Sidney was found guilty of high treason,
and adjudged to die ! But the principles for which
he suffered did not die with him. A few years later
they were asserted, and triumphantly maintained, in
that Revolution which drove the tyrant James from
his throne. The king was *deposed*, and called *to
account* by the people ; and not only was the *general
insurrection*, which Sidney had truly held to be no
rebellion, solemnly legalized, but the original compact
between the monarch and his subjects was recognized
by act of Parliament. It was not until after this
memorable event, during the reign of William and
Mary, and in the year 1698, that the " Discourses on
Government" were first published, and read by English statesmen.

The name of Algernon Sidney is not an obscure
one. Associated with that of Russell, as a martyr
for liberty, it has come down with honor to our day.
Yet the remark previously made holds true, that we
are able to derive from general history but an imperfect view of the career, the opinions, and the cha-

racter of this eminent republican. Tradition, rather than history, has preserved the memory of his virtues and his genius. Hume makes mention of him as a " singular person," wedded to his one idea of a republic. He gives a very fair and impartial account of his trial and condemnation, which he justly considers a blemish upon the administration; but, it is evident that Hume, if he understood, was not the man to appreciate such a character as that of Sidney. Other historians occasionally allude to him; but with the exception of his trial, we find nowhere any circumstantial account of his private life or public career, save in the brief and imperfect sketch by Collins in his " Memoirs of the Sidneys," printed in 1746, and in the narrative of an enthusiastic admirer, Mr. Meadley, published in London in the year 1813; a work, we imagine, never much known among us, and now almost forgotten on this side of the Atlantic. To these may be added the " Brief Memoir" by Richard Chase Sidney, also published in London, containing the substance of Meadley's narrative, with a short account of Sidney's trial, and a description of Stephanoff's celebrated painting of that event. These, we believe, are all the writers who have as yet undertaken to sketch the life of this celebrated man. The materials for a complete biography are, therefore, not very abundant. The most valuable, as well as reliable, are those which are to be found in the large volume containing his " Discourses," published at the same time with Harrington's " Oceana." In this volume we find all his letters which had then been discovered,*—the paper containing his defence, which he delivered to the sheriff on Tower Hill—his admirable " Apology," written just before his execution, and a minute and circumstantial account of his trial and condemnation. From these papers, together with the account of such writers and historians as have made mention of him, we are to gather the facts necessary to present a connected account of his life and public career, and which will enable us the better to appreciate the character of his genius, the constancy and heroism of his nature, and the singular inflexibility of his purpose and opinions.

* The two works above mentioned contain extracts from other letters of Sidney, discovered subsequently to the publication of the edition of 1772.

CHAPTER I.

Family of Sidney—His Birth and Early Education—Travels with his
Father on the Continent—Goes to France—Returns to England in
1641—Commencement of the Civil War—Appointed to the Command
of a Troop in Ireland—Serves in Ireland—Returns to England in 1643
—His Political Sentiments at this Time—Enters into the Service of
Parliament—Appointed a Colonel under Manchester—Battle of
Naseby—Sidney Wounded, and sent to London—Appointed Governor
of Chichester—Retires from Active Service—Progress of the Civil
War—The Independents get Control of the Army—Sidney ap-
pointed Colonel under Fairfax—Elected Member of Long Parliament
—Goes with his Brother to Ireland—Appointed Lieutenant-General
and Governor of Dublin—Service in Ireland—His Return—Receives
the Thanks of Parliament—Appointed Governor of Dover Castle—
Reflections on his Military Career.

THE family of ALGERNON SIDNEY* was one of the most
ancient and honorable in England. It was a branch
of the old Norman aristocracy. His ancestor, Sir
William Sidney, in the reign of Henry II., had accompanied the king from Anjou, as his chamberlain. A

---

* The name is " *Sydney*" as found subscribed to his published letters.
It is so also subscribed by Sir Philip Sidney to his will. Sir Philip, as
a correspondent, wrote it "Sidney" or "Sydney," as the fancy of the
moment prevailed with him. The former appears to be the modern
orthography, which I have preferred to retain. :

lineal descendant of this Sir William Sidney, of the same name, was tutor to Edward VI., who, in the year 1552, rewarded his services with the forfeited park and manor of Penshurst in Kent. This was the family seat of the Sidneys. Here resided Sir Henry Sidney, the son and heir of the last Sir William, for many years Governor of Ireland, and a name honorably mentioned in history. His eldest son was the celebrated Sir Philip Sidney, author of the pastoral romance of Arcadia, the favorite of Queen Elizabeth, and nephew to Dudley the powerful Earl of Leicester, who feasted the Queen in his castle of Kenilworth, and, it said, aspired to the hand of his royal mistress.

Sir Philip Sidney was mortally wounded at the battle of Zutphen, and dying a few days afterwards, the family estate passed to his brother Robert, who was created by James I. Baron Sidney of Penshurst, and subsequently Viscount Lisle and Earl of Leicester. This nobleman was succeeded in 1626 by his son Robert, the second Earl of Leicester of this family, and the father of Algernon Sidney. Lord Leicester was married in the year 1618 to Dorothy, eldest daughter of the Earl of Northumberland. He was a nobleman of great distinction, and much employed in diplomatic and other public business during the reign of Charles I.

Algernon Sidney, born in the year 1622, was the second son of this nobleman. He was named after his maternal uncle, Algernon,* Lord Percy. His

---

* The name seems originally to have been written *Algernoon.*

early education, the best and most accomplished that the times afforded, was carefully conducted by his father, who himself was a man of extensive and varied acquirements. In 1632, the Earl of Leicester was sent ambassador to Denmark. He took with him his two eldest sons, Philip, Lord Lisle, and Algernon, in order that he might the more carefully superintend their education. After an absence of three months, during which time he visited various courts and cities on the continent, he returned to England. In the year 1636 he was appointed ambassador extraordinary to France. Still pursuing his design of personally superintending the education of his sons, and of giving them every advantage of study and travel, he again permitted them to accompany him on his mission. The mind of young Sidney was rapidly maturing, and the progress he made in his studies repaid the utmost care and attention of his father. He was distinguished, even at this early period of life for his placid and manly temper and his sprightly wit. In a letter written about this time by his mother to her husband, she mentions with evident pride the favorable reports that some friends who had lately returned from Paris brought with them concerning her son, that " he had a huge deal of wit, and much sweetness of temper." The serenity of temper and the calm and placid disposition which characterized Sidney in his later as well as his earlier years, are said to have been strikingly exhibited in the features of his portrait at Penshurst, painted at Brussels, in 1663, and forwarded thence by him to his father.

The Earl of Leicester remained several years in France. During this time Algernon visited Rome, then under the government of the Pontiff Urban VII., where he resided some time. In 1639, the earl returned to England on a temporary visit, and was present at the marriage of his eldest daughter Dorothy, the *Sacharissa* of the poet Waller.* This lady was married to Lord Spencer, afterwards Earl of Sunderland, who was killed in the civil wars at the battle of Newbury. His son, the nephew of Sidney, was that Earl of Sunderland who was distinguished in the councils of Charles II. The celebrated Marquis of Halifax, whose name is so well known as a statesman and politician of the same reign, was also a nephew of Sidney by marriage.

The Earl soon after returned to Paris, where it seems his son Algernon remained, closely engaged in the prosecution of his studies. Being designed for the army, an application was now made on his behalf by his uncle, the Earl of Northumberland, to the Prince of Orange, for a commission in the Dutch service, but the commission having been previously disposed of, young Sidney was obliged to remain without employ-

* Dr. Johnson states that Waller's verses did not subdue the high-born and beautiful lady, who rejected the addresses of the humble poet with disdain. In her old age, meeting somewhere with Waller, she asked him when he would again write such verses upon her. " When you are as young, Madame," said 'he, "and as handsome as you were then "

ment in Paris, till the final return of his father to England, in the autumn of the year 1641.

It was at this period, the most eventful crisis in English history, that his active life commenced. The Long Parliament had been in session a year, and the seeds of that great revolution which was about to convulse England were fast taking root. Pym had brought forward his famous accusation against the Earl of Strafford, Lord Lieutenant of Ireland, and the head of that unfortunate minister had rolled from the scaffold, a victim to the popular justice, or the popular vengeance. The successor chosen to take the place of Strafford in the government of Ireland, was the Earl of Leicester. Various causes combined to delay the departure of that nobleman for Ireland, notwithstanding his presence was imperatively demanded there. The Irish rebellion, as it was called, had broken out. It was general, terrific, and devastating. Almost the entire English population were massacred under circumstances of horrid barbarity and cruelty. The Earl of Leicester, then, according to Hume, in London, being prevented himself from repairing to the scene of action, dispatched his eldest son, Lord Lisle, in command of his own regiment, to reduce the insurgents. In this regiment, Algernon Sidney, then in his nineteenth year, had command of a troop. This was his entrance into military service. In various actions and skirmishes fought with the insurgents, he is reported to have behaved with extraordinary spirit and resolution. The war, however, dragged slowly along. Sid-

ney and his brother awaited in vain the appearance of
their father in Ireland. - The king had too much upon
his hands at home to prosecute vigorously the war
against his subjects across the channel. He had
already unfolded the royal standard against his Parliament, and the civil war had actually commenced on
the 22d of August, 1642. Sidney's maternal uncle,
the powerful Earl of Northumberland, adhered to the
cause of the Parliament, his father to that of the
king. After a year's delay, Leicester obtained his
dispatch for Ireland. Preparing to embark, he received a peremptory order to remain. Another year's
delay ensued ; Leicester was deprived of his government, upon which he retired to Penshurst, where he
remained in seclusion during the rest of his life.

Meanwhile, it seems, Lord Lisle and Sidney, from
the activity and zeal displayed by them against the
insurgents, had incurred the jealousy of the advisers
of the king. Finding a longer service in Ireland irk-
some, they obtained leave of the king, with the permission of their father, to return to England.

On arriving at Chester, in August, 1643, some of
their horses were taken from them by the royalists,
which caused them immediately to put out again to
sea. It appears they were suspected by both parties,
for on their second landing, at Liverpool, they were
detained, with their arms and property, by the Commissioners of the Parliament. A letter written at
this time by Sidney to one Bridgeman, a royalist, at
Chester, demanding a restoration of their horses, re-

2

veals his intention of proceeding at once to his father at Oxford, then in the hands of the king. This letter being discovered, fresh instructions were given by the Parliament to detain the brothers in custody, and they were subsequently sent up under arrest to London. The king spoke very harshly and severely of their conduct, and even intimated that the whole affair was a contrivance on the part of the brothers. This accusation, doubtless, had a tendency to fix their sentiments the more strongly in opposition to the royal cause.

Thus far Sidney had taken no active part in the struggle between the king and the Parliament; we are therefore left in some doubt as to his sentiments in respect to the merits of the controversy prior to his return to England. At the beginning, of his service in Ireland, the struggle had not yet commenced. Even after the royal standard had been raised at Nottingham, the reduction of the Irish insurgents was the common object of both parties, the Parliament as well as the king. It is not therefore to be inferred from his service in Ireland, that he was a partisan of the king. On the contrary, various circumstances would lead to a directly opposite conclusion. The character of Sidney was already formed and his opinions, always firm, even as has been charged, to obstinacy, were matured. It is not to be supposed that he wavered for a moment in his choice between the popular and the absolute party, far less that he adhered to the king, and subsequently changed sides to the Parliament. In corroboration of this opinion, that Sidney was from the first an advocate of the popular cause, his own solemn declaration may be cited as found in the able paper he drew up immediately before his execution.*　He commences by saying, that from his youth up he endeavored to uphold " the *common rights of mankind*, the laws of the land, and the true Protestant religion, against corrupt principles, *arbitrary power*, and popery." And then adds—" I am no ways ashamed to note that from the year 1642 till the coming in of the king, I did prosecute the above principles."

On arriving at London, Sidney and his brother gave in their adhesion to the Parliament, and actively enlisted in behalf of the popular cause—a cause to which the former at least never proved recreant to the day of his death.　Sidney at once volunteered his services in the parliamentary army, and on the 10th of May, 1644, the Earl of Manchester appointed him to the command of a troop of horse in his own regiment. The war between the king and Parliament was now carried on with great animation on both sides.　Thus far indeed, success seemed to favor the royalists. The great parliamentary leader, Pym, was dead. Hampden had fallen in battle.　Waller had been routed, and his army dispersed.　Bristol had opened her gates to the victorious arms of Prince Rupert, and Gloucester was invested, but still held out under the heroic Massey, against the arms of the king. Such was the aspect of affairs during the campaign of

* His " Apology in the Day of his Death."

1643. Toward the close of that year, however, matters were a little improved. The army under Essex marched successfully to the relief of Gloucester. One or two spirited and brilliant actions fought by Fairfax and Cromwell—names then fast rising to distinction—turned the scale of battle in that quarter against the royalists. The genius and address of Vane had succeeded in carrying, with the Scottish commissioners, "the Solemn League and Covenant," in pursuance of which, early in the year 1644, an army of twenty thousand Scots had crossed the Tweed to the assistance of the Parliament. Still it must be admitted that this campaign opened under unfavorable auspices to the parliamentarians

It is at this period that we find Sidney joining the army under the Earl of Manchester, who was then levying a force in the eastern counties to oppose the victorious royalists. He had collected a body of fourteen thousand men. Oliver Cromwell, already the greatest soldier of the age, served under him as Lieutenant-General, with his own troop of stern and determined men, the nucleus of that famous army which he afterwards commanded in chief, whose proud boast it was that no enemy had ever seen their backs. We do not design, however, to trace the conduct of the war, or even of this campaign, further than as connected with the career of Sidney. It is stated that he was in several actions, in all of which he conducted himself with great gallantry. We do not, however, find any positive mention made of but one—the battle

of York, or more properly speaking, the battle of Marston Moor, fought near that city. This was one of
the most important and best contested actions of the
war. The number of combatants was greater than in
any preceding action, and the result was decisive.
Lord Fairfax and his more illustrious son, Sir Thomas
Fairfax, had been ordered to join the Scottish army,
under Leven, and after the juncture had laid siege to
the city of York, a place of the greatest importance
to the royalists. Here, by a brilliant movement, the
army, under Manchester and Cromwell, had effected a
junction with that of Fairfax. The combined armies
numbered not far from twenty-five thousand men.
The Earl of Newcastle, the most accomplished and
able commander of the royalists, held the city against
the besiegers. A series of irregular sorties and attacks
had been made, but without decisive success, though
it was evident that unless relief arrived, the city must
capitulate. But relief was nearer than the garrison
imagined. Suddenly Prince Rupert, at the head of a
brilliant army of 20,000 men, appeared in sight of the
walls of York. Fairfax attempted to intercept their
march, but failed, and the glittering pikes of Rupert's
cavaliers were soon after seen defiling through the
narrow gates of the besieged city. All hopes of the
reduction of the city were of course at once abandoned. The parliamentary army raised the siege and fell
back. Meanwhile a difference of counsels arose in
each army. The fiery and impatient Rupert was for
giving immediate battle, but the cooler and more skil-

ful Newcastle counselled delay. Rupert, headstrong
and violent as ever, relying on the express commission
of the king, and arrogantly assuming an air of superiority over his associates, determined to take the responsibility of some daring achievement upon himself
and gave orders for action. Newcastle listened in
silence, and smiled in scorn at Rupert's vaunted
boasts over the inferiority of his adversaries, and those
adversaries the soldiers of Fairfax and Cromwell! He
was advised to take no part in an action where the command was taken from him; but he declined the advice, and going into the action, as he said, a volunteer,
he resolved to die as he had lived, a loyal subject.
Such instances of chivalric spirit and high-toned
honor, go far to redeem a cause that has very little
else in it to enlist the popular sympathy.

In the parliamentary army a like difference of
opinion existed. The cautious Scottish commanders,
who had not yet learned the temper and mettle of
Fairfax's pikemen and Cromwell's Ironsides, were for
retreating. Not so most of the English officers, who
had declared for battle. It may well be imagined that
none was more ardent and eager for action than
young Sidney. These counsels, however, were tem-
porarily overruled, and the parliamentary army abandoning their position, slowly and sullenly retreated on
the road to Tadcaster. Scarcely had they marched
eight miles from the city of York, when several troops
of Rupert's cavalry assailed the rear of the retreating army. The parliamentarians found themselves

obliged to fight; the command to halt ran along the lines, and countermanding the order to march, the army fell back upon Marston Moor. That night, 50,000 of the best soldiers in England, on both sides commanded with equal valor, under the lead of the most renowned generals of the nation, lay encamped near the field of Marston Moor ready to commence a contest that should decide the fate of the monarchy. In the one camp, dimly through the starlight, were to be seen the banners of Newcastle, Rupert, and Goring, around which rung out the notes of gayety, and the festive and joyous voices of the cavaliers already anticipating an easy victory. In the other, the blue banner of the covenanters drooped lazily from its staff, around which clustered Leven's Scottish infantry; the ever vigilant Fairfax, and the cool and steady Manchester, were making their preparations for the morrow; while from Cromwell's encampment arose the constant voice of pious exhortation, of psalmody, and of prayer. On the morning of the 2d of July both armies prepared for action. A large ditch or drain ran in front of a portion of the army of the parliament. The centre was under the command of the Lords Fairfax and Leven. On the right, which was broken and somewhat protected by natural fences and lanes, Sir Thomas Fairfax was stationed. Cromwell and Manchester held the left, which was a barren waste terminating in a moor. On the other hand, Prince Rupert himself took his position opposite Sir Thomas Fairfax, while Cromwell and Manchester on the left, were opposed by several infantry brigades supported by Goring's cavalry.

At five o'clock in the afternoon the arrangements were completed; the battle commenced at seven. Manchester's infantry moved upon the drain, where, while vainly endeavoring to form, they were mowed down in heaps by a murderous fire from the royalist musketeers and cannon. Goring immediately prepared to charge with his cavalry, and rapidly advanced for that purpose; but, ere he could approach the disordered ranks of Manchester, a terrible assailant encountered him. The horse of Cromwell had wheeled round the right of the ditch, and fell full upon Goring's flank. The charge, though momentary, was decisive. Goring's cavalry were routed, and fled in every direction. Cromwell turning upon the cannoniers, sabred them at their guns, and completing the total defeat of the right wing of the royalists, marched leisurely back to his position. It was at this point of the army that Sidney, now raised to the rank of colonel, commanded. Honorable mention is made of his conduct during the action, in the old parliamentary chronicles of the day. "Colonel Sidney, also, son to the Earl of Leicester, charged with much gallantry in the head of my Lord of Manchester's regiment of horse, and came off with many wounds, the true badges of his honor." It is stated in the annals of the day, that after Sidney had been dangerously wounded and was within the enemy's power, a soldier stepped out of Col. Cromwell's regiment, and rescuing him from his perilous position, carried him to a place of safety. Sidney desired to know the name of his preserver in order that he might reward him, but the soldier, one of those stern zealots whom Cromwell had gathered around him, told him that he had not saved him for the sake of obtaining any reward, and refusing to disclose his name, returned to his place in the ranks.

Meanwhile, on the right wing, Fairfax had been driven back under the impetuous charge of Prince Rupert, who, believing the day won, followed up his advantage too eagerly and too far. Turning to break the centre of the parliamentary force, and complete what he believed to be his victory, he suddenly encountered Cromwell, who had simultaneously charged and defeated the centre of the royalists. The shock was tremendous, and for a while the battle raged with intense fury. Cromwell, though wounded in the neck, still kept the field, and urged on in person his stern and enthusiastic followers. The result of such a contest could not long be doubtful. The troopers of Cromwell soon swept in triumph over the bloody field. Rupert was driven back with great loss, and the victory declared decisively for the parliamentarians. At ten o'clock in the evening the action was at an end. The victory was complete. Besides the slain, fifteen hundred royalist prisoners were taken, together with all their artillery, baggage, and military stores. The appearance presented by the field is strikingly described by an accomplished author, whose narrative of a battle which has been differently related, has been in the main followed here.* "It was 10 o'clock, and by the melancholy dusk which enveloped the moor, might be seen a fearful sight. Five thousand dead bodies of Englishmen lay heaped upon that fatal ground. The distinction which separated in life these sons of a common country seemed trifling now! The plumed helmet embraced the strong steel cap, as they rolled on the heath together, and the loose love-locks of the careless cavaliers lay drenched in the dark blood of the enthusiastic republican." Soon after York opened her gates, and a large part of the north of England submitted to the authority of the Parliament.

The same authority which makes such honorable mention of Col. Sidney's heroism and gallantry in this battle, informs us also that he was afterwards sent to London, "for the cure of his wounds." We do not find it stated how long he remained there, or when he became able to resume his command. Probably he did not serve in the army again during that campaign. On the 10th of May, of the following year, as appears by his father's manuscripts, he was appointed governor of Chichester, and a day or two afterwards, he wrote to Sir Thomas Fairfax, stating that he was about to go down to enter upon his charge, after which he should wait upon him to deliver up his regiment. "I have not," he adds, "left the army without extreme unwillingness, and would not persuade myself to it by any other reason than that, by reason of my lameness I am not able to do the Parliament and you the ser-

* Forster's Life of Cromwell.

vice that would be expected from me." From this it would seem that the wounds he had received at Marston Moor had hitherto disabled him from active service in the field.

Notwithstanding the brilliant victory of Marston Moor, the campaign of 1644 was brought to an indecisive close. It had become evident that the old chiefs of the army, Essex, Manchester and Sir William Waller, whatever their merits and claims, were not the men to bring the war to a successful termination. These leaders of the Presbyterian interest, were the advocates of moderate councils and moderate actions. Unwilling to push matters with the king to the last extremity, they were warring against his *prerogative*, not against his *person*. Essex's commission ran in the name of the *King and Parliament*, and contained a clause relative to the safety of his majesty's person. The primary object of the Parliament undoubtedly was, to defend its privileges, not a total change of government. But a new and more energetic class of men had sprung up into notice, into whose hands the control of the revolution was about to pass. They were the leaders of the Independents, the *Republicans* of the revolution, such men as Cromwell, Ireton and Fairfax in the army, and Vane, St. John, Marten and their associates in the Parliament.

No class of men have been more misrepresented, and the public actions of none have been less thoroughly understood. It should be the province of biography as well as history to do justice to their motives and the great deeds they achieved. These men were not troubled with any nice distinctions between the lawfulness of a war against the king's prerogative, and war against his person. Their actions were based upon the broad and fundamental doctrines of human rights, which Sidney afterwards inculcated in his writings—the right of insurrection against tyranny and oppression—the right of a people to frame their own government, to alter or abolish it at pleasure, and to-call their rulers to account—the right, in short, which more than a century after, was asserted in the American Declaration of Independence—entire civil and religious liberty. To these doctrines Sidney adhered, and for them he afterwards perished on the scaffold.

Cromwell, indeed, from the first, with his penetrating and masculine intellect, had appreciated the true merits, and anticipated the ultimate issue of the contest. In one of his earliest speeches to that remarkable body of stern and determined men whom he gathered around him—men whose martial ardor and courage were elevated into a kind of religious enthusiasm—he stated the point at issue clearly and distinctly. He declared to them that if he " met King Charles in the body of the enemy, he would as soon discharge his pistol upon him as upon any private man, and for any soldier present who was troubled with a conscience that would not let him do the like, he advised him to quit the service he was engaged in." Vane, too, in Parliament, thoroughly understood the

nature of the controversy, and that it was the entire
overthrow of the monarchy, not the mere limitation of
the power of the king, that was to be regarded as the
true end of the struggle.   So, too, it appeared to Sidney ; and with the ardor and enthusiasm of his nature,
he entered heartily into the boldest measures of the
popular party, and never for a moment ceased to be
their champion even when Cromwell himself proved
recreant to his republican principles ; and when liberty
and truth were finally proscribed from England, he
proved his devotion to the faith of his life, by encoun-
tering voluntarily exile and banishment.

Not only had the Independents, or the Republicans,
laid hold of the grand idea of civil liberty in government, which we understand by popular sovereignty,
but they were far in advance of that age in their doctrines of freedom of worship and liberty of conscience.
The Presbyterians, it is well known, insisted upon a
conformity of religious worship, to be established by
the state.   Their own system was to take the place of
that of Laud and the Church of England. Sidney and
Vane, on the other hand, advocated the great doctrines
of religious as well as civil freedom—universal toleration in matters of belief, and full liberty to every man
to worship God as his own conscience might dictate.

These were some of the ends now to be accomplished by the revolution ; but to reach them it was
necessary that the revolution should pass out of the
hands of the Presbyterian majority. This was the
work of Vane and Cromwell, a work in which Sid-

ney heartily co-operated. The first great step to be taken was to re-organize the army—to dismiss from the service those in command who scrupled to "discharge a pistol upon the king," and to entrust the work of subduing the royalists to surer and less punctilious hands. To effect this, Cromwell, on the 9th of December, 1644, introduced in Parliament his famous "self-denying ordinance," providing that no member of either house should hold under the authority of Parliament any office, civil or military, during the war. Vane ably supported the bill, which passed the Commons, but failed in the House of Lords. The following month, however, a substitute was proposed and carried, whereby every member of Parliament was thenceforth discharged from whatever office civil or military he then held. This law of course brought in the resignations of Essex, Waller, Manchester, and all the old parliamentary officers, including Cromwell himself. But it was not the purpose of the Parliament to deprive itself of the services of the future Lord-General. In the army of the "new model," which was immediately organized, Sir Thomas Fairfax was appointed general-in-chief, and Skippon major-general. The name of the lieutenant-general was left blank ; the blank was afterwards filled with the name of OLIVER CROMWELL. Sidney was one of the twenty-six colonels appointed in the new army. Among these subordinate officers also were Ireton, Desborough, and Harrison, destined afterwards to become famous in the history of the Commonwealth.

It is unnecessary here to sketch the further history of the military operations between the king and the Parliament. As has been just mentioned, Colonel Sidney, on account of his lameness, reluctantly gave up the command of his regiment in Fairfax's army, and retired to the government of Chichester. We do not find that he was in the field during the campaign of 1645, nor present at the decisive battle of Naseby, which prostrated the power of the king and established the supremacy of the people of England through their Parliament.

In the month of December of this year, Colonel Sidney was elected a member of the House of Commons from the borough of Cardiff, as will presently be noticed in our sketch of his parliamentary career. Soon after, the House of Commons, on the recommendation of Sir Thomas Fairfax, and in consideration of his valuable services, voted him two thousand pounds in payment of his arrears. In January, 1646, his brother, the Lord Lisle, was appointed lord lieutenant of Ireland, and was ordered to that country to make head against the Marquis of Ormond, who had succeeded the Earl of Leicester in the government, by the king's authority. The same delays that had attended the departure of the Earl of Leicester attended that of Lord Lisle. His commission was not signed till April following, and it was not till the first of February, 1647, that he actually embarked. On the 6th of July, in the preceding year, Sidney received a commission from his brother for the command of a

regiment in this expedition.   His attendance in parliament was dispensed with by a resolution of the
House of Commons ; and having completed his preparations, he accompanied Lord Lisle into Ireland.
It appears, by the journal of his father, that the committee of government at Derby House had invested
Sidney with the responsible command of lieutenant-
general of the horse in Ireland and governor of Dublin.   He did not, however, long discharge the duties
of this new place.   The commission of Lord Lisle ran
only for one year from its date, and the influence of
his jealous rival, Lord Inchiquin, succeeded in preventing its renewal by the Parliament.   Thus after a service of less than two months, Lisle's commission
having expired, he returned to England.   The partizans of Inchiquin now resolved to supersede Sidney,
and finally succeeded in getting one Colonel Jones
appointed governor of Dublin in his place.   It appears
from the Earl's manuscripts, that on the 8th of April,
1647, a motion was made in Parliament that Colonel
Jones should be made governor of Dublin in place of
Algernon Sidney, and that the motion was seconded
by old Sir Henry Vane* on the ground, that Lord
Lisle having been recalled, it was not proper that so
important a place as Dublin should be left under the
government of his brother.   The resolution was opposed by William Armyn and others, who urged that
if they had ill-used one brother, it was no reason why

* Father of the celebrated Sir Henry Vane the Younger, and formerly
one of the secretaries of Charles I.

they " should do injustice to the other, who had *so well deserved of them;*" but, the House being thin, and many of Colonel Sidney's friends absent, the motion was carried, and Jones appointed governor of Dublin. That it was no want of good conduct which induced the House to supersede him, appears from its subsequent action. It was thereupon moved " that some recompense might be given to Algernon Sidney *according to his merits,*" which was agreed to unanimously.

On his return to England the first of May, he immediately repaired to London, where he received the thanks of Parliament for his good service in Ireland. Subsequently he was appointed governor of Dover, where he remained some time in the discharge of his duties, and on the 13th of October, 1648, was promoted by an ordinance of Parliament to the honorable title of lieutenant. His name was regarded as of good omen among the learned enthusiasts of the day, as, when written in the Hebrew character, with a slight variation, it might be translated, "He is against strange men that destroy the cause."*

Here properly closes the sketch of Colonel Sidney's military career. Henceforth we find him a prominent member of the Long Parliament up to the period of its final dissolution. His services as a soldier form the least distinguished portion of his career. Though valuable in their sphere, they were unobtrusive and modest. The young parliamentary colonel of twenty-

* Meadley's Memoirs.

four, unfurled his banner at the head of his regiment
in Fairfax's army, inscribed with his simple and ex-
pressive motto, so characteristic of him who had
chosen it, *Sanctus amor patriæ dat animum*, with no
higher aspiration than simply to do his duty, while
his more ambitious but not more gifted associates,
Ireton, Fleetwood, Lambert, and Desborough, were
pushing themselves forward to distinction and fame.
That Sidney while in the army did discharge his duty
with fidelity, and that he performed many valuable
services, is proved in the approbation his conduct received from his cotemporaries, in the thanks of the
Parliament, in the honorable mention that is made of
his gallantry on their records, and especially in the
undying enmity that was afterwards manifested toward
him by Charles II. and his court on the restoration of
the monarchy. As a soldier he was distinguished by
the same chivalrous ardor and undaunted bravery
which marked the character of his illustrious kinsman,
Sir Philip Sidney, who fell on the field of Zutphen.
Bishop Burnet, who knew him personally, but who
has not done full justice to his character, speaks of
him as " a man of the most extraordinary courage—
a steady man even to obstinacy."* These attributes

* The whole passage reads as follows :—" A man of the most extraordinary courage—a steady man even to obstinacy—sincere, but of a rough
and boisterous temper that could not bear contradiction. He seemed to
be a Christian, but in a peculiar way of his own; he thought it was to
be like a divine philosophy in the mind; but he was against all public
worship and everything that looked like a church. He was stiff to all
republican principles, and such an enemy to everything that looked like
a monarchy, that he set himself in high opposition against Cromwell'

of the soldier, united as they were in Sidney, with a singularly clear and rapid judgment, an inflexible constancy of purpose and firmness of temper, might, under circumstances more favorable to the development .of his military genius, have placed him high among the lists of the generals of the Commonwealth. But unforeseen events closed to him the path to exalted military command in the army that Cromwell commanded. He left it to take his place with Vane and St. John in the councils of the nation, among the ranks of the republicans in Parliament, where his presence was most needed and his place could be less easily supplied.

when he was made Protector. *He had studied the history of government in all its branches beyond any man I ever knew.* He had a particular way of insinuating himself into people that would hearken to his notions and would not contradict him."

CHAPTER II.

The Long Parliament—Its history—Difficulty attending the election of new members—Sidney elected from Cardiff—Does not take an active part in its deliberation—Events which led to the trial of the King—Conference with the King at the Isle of Wight—Treacherous conduct of Charles—"Pride's purge"—Proceedings to bring the King to trial—Sidney nominated one of the commissioners—Declines to sit—His reasons—His opinions of the King's guilt—Reflections on the trial and execution of the King—Conduct of the judges—Sidney retires to Penshurst—Returns to London after the King's death—Resumes his seat in Parliament and sustains the government—Establishment of the Commonwealth—Installation of the new Council of State—Sidney opposes the "test" oath in Parliament—Difficulty with Cromwell—Question respecting the dissolution of Parliament—Sidney a member of the committee to which it was referred—Labors of the committee—Subject referred to committee of the whole—Difficulty between Sidney and his officers—Resigns the command of Dover—Visits Holland—Quarrels with the Earl of Oxford—Returns to England and resumes his parliamentary duty—Appointed on various committees—His colleagues—Vigor of the Commonwealth government—Sidney's account of it—Ambition of Cromwell—His hostility to Sidney—Contest between the military and civil power—The republicans oppose Cromwell—Plan of the republicans to dissolve parliament and call a new one—Plan of Cromwell—Vane's bill—Is defended by Sidney—Crisis in public affairs—Long Parliament dissolved by Cromwell—Sidney forced out—Retires to Penshurst—Refuses to take any further part in the government—Cromwell—Vane.

THE name of Algernon Sidney is closely connected

with the history of the Long Parliament. He became a member of it in the latter part of the year 1645, and though sometimes absent on military and other duties, he continued to retain his seat until its dissolution by Cromwell, and re-assembled with it on the abdication of the Protector, Richard Cromwell. This famous body, whose achievements are so remarkable in English history, assembled at Westminster, in November, 1640. The House of Commons numbered about five hundred members, chief among whom, on the popular side, were Pym, Hampden, and Hollis, St. John, Marten, and Vane. One of the first acts of the Commons was the impeachment of the Earl of Strafford, who was tried by the House of Lords, and notwithstanding the strenuous efforts of the king, was condemned and executed. On the rupture between the king and Parliament, many members of both Houses who favored the royal cause, left their places, and never afterwards met with the Parliament. When the royalist members assembled at Oxford in 1644, there were found to be rising of one hundred and eighteen who adhered to the cause of the king. The Commons at Westminster at the same time ordered a call of the House, and two hundred and eighty members answered to their names, while one hundred more were excused as being absent in the service of the Parliament.

It appears thus that the great majority of the members adhered to the popular cause. Some had voluntarily retired, and some had been expelled or declared unable any longer to sit, the House exercising its revolutionary right of declaring the eligibility of its own members. Still it was desirous for many reasons that the popular representation should be preserved entire, and that the places of such members as were dead or absent, and ceased to act, should be filled by their constituents. To this question the attention of the best and most eminent of the republican leaders had been for some time directed. It was found at first that a difficulty existed. The writ authorizing a new election, had always been under the great seal; but the lord keeper, in 1642, had carried it off to the king, at York, and the House of Commons could not yet bring itself to overleap and disregard the customary forms of the monarchy. No action was, therefore, taken upon the subject, until the 30th of September, 1644, on which day it was voted that the House should, at a future time specified, take the subject into consideration. Still nothing decisive was done that year. Parliament yet hesitated, hoping, doubtless, a reconciliation with the king and a reunion of its members. Meanwhile, the great change already mentioned, took place in the army; the republicans—the men who clearly foresaw the inevitable issue of the contest—the true statesmen of the age, began to make their influence felt upon the government. The battle of Naseby, so hopelessly fatal to the fortunes of the king, placed the day of reconciliation, if possible, still further off, and strengthened the cause of the popular leaders. Vane, St. John, Marten, and their associates in parliament, who had been diligently urging forward this measure of filling up the representation, were now enabled to act. A petition came up from the borough of Southwark, praying that the people might be authorized to elect two representatives in place of one who had died, and one who had been disabled by a vote of the House. On the 21st of August, 1645, the initiative step was taken. A majority of the Parliament decided that new writs should be issued for Southwark and one or two other places. This example was speedily followed, and during the remainder of that year, no less than one hundred and forty-six vacant seats were filled by new elections among the people. Under these new elections Algernon Sidney, in December of that year, was returned a member of the House. The ranks of the republicans were also recruited with other distinguished and enlightened statesmen ; the able and accomplished Ireton was chosen, the resolute and straightforward Fairfax, the honest and open Ludlow, Blake, the illustrious admiral, who afterwards so nobly sustained the flag of the commonwealth on the ocean, Hutchinson, Skippon, Massey, and other earnest and zealous republicans. These men infused new life and energy into the councils of the nation, and brought the struggle with the king to a speedy close.

Colonel Sidney does not appear to have taken a very active part in the proceedings in Parliament for two or three years after his election. He preferred the more stirring scenes of the camp and the field.

We have seen that during the latter part of the
year 1646, he was busily employed in preparation for
the expedition to Ireland, and for that purpose his attendance in Parliament was dispensed with, by a resolution of the House of Commons. After his return to
England, his military duties, as governor of Dover,
occupied his principal attention up to the time of
the trial and execution of the king. It became
evident then that the Revolution had reached its
crisis, and that the great popular battle was thenceforth
to be fought upon the floor of the Parliament, and not
upon the field. Sidney thereupon took his seat, and
participated actively in the duties of the House, as
one of the warmest supporters of the new commonwealth.

It is unnecessary in this place to trace the events
which led to the trial, the condemnation, and the execution of the king. It is enough to say that Charles
Stuart had betrayed the national cause, had endeavored to subvert the liberties of his subjects, and had
proved faithless to his engagements with the Parliament. Discarding the absurd maxim that "the king
can do no wrong," we may safely, in our day, pass
the judgment upon him that he was a greater criminal
than Strafford had been, and no one, we think, can
approve the condemnation of that ill-fated nobleman,
without conceding the abstract justice of the sentence
which adjudged Charles to the scaffold. The king
for some time previous to his trial had been a captive
in the hands of the Parliament. The Presbyterian

majority, who then ruled the Parliament, were desirous of an accommodation with the king, and of re-
placing him upon the throne, contrary to the wishes
of the republicans, upon certain conditions and concessions made by him to the liberties of the people.
Charles had his crown already within his grasp, but
his arbitrary and tyrannical disposition, united with
his duplicity and falseness, lost him not only his
throne but his life.

The memorable conference between the king and a
committee of the Parliament at the Isle of Wight, commenced on the 18th of September, 1648, and was
spun out for more than two months. Vane was a
member of this committee, and speaks of Charles in
these negotiations as " a man of great parts and abilities." But notwithstanding his abilities, he seems to
have been attended here more than at any other
period of his life, by his evil genius, which was
already weaving the web of his destiny. Little could
the misguided monarch, as he obstinately refused the
concessions demanded of him, little could he then anti-
cipate the scene that in less than three months would
be revealed to his wondering eye—the scaffold shroud-
ed in black at Whitehall, on which stood the masked
headsman with his fatal axe ! The king made several
concessions, with the secret reservation to retract
them. He obstinately refused, however, notwithstanding the entreaties of Hollis and the Presbyterians, to
yield full freedom of religious worship, or to treat on
any other basis except that his friends should be fully

3

indemnified for their losses. These terms were anything but satisfactory to the republicans, yet the Presbyterian majority, weary of the war, were disposed to
accede to them. On the 1st December, the commissioners made their report to the House. A resolution proposed by the Presbyterians, that the king's
answers furnished a ground " for the settlement of the
kingdom," supported by Prynne and Hollis, and
opposed by Vane, was finally carried by a vote of one
hundred and forty to one hundred and four. But the
republican minority in the house were sustained by a
formidable ally. The ARMY, headed by Cromwell,
was republican, and an ominous voice had already
come up from it in the shape of an address to the Parliament calling for the prosecution of the king. The
day after the vote the Parliament was " purged" of a
portion of the Presbyterian majority by Col. Pride's
regiment, and the power of the state passed wholly
into the hands of the republicans

It does not appear that at the time of "Pride's purge,"
Sidney was in attendance in the House. Many of the
best of the republicans, among whom was Vane, we
know disapproved of this unjust and outrageous interference of the army with the rights of the people's
representatives, and it is not to be doubted that Sidney was one of these. The act was a high-handed
outrage, and the first great error committed by the
republicans. It was quickly followed by another,
which indeed was its inevitable result, the execution
of the king. On the 2d of January, the Commons

passed the significant resolution, preparatory to the overthrow of the monarchy : " That the Commons of England in Parliament assembled do declare, that THE PEOPLE are, under God, the original of all just power." An ordinance for creating a " high Court of Justice," and appointing Commissioners for the trial of the king, had been introduced some days before, was read a third time on the 6th, and was passed. The number of the Commissioners named in it was one hundred and thirty-five. They comprised all the illustrious republicans of the times, except Sir Henry Vane, who had retired from Parliament after " Pride's purge," and refused to share further in the proceedings. Colonel Sidney and his brother, Lord Lisle, were both named members of the Commission to try the king. Neither one of them, however, thought proper upon it. Sidney, it seems, attended with Fairfax the first meeting of the Commissioners in the painted Chamber, and expressed himself dissatisfied with the whole proceeding. His own account of his share in the transaction we find stated in a letter written by himself to his father after the restoration :

" I was at Penshurst when the act for the king's trial passed, and coming up to town I heard my name was put in. I presently went to the painted Chamber, where those who were nominated for judges were assembled. A debate was raised, and I did positively oppose Cromwell and Bradshaw and others who would have the trial to go on, and drew my reasons from these two points :—First, the king could be tried by no court. Secondly, that no man could be tried by that court. This being alleged in vain, and Cromwell using these formal words, ' I tell you we will cut off his head with the crown upon it,' I replied, ' you may take your own course, I cannot stop you, but I will keep myself clean from having any hand in this business,—and immediately went out of the room and never returned. This is all that passed publicly, or that can with truth be recorded or taken notice of. *I had an intention* which is not very fit for a letter."

The " intention" spoken of by Sidney, Sir James Mackintosh conceives, and with good reason, to have been to procure the concurrence of both Houses of Parliament in the deposition of the king. Clarendon says that among the enemies of the king there were three opinions ; one was for deposing him, another for secret assassination, and a third for bringing him to public trial as a malefactor. The plan for " assassination" may be set down as one of the many fictions of this royalist historian, but the other two were doubtless discussed among the republican leaders, who finally resolved to bring the king to trial as a criminal. Unquestionably Sidney in opposing a public trial shared the wiser and more statesmanlike views of Vane, and favored the deposition of the king.

It will be observed, however, that while Sidney doubts the power of the court, or of any court, to bring Charles Stuart to trial, he does not utter a word or intimate a doubt as to his guilt, or the justice of his sentence. Indeed he never hesitated to approve and justify the sentence. And even after the restoration, when the minds of the royalists were poisoned against him, far from attempting to ingratiate himself by any base " compliance with the times," he frankly answered an inquiry of his father on the subject, " I do avow that since I came into Denmark, I have many times *so justified that act*, as people did believe I had a hand in it; and *never did disavow it* unless it were to the king of Sweden and Grand Maître of Denmark who asked me privately."

We do not here design to discuss either the justice, or the wisdom and policy, of this daring act—the " boldest hitherto done in Christendom." It has been often condemned as a gratuitous and wanton cruelty, and the motives of the resolute and determined men who wrought it have been traduced and assailed. Time, and the progress of liberal sentiments, which have fully vindicated its justice, have also vindicated the motives of the men who sat with John Bradshaw in that judgment seat. The policy and statesmanship of the act is more questionable. Doubtless it inculcated a terrible and lasting truth, one not easily forgotten by princes and rulers, that however monarchs might theorize on their " divine rights," yet practically the power dwelt in the hands of the people, but its results proved it a lamentable political error, and demonstrated the superior wisdom of the course preferred by Vane and Sidney. It opened the way to the aspiring ambition of the successful soldier who, so soon after, subverted the liberties of the commonwealth. It obliged the new government to lean for support upon the army rather than upon that moral power which, in a free state, is always wielded by the civil authorities, and centers in the bosom of the national representation. Finally, the scene itself, so sudden, so startling, so tragic, united with the pious constancy and fortitude of the sufferer, shocked the minds of a people constitutionally loyal, like the people of England, and had the effect of producing more than any other single cause that powerful reaction in public sentiment against the new government, which, eleven years after, manifested itself in those shouts of acclamation which greeted the arrival of the second Charles, a wanderer, recalled from exile, to be raised without conditions to the throne of his ancestors. All then that remains is the stern, severe, naked justice of the act, the sublimity of the spectacle displayed by those men of stout hearts and resolute minds, and the moral lesson inculcated, which has not been lost to the world.

The king was executed on the 30th day of January, 1649. It is to be remarked that of the one hundred and thirty-five judges appointed to try him, seventy-one was the greatest number ever present at the trial. Most of the rest, like Fairfax and Sidney, were designedly absent. Sixty-three were present when sentence was pronounced, and the names of fifty-nine are found attached to the death warrant. Among these, besides Oliver Cromwell whose signature is next to that of the president, are to be found the names of those well known and steady republicans, Bradshaw, Ireton, Fleetwood, Marten, Scot, and Ludlow ; and Whalley, Dixwell and Goffe, who subsequently fled to the colonies of America, and died in exile in the then wilderness of New England.

During these proceedings, Sidney, with his brother, Lord Lisle, left London and went to Penshurst. They remained there several days, and until after the condemnation of the king. Having openly opposed the proceedings in the Painted Chamber, Sidney did not choose to lend even so slight a sanction to them as might be inferred from his presence in the Capital. But as has been before mentioned his objection proceeded rather to the form of the proceeding, and his reluctance to bring Charles to the scaffold, than from any doubt of his guilt, or from any want of sympathy with his republican associates. That he heartily concurred in the abolition of royalty and the establishment of a free commonwealth, is evident from the fact that he immediately returned to London and took his seat in Parliament, where he at once zealously co-operated in all the measures proposed to sustain the new government.

Sidney now applied himself as closely to the business of the House as the duties of his military place, which he still retained, would permit. The new government which came in after the king's death, was strictly a commonwealth. The House of Lords was, by a formal vote, abolished, and the next day, by another vote, the " kingship" was declared " unnecessary, burdensome and dangerous to the liberty, safety, and public interest of the people." The sole legislative, as well as executive power, was therefore vested in what remained of the House of Commons. The religious government of the nation was settled, establishing the Presbyterian form, but depriving it of all temporal power or pretensions; and religious toleration became the order of the day in place of the rigid coercive power which had so long been wielded by the ancient hierarchy of England. In a very few days most of the vestiges of the monarchy were swept away. The great seal was broken to pieces and a new one devised. The name of the King's Bench was changed to that of Upper Bench. Even the king's statues at the Royal Exchange and other places were taken down, and Harry Marten's inscription placed on their sites.

Exit tyrannus regum ultimus.

It soon, however, became apparent to the statesmen of the Commonwealth that an executive power of some description was necessary in the new government. For this purpose a committee of five was appointed to name a council, to consist of forty persons, to act as the executive power, whose authority was to continue for one year. The new council was installed on the 17th of February. The illustrious Bradshaw was chosen its president. Besides Cromwell, it comprised nearly all the eminent republican leaders of the time, Ireton, Ludlow, Marten, St. John,

Hazelrig, Harrington, Scott, Lisle, and Hutchinson.
Some of the nobility were also members; the Earls
of Denbigh, Mulgrave, Pembroke, and Salisbury, and
the Lords Fairfax and Grey. Vane also was
chosen a member, at the earnest solicitation of Cromwell, it is said, whose ambitious aspirations had
not yet taken form and shape; but he did not present
himself till nine days after. He found an obstacle to
his being sworn into the council, by reason of a resolution proposed in the House, that no person should be
a member without expressing his approbation of all
that had been done on the king's trial. Vane refused
to take the test. It was upon this occasion that Sidney, sensible of the importance and value of such
services as Vane's, in the executive council of the
new government, opposed this test in the House with
great warmth and animation. Among other things
he observed, that "such a test would prove a snare to
many an honest man, but every knave would slip
through it." This cutting, and perhaps imprudent
sarcasm was construed into a personal affront by
Cromwell, Harrison and others, and a violent debate,
which occasioned great excitement, ensued, it being
contended that Sidney had called all those knaves
who subscribed to the test. The experienced Harry
Marten, one of Sidney's warmest friends, at length
quieted the turmoil, and put an end to the debate, by
one of his quick-witted and good-natured explanations.
He declared that Sidney had only said that every
knave *might* slip through, not that every one who *did*

3*

slip through was a *knave*. Sidney in the letter to
his father, already mentioned, alluding to this circumstance, declares his own conviction that it was much
against his interest, as it made Cromwell, Harrison,
Lord Grey of Groby, and others his enemies, who
from that time, continually opposed him.

The opposition of Cromwell and his satellites, however, as we shall presently see, was not only against
Sidney, but against Vane, Bradshaw, Ludlow, and
the noblest minds among the republicans who stood in
the path of his ambition.

The first great question which the House and the
executive council encountered, was that of the succession, and of regulating the election of future parliaments. The "Rump Parliament," as it is called, has
been accused of the desire of perpetuating itself, after
all its power and influence had departed. The charge,
so far as the leading members of the republican party
are concerned, is unfounded. Cromwell, in forcibly
dissolving the Long Parliament, acted the part of a
military tyrant and usurper, as he was, by overturn-
ing the civil authorities at the very moment the Parliament was about peacefully to dissolve itself, and to
call another elected, by the suffrages of the people.

The dissolution of the Parliament. the calling of
another, regulating the succession of parliaments, and
fixing the ratio of representation, had been primary
and important objects with the statesmen of the new
Commonwealth. Only three months after the installation of the executive council, on motion of Vane,

the question for the dissolution of the present Parlia-liament came up in connection with the subject of calling future parliaments and regulating the elections. On the 15th of May, the whole matter was referred to a committee of nine persons, of which Vane was the chairman. Of this committee Col. Sidney was a member. It was directed to sit every Monday and Friday, until its laborious duties were completed. The first report of this important committee was not made till January of the next year, and then only partially acted on. The labors of the committee were again resumed, and through this and the following year it would seem to have met more than fifty times; still no decisive result was attained. The subject was finally referred to the committee of the whole House, where, by the labors of Vane, Sidney, and other true and tried patriots, a bill for the peaceful dissolution of the Long Parliament, the calling of another, and fixing the representation, was matured and about to pass at the very moment when Cromwell introduced his soldiers on the floor of the House, and turned out its members at the point of the bayonet. The provisions of this bill will be presently noticed.

Col. Sidney though an influential member of this important committee, was absent from many of its deliberations. On the 13th of July, he was continued by resolution of the House in the government of Dover Castle, and his time seems to have been divided between his military and civil duties. The following winter he became involved in an unfortunate dispute with his officers in the garrison at Dover. A court martial was at once convened, but thinking himself unfairly treated, he appealed to Parliament for redress, who appointed a committee to investigate the matter, and in the meantime ordered the proceedings of the court martial to be stayed. Notwithstanding this, the court martial continued to sit, till the Parliament noticing their refractory conduct, summoned three of its officers to the bar of the House. The matter was finally referred to the Council of State, who on the 28th March, 1652, gave Sidney the redress he asked, and restored him his horses and other property of which he had been deprived.

Having resigned his military command, and nothing of great importance being before the Parliament, Col. Sidney went over on a visit to the Hague. Here, on the 19th of April, his impetuous temper drew him into a quarrel with the Earl of Oxford at a play. Sidney conceiving himself insulted by the Earl, sent him a challenge, and the parties proceeded at once to Flanders, with their seconds, to settle their dispute by single combat. The duel was prevented by the interference of some friends, who promptly followed and intercepted the parties on their way to Flanders.

In the autumn of 1651 Col. Sidney returned to England, and being now freed from his military engagements, he devoted himself with great assiduity to his duties in the house. During the remainder of this, and the following year, he performed various important services, particularly in his duties upon the committees. He was upon two committees for promoting the union with Scotland, to accomplish which Vane was subsequently sent as a commissioner into that country, after the battle of Dunbar. He was also a member of the committee charged with effecting various important alterations in the practice in courts of law. Upon this committee there were several of his associates who were not members of Parliament. The celebrated Sir Matthew Hale, the most profound and accomplished jurist of the age, was a member of it. He seems also to have had some singular associates who appear to have been very little qualified for the work. Among these may be mentioned Major-General Desborough and the famous preacher Hugh Peters, formerly minister at Salem in Massachusetts, and afterwards the chaplain of Cromwell, who, according to Whitlocke, " understood little of law, was very opinionative, and would frequently mention some proceedings of law in Holland wherein he was altogether mistaken." The committee met several times in the House of Lords; but, considering the nature of the times, and the discordant materials of which it was composed, it is not wonderful that little was effected by its labors. Among other resolutions passed in the committee, the following may be taken as a specimen : " If the defendant in a personal action before pleading, tender satisfaction to the plaintiff, with cost of suit, and it appear afterwards at the trial to the jury sufficient, and not accepted of, the plaintiff to lose his own and pay the other's costs of suit."*

Sidney was chairman of the committee on a bill for satisfying those adventurers who had lent money to assist the government in suppressing the Irish insurgents on an assignment of the confiscated lands. This bill included the subject of the arrears due to the army employed in that service, and the encouragement of Protestant settlers in Ireland ; and after a laborious investigation of several months, Sidney reported the proceedings complete to the House. Finally, on the 25th of November, 1652, he was elected a member of the Council of State, and remained in discharge of the executive duties of the government until its overthrow by Cromwell the following April.

No one can deny in looking at the administration of the government of the Commonwealth during the period between the death of the king and the dissolution of the Long Parliament, that it was conducted with unparalleled vigor and ability. It is a common mistake to attribute the power which, at this period, England wielded at home and abroad, and the proud eminence she attained among civilized nations, solely to the skill and genius of Oliver Cromwell. Surely the statesmen who guided the vessel of the Commonwealth through the rocks on either side into a place of comparative safety, before the helm fell exclusively into the powerful hands of the great soldier, may

* Roscoe's Lives of Eminent British Lawyers, Sir Matthew Hale.

CHAPTER II. 63

justly claim at least, to divide the glory of the achievement. We see not why the names of such men as
Vane, and Bradshaw, and Algernon Sidney, who sat in
the legislature and in the executive councils of the state,
and who so successfully conducted the foreign as well
as the domestic administration, while Cromwell was
fighting his battles of Drogheda, Dunbar, and Worcester, should be comparatively forgotten, and their
glory eclipsed by the halo which surrounds the name
of the victorious general of the Commonwealth.
Nothing so contributed to increase the power and
exalt the fame of England abroad, during this period,
as her splendid maritime successes. With these, certainly, Cromwell had little to do. The first war with
the Republic of Holland was commenced and virtually
brought to a close during the Long Parliament. Sir
Henry Vane was then at the head of the naval department; and, notwithstanding the comparatively
small naval force at the command of the English government, the unparalleled skill and exertions of that
great statesman, aided by the united efforts of the Parliament, soon raised the navy of the Commonwealth
to a position to contest successfully with her rival the
dominion of the seas. The Parliament selected one of
its members, hitherto known only as a plain but inflexible republican, destined to become famous as a
hero, BLAKE, to the command of the fleet, and to contest with such captains as Van Tromp and De Ruyter,
the supremacy of the ocean. The result proved the
wisdom of the choice. We quote the words of Sid-

ney himself, as found in one of his discourses, in vindication of the fame of that government of which he was a member. A nobler and a juster eulogy was never pronounced on the deeds of the republican statesmen of the Long Parliament.

" When Van Tromp set upon Blake in Folkestone Bay, the Parliament had not above thirteen ships against three score , and not a man who had ever seen any other fight at sea than between a merchant ship and a pirate, to oppose the best captain in the world, attended with many others, in valor and experience not much inferior to him. Many other difficulties were observed in the unsettled state—few ships, want of money, several factions, and some, who, to advance particular interests, betrayed the public. But such was the power of wisdom and integrity in those that sat at the helm, and their diligence in chosing men only for their merit, was blessed with such success, that in two years our fleets grew to be as famous as our land armies ; the reputation and power of our nation rose to a greater height than when we possessed the better half of France, and the kings of France and Scotland were our pensioners. All the states, kings, and potentates of Europe most respectfully, not to say submissively, sought our friendship ; and Rome was more afraid of Blake and his fleet than they had been of the great king of Sweden when he was ready to invade Italy with a hundred thousand men."

Warburton calls the members of the Long Parliament " a set of the greatest geniuses for government the world has ever seen embarked together in one common cause." Even Hume himself, notwithstanding his strong political bias, and the injustice he has elsewhere done the republicans of the Commonwealth, bears involuntary testimony to their great ability in the administration of the government. Speaking of the period of the battle of Worcester, when the Republic had an army of eighty thousand soldiers on foot, he says: " The vigor of the Commonweath and the *great capacity of those members who had assumed the government*, never, at any time, appeared so conspicuous."

But the days of the Long Parliament were drawing to a close. The men who bore rule in its councils, were the men who stood in the path of Cromwell's ambition. One of these was Algernon Sidney, who continued firmly attached to the cause of the Parliament and the Commonwealth, side by side with Vane and his noble associates, to the last. It has been mentioned, that Sidney early encountered the ill-will of the lord general, nor does it appear that he ever was reinstated in his good opinion, even while Cromwell was yet acting in perfect unison with the republican leaders in Parliament. Sidney had been strongly recommended by Ludlow to Cromwell for the appointment of general of the horse in Ireland, and as the second in command to the gallant General Ireton in the government of that kingdom; but Cromwell could not overcome his dislike to Sidney, and under the pretence of his being related to some of the royal party, appointed Ludlow himself to that station. At the time of Sidney's accession to the Council of State, Cromwell was weaving that web of intrigue, and meditating those schemes of fatal ambition, which ended in the overthrow of the Commonwealth. Other eyes besides those of Sidney were now bent upon the aspiring soldier, and his course was watched with intense anxiety by all the true and tried republicans in Parliament. Even his old friend, Harry Marten, who had stood by him in the matter of the "purge" of Parliament, now looked upon him with distrust, and prepared to separate from him for ever.

The decisive battle of Worcester, the "crowning mercy," as Cromwell styled it, was fought the preceding fall. The royalists were utterly subdued ; the young king was a fugitive and a wanderer, and no power in England was left to challenge the supremacy of the government. Cromwell was again in London, and in attendance in the Parliament. From that point is to be traced the first manifest development of his unworthy and criminal ambition. It is not our intention here to follow the progress of the quarrel which fell out between the Parliament and the army, or rather its general, Cromwell. It originated in the sound policy of the Parliament of reducing the army to the peace establishment, and thus annulling the military power—a measure extremely distasteful to Cromwell and his officers, by whom it was strenuously resisted. It is unnecessary to say that Sidney co-operated heartily with Vane in advocating the measure, and thus made wider the breach between himself and the lord general.

The crisis between the civil and military powers, however, turned upon another but a kindred point of controversy. Both professed to be desirous of a speedy dissolution of the old Parliament, but both were not so eagerly anxious for the convocation of a new one. The conferences toward the close of the year 1652, between the lord general and his principal officers, and some of the more yielding republicans, such as his kinsman St. John, and Sir Arthur Hazelrig, preclude every other conclusion save that Cromwell was aiming at, if not conspiring to obtain, the chief authority in some form or shape. The plan he finally settled upon was the dissolution of the old parliament, leaving the powers of government in the hands of a few " select persons," or in other words, a military commission, which he knew he could mould to his own purposes. Not so Sidney and the republicans. They desired the dissolution of Parliament by an act of their own ; and by the same act the convoking of another as the sovereign power in the state, based upon the broad principle of POPULAR SUFFRAGE and EQUAL AND JUST POPULAR REPRESENTATION. This bill had been reported by Vane to the House from the committee of which Sidney was a member; and after being kept in committee of the whole, and discussed at intervals for a period of eleven months, was sent back to the same committee to be perfected. Before the labors of the committee were completed, Vane had procured a vote of the House, that the period of the dissolution should be fixed for the 3d of November, 1653. In April of that year, the bill, as it had been agreed upon in the committee, was brought up before the House for action. Its discussion brought with it the final crisis—the open rupture with Cromwell—the dissolution of the Parliament—the overthrow of the Commonwealth. This bill, so distasteful to Cromwell, and which, at the moment of the dissolution of the House, he snatched from the hands of the clerk and destroyed, provided for the dissolution of the present Parliament, and the calling of another, to be elected by the suffrages of the qualified voters of the whole . people. The number of representatives fixed was four hundred. The inequalities of representation which existed in former parliaments were carefully avoided. Ludlow, in his "Memoirs," says, that some boroughs, with scarcely a house in them, chose two members, and that the county of Cornwall elected forty-four, while Essex, bearing as great a share in the payment of taxes, sent no more than six or eight. The same excellent authority adds, that the present bill provided that the members of Parliament should be "chosen by the several counties in as near a proportion as was possible to the sums charged upon them for the services of the state, and all men admitted to be electors who were worth £200 in lands, leases, or goods." The effect of this truly radical reform bill, may be estimated by a comparison of the counties just named, Cornwall and Essex. It gave the former ten, the latter fourteen members. It may also be mentioned that the £200 qualification clause was not the original proposition of Vane and his friends. The sole qualification they proposed was a freehold in land, or other profits of the yearly value of 40s., or a leasehold estate for life of the value of £5, or for twenty-one years of the value of £20. These provisions were, however, opposed by Cromwell, who succeeded in defeating the friends of the bill on several divisions, and procured the higher qualification to be inserted.*

The contest was thus narrowed down between Cromwell and his officers on the one hand, and between Vane, Sidney, and the republicans in Parliament on the other, to this point, namely, whether the House should be dissolved, leaving the powers of government in the hands of Cromwell and his military cabal; or whether it should be dissolved, and another chosen by the suffrages of the people, installed in its stead. It is not to be wondered at, that the latter course was distasteful to the future dictator. A free Parliament stood between him and the supreme authority; and he resolved, at all hazards, and at every sacrifice of principle to effect his object.

The scene of the final dissolution of the Long Parliament was enacted on the 20th of April, 1653. About one hundred members had assembled. Algernon Sidney sat at the right hand of the Speaker, Lenthall. With Vane, Marten, Scot and the principal members, he had been there from an early hour. The

* Forster's British Statesmen, Life of Vane.

act for the "new representative" had arrived at its
last stage, and after a powerful speech from Vane, was
about to pass into a law. At this stage of the proceedings Major General Harrison, then one of Cromwell's allies, arose to make a speech, evidently for the
purpose of gaining time. Meanwhile, Colonel In-
goldsby was despatched in haste to the lord general,
who was sitting in council with his military cabal, at
Whitehall. Rushing without ceremony into the presence of Cromwell, he exclaimed, "If you mean to
do any thing decisive you have no time to lose!" The
General immediately rose, ordered a party of soldiers
to the House of Commons, and himself, with Lambert and a few others, repaired thither. The ir-
resolution of Cromwell is strongly marked in his
conduct that day in the House. Like Cæsar, he hesitated before he crossed the Rubicon; but Rome and
empire lay beyond. As if in mockery of the outrage
he was about to commit, he had laid aside every ves-
tige of the soldier, and appeared "clad in plain black
clothes with gray worsted stockings." On entering
the hall, he "sat down as he used to do, in an ordinary place." He listened attentively to Vane, who
was urging with warmth and eloquence the necessity
of dispensing with certain immaterial forms and proceeding at once to the final vote upon the bill. "Now
is the time," whispered Cromwell to the misguided
Harrison. "*I must do it!*"

"The work, sir, is very great and dangerous," was
the cautious reply of Harrison.

" You say well," answered Cromwell, and sat still for another quarter of an hour.

It appears that the Speaker was actually about to put the question,* when Cromwell suddenly started to his feet and commenced a strange and incoherent harangue against the Parliament and the proceedings of the members. He soon succeeded in lashing himself into a passion ; but he had to deal with resolute and undaunted-men, who were not to be awed by the words or the frown of the dictator. Vane, Marten and Wentworth successively rose to answer, but their voices were lost in the confusion. At length, Sir Peter Wentworth made himself heard, and hurled the scathing denunciation at Cromwell—" that he had never heard such unbecoming language in Parliament —language the more shameful as it came from their servant ; that servant whom they had so highly trusted and obliged, and whom, by their unprecedented bounty they had made what he was."

At these words Cromwell thrust on his hat and sprang to the centre of the floor. Eye-witnesses have described† the shameful scene which followed —a scene humiliating to the greatness of the victorious general of the Commonwealth, in which the

---

* Sir Arthur Hazelrig, a member present, says : " We were laboring here in the House on an act to put an end to that Parliament and to call another. I desired the passing of it with all my soul. *The question was putting for it*, when our General stood up and stopped the question, and called in his Lieutenant with two files of musketeers, with their hats on their heads, and their guns loaded with bullets."

† Sidney, Ludlow, Hazelrig.

coolness and calm self-reliance of the conqueror of Worcester and Naseby fight, seemed to have degenerated to the rant and bluster of a common brawler. He paced the floor—he stamped and raved like a madman. He applied the vilest epithets and used the most ignoble language. When Vane courageously rose and succeeded in making himself heard for the last time, Cromwell sternly interrupted him :— " You might have prevented all this, but you are a juggler, and have not so much as common honesty." Then cutting short his discourse, he exclaimed, " You are no Parliament. I say you are no Parliament! I'll put an end to your sitting. Begone! Give way to honester men." He stamped with his foot as he spoke ; the door was flung open ; his musketeers filed into the hall, and drove out the members at the point of the bayonet. As they passed along, Cromwell, now excited beyond control, singled out individually those whom he had most reason to hate and loaded them with opprobrium and insult. One he called, by name, an adulterer, another he accused of embezzlement, a third of fraud and injustice. As Vane passed by among the last, protesting with earnest voice, " This is not honest ; yea, it is against morality and common honesty," Cromwell spoke in a harsh and troubled tone, unable to hurl any personal accusation against his most formidable rival— " Sir Harry Vane ! Sir Harry Vane ! The Lord deliver me from Sir Harry Vane !"

During the whole of this remarkable scene, Sidney

remained firm at his post; but finally, with his associates, was obliged to succumb to force and violence.
From the journal of his father, Lord Leicester, penned, undoubtedly, on the relation of Sidney, we quote
the closing scenes of this singular drama: "Then
the general, pointing to the speaker in his chair, said
to Harrison, 'fetch him down.' Harrison went to the
speaker and spoke to him to come down, but the
speaker sat still and said nothing. *Take him down,*
said the general; then Harrison went and pulled the
speaker by the gown, and he came down.* It hap-
pened that day that Algernon Sidney sat next to the
speaker on the right hand. The general said to Harrison, 'Put him out.' Harrison spake to Sidney, but he
said he would not go out, and sat still. The general
said again, 'Put him out.' Then Harrison and Wors-
ley (who commanded the general's own regiment of
foot) put their hands upon Sidney's shoulders, as if
they would force him to go out. Then he arose and
went towards the door. Then the general went

---

* Lenthal's firm conduct on this occasion is corroborated by other testimony. He told Harrison, says Ludlow, "that he would not come down
unless he was forced. 'Sir,' said Harrison, 'I will lend you my hand,"
and thereupon putting his hand within his, the speaker came down."
Sir Arthur Hazelrig gives the following description: "The speaker, a
stout man, was not willing to go. He was so noble that he frowned,
and said he would not go out of the chair till he was plucked out,
which was quickly done, without much compliment, by two soldiers."
The resolution displayed by Lenthal on this occasion, is somewhat remarkable, inasmuch as he was a man of little decision of character.
Sidney's courageous conduct was characteristic, and such as he never
failed to display on all occasions when he had a right to sustain, or a
duty to discharge.

towards the table where the mace lay, which used to
be carried before the Speaker, and said—' Take away
these baubles.' So the soldiers took away the mace."
And thus closed that famous Parliament which had
wrought such great achievements for the liberties of
the people of England. The lord general seized the
act of dissolution from the hands of the secretary,
locked the door, and carried back the keys with him
to Whitehall, himself now the sole depository of the
power of the Commonwealth.

Sidney immediately retired in disgust to his father's
residence at Penshurst. Thenceforth he refused to take
any part in Cromwell's usurped government, or in
the slightest degree to countenance it. It was not
until the reassembling of the Long Parliament, after
the death of the Protector Richard, that he again appeared upon the scene.

The personal history of Algernon Sidney, as has
been seen, like that of almost every public man of that
period, is connected with the history of the great man
of the age, Oliver Cromwell. In tracing it we have
had frequent occasion to speak of Cromwell, though
not always in the flattering and eulogistic terms which
have of late been so much in vogue among a class of
his admirers. A brief digression from our main subject may not be out of place here, in order to correct
any erroneous impression as to the character of this
really great and extraordinary man, which may have
been left by the relation of his connection with the dissolution of the Long Parliament.

Cromwell is certainly one of the most striking and remarkable personages in history. His biography has been so often written, and is so familiar to the general reader, as to render it superfluous, even were it proper, to glance at it here. He had been wild and dissipated in his youth, but on a sudden abandoned his dissolute course of life, and adopted the tenets and rigid morality of the strictest sect of the Puritans. His religious professions which have called forth so many contradictory opinions were doubtless sincere; yet though his enthusiasm was deep and stern, his mind was too vigorous and well balanced to suffer it to lead him into those wild rhapsodies which heated the imaginations of so many of the leading Puritans.

We think it may safely be asserted that Cromwell was neither a hypocrite nor a fanatic. Yet, while always keenly sensitive to religious emotions, he did not scruple, when occasion required, to make use of his reputation for sanctity and godliness, for secular purposes. In the midst of his most pious professions, and perhaps of his most devout feelings, he was always the clear-headed, far-seeing, practical man of the world, not disposed to stick at a point of metaphysics or abstract theology in gaining an end. Perhaps it is true that in his later career, ambition and the lust of power may have shared far more of his thoughts than did his devotional meditations. This may serve to explain the meaning of the question put by him to one of his chaplains on his death-bed, when his mind returned to those deep and earnest thoughts on which it had so intently dwelt in former years—whether it were "*possible for one to fall from grace and be finally lost ?*" And upon being answered in the negative, he replied—"*Then I am safe, for I am sure I was in grace once.*"

The sincerity of Cromwell's political actions and professions in the earlier portion of his public career, we have as little reason to doubt. While he yet acted with Vane, Sidney, Marten, and Bradshaw, he was sincerely and truly a republican. Perhaps his mind was among the very first to penetrate clearly into the future, and to appreciate the merits of the question at issue. But the political honesty of Cromwell was not proof against temptation. That he betrayed the popular cause, and proved recreant to his republican principles, is true. It is not impossible, as some of his admirers have claimed, that he may have been perfectly sincere in his views of public policy, which led to his concentrating in his own hands the powers of the state, and that he was, if such a thing be possible, an *honest* usurper. The obvious inference, however, from the facts of his history, seems directly the reverse of this. Like every crafty and ambitious statesman, Cromwell was not a stranger to diplomacy and intrigue. Sometimes he found it necessary to avail himself of the arts of dissimulation, in which he was a profound adept. He habitually concealed his well-laid plans, but generally endeavored to give a plausible explanation of his actions. Nor were his explanations at all times true ones. All this, however, may be reconciled without the assumption that he acted throughout upon a plan of systematic hypocrisy, for there will be found running through these explanations, tedious and verbose as they are, a subtle and plausible logic that may well have imposed upon his own mind as it did on others, and have silenced, if it did not entirely satisfy, his own scruples. Cromwell, doubtless, carried his arts of dissimulation too far. In his eagerness to justify his conduct and prove the purity of his motives, he occasionally descended to what the world might, with some propriety, call falsehood.* Yet to say that his whole public career was but the manifestation of a preconcerted system of hollow-hearted duplicity and falsehood, is ascribing a littleness to the character of this really great man which we think the facts of history do not warrant.

Cromwell was more than forty years of age when he first entered into public life. The great capacity of the man was known to few—indeed to none save, perhaps, his kinsman John Hampden, who knew him well.

* Among the other moral inconsistencies in this singular character, may be mentioned the fact stated by Noble, that notwithstanding the warmth of his religious zeal, and the severe outward propriety of his conduct, the Protector is known to have indulged in several not very reputable intrigues with ladies of his court. The Lady Dysert, afterwards Duchess of Lauderdale, and the wife of General Lambert, are mentioned as his favorites. These ladies were the very reverse of each other in manners and accomplishments. Lady Dysert is described as " beautiful, witty, learned, and full of intrigue." Mrs. Lambert, on the contrary, though a woman of pleasing attractions, was a bit of a Puritan, and " employed herself only in praying and singing of hymns."

Almost on his first appearance in parliament, Lord Digby inquired of Hampden who that sloven was whom he had just heard speak in the House. Hampden answered—"If we ever come to a breach with the king, which God forbid! In such a case, I say that sloven will be the greatest man in England!" And well was the opinion of Hampden justified, and admirably was his prediction fulfilled. The sagacity of Cromwell, his prodigious energy of character, his rugged, robust manhood, were all brought into advantageous employ during the civil war. He became the first soldier of the age. Subsequent events proved, as in the case of Napoleon, that his capacity was equally as great in the administration of government as in war. When once he had usurped the supreme authority, it is but just to his memory to say that he held the reins with a strong and steady hand; that he governed wisely and well. England enjoyed more of liberty, civil and religious, under the Protector, than she had ever known in the days of her kings. Religious toleration was guarantied, and the right of conscience respected; even the persecuted Jew, the outlaw of civilization, who for ages had been under the ban of society and government, was no longer proscribed, but was brought within that wise and comprehensive system of toleration which the Protector so liberally favored. The administration of Cromwell proved that he had a genius for government—that he was no vulgar usurper, but, like Napoleon Bonaparte, was a man gifted with that vigor of intellect and those great

mental endowments which enabled him to wield despotic authority for the glory and advantage of his
country. The government so wisely administered by
the Long Parliament, lost not a whit of its resistless
energy when it passed into the hands of the Protector.
He made the British name renov.ned all over the
world. His victorious armies defended the Protestant faith. His fleets swept the sea. His threat at
once made the Sultan and the Roman Pontiff tremble.
At his feet both France and Spain were suppliants.
Not a moment, from the time of Cromwell's accession
to the supreme authority, to the day of his death, did
England cease to rise in the scale of European politics ;
not a moment did she pause in her splendid career,
until Cromwell nearly realized his proud boast that he
would make the name of Englishman as much honored as that of Roman had been.

Yet notwitstanding the vast capacity and splendid
achivements of this celebrated man, the errors (to call
them by no harsher name) of his political course are
too glaring to be concealed. His conduct upon the
trial of the king may be entirely justified by the same
liberal judgment that absolves Bradshaw and his noble
associates. Up to this time we have every reason to
believe that he was sincere and honest in his
attachment to the popular cause. Ambition and the
lust of power had not yet found a chance to tamper
with his conscience. It was not until after his Irish
campaign, after his splendid victory at Dunbar, after
his " crowning mercy" at Worcester, which completely

annihilated the power of the enemies of the Commonwealth in the three kingdoms, and made him the idol
of the army, that Cromwell was seduced from his alle-
giance to the popular cause, and was drawn away to
follow the path of ambition which his splendid successes had laid open before him.   The forcible dissolution of the Long Parliament was the first palpable
manifestation of the new policy he had adopted.   It
gave the friends of republicanism distinctly to understand that he had formally cut loose from the common
cause, and meant to trample under his feet the rights
of popular representation.   At this point the best and
truest friends of the Commonwealth, Sidney, Vane,
Bradshaw, and Marten abandoned him.   The parliament which he and his officers summoned, themselves
nominating the members, known in history as " Bare-
bones Parliament," he found useless.   He resolved to
dissolve it.   The majority of the members fell in with
his plan and tendered him their resignation.   The
minority, among whom was General Harrison, the
same that had assisted to pull Sidney and the Speaker
from their seats, refused.   The scene of the Long Parliament was re-enacted.   To the summons of Colonels
Goffe and White to disband, Harrison, now no longer
the dupe of Cromwell, asked these officers for their
warrant ; " they returned no answer, but went and
fetched two files of musquetiers, and did as good as
force them out."   A few days after, General Lambert,
in the name of THE ARMY *and* the three nations, invested Cromwell with the title and dignities of Lord

Protector of the Commonwealth, and published an instrument of government, how sanctioned or by whom written was best known to Cromwell himself. Such was the natural sequel to the forcible dissolution of the Long Parliament, and such the manner in which Cromwell usurped the supreme power. This step once taken, his whole subsequent career is explained. He stood before the world confessedly an usurper, holding his power by the sword, and the might of the omnipotent dictator made the right when he forced a portion of one of his parliaments to sign a pledge of fidelity to his person and government—when he dissolved another at his own pleasure, because he could not control it—when he turned an hundred of its members out of doors—when he threw Vane, and Marten, and Bradshaw into prison, and when he quartered his military governors and their satellites over England. The wisdom of his civil administration, the genius displayed in his foreign policy, the glories of his government at home and abroad, cannot conceal these things, nor convince us that Oliver Cromwell did not prove untrue to the great trust which the battles of Dunbar and Worcester placed in his hands, and did not sacrifice the liberties of his country to unholy ambition. It was the melancholy and oft repeated lesson of successful resistance to tyranny, followed by military usurpation. The Revolution, it is true, wrought great things for the general cause of freedom, yet on the whole it was a failure : but what might not that revolution have done for the people of England, if the great soldier had remained steadfast and true to the cause of the people and liberty !

A widely different character was that of Sir Henry Vane, commonly called the younger, one of the noblest and brightest names in the roll of British statesmen. Vane, like Sidney, was a descendant of one of the oldest families of the English nobility. Like Sidney he was also a dissenter from the Church of England, and embraced the doctrines of the Puritans. Like Sidney he was a member of the Long Parliament, but refused to sit in judgment on the king. Like Sidney he boldly faced Oliver Cromwell in his march to absolute power. Like him he remained steadfast and faithful to the end to the cause of civil and religious freedom, and dying like him, upon the scaffold, proclaimed his entire faith in the principles of his whole life, and his bright anticipations for the future. " I die in the certain faith and foresight that THIS CAUSE shall have its resurrection in my death. My blood will be the seed sown by which this glorious cause will spring up which God will speedily raise."

The profound intellect of Vane, and his genius as a statesman, as well as the beautiful consistency and purity of his character, have rarely been appreciated. The English historians of the school of Clarendon and Hume have done less justice to his memory than to that of almost any other public man of the age Clarendon, his bitter personal enemy, is indeed forced to concede his great capacity—that he was a man of " extraordinary parts, a pleasant wit, and a great understanding ;" but Clarendon's mind, distorted by personal and party prejudice, is unable to conceive, or if it does, has not the magnanimity to describe, the character of Vane in anything like truthful colors. He accuses him of possessing "rare dissimulatiou," and if not superior to Hampden, of being "inferior to no other man in all *mysterious artifices.*" The political bigot Clarendon accuses the most liberal-minded of his contemporary statesmen of religious fanaticism, and even does not hesitate to utter or insinuate, what he must have known was the grossest of calumnies, that Vane believed himself *inspired*, and that he was the person " destined to reign over the saints a thousand years."* Such are the sources from which English history is derived. Clarendon, speaking of Vane's celebrated and successful negotiations with the commissioners of Scotland, to induce that nation to unite with the Parliament, says—" There need no more be said of his ability than that he was chosen *to cozen and deceive a whole nation* which excelled in craft and cunning, which he did with notable pregnancy and dexterity." Hume, following Clarendon, was by no means insensible to the greatness of Vane as a statesman, and speaks of his splendid parliamentary talents and his capacity for business ; but Hume could not let pass the opportunity of depreciating the honest republican and the devout Christian. His writings, he tells

* A wild but small sect of enthusiasts, o′ whom General Harrison was one, believed that " King Jesus" was about to appear and reign on earth for a thousand years. They were called " Fifth Monarchy men."

us, are "absolutely unintelligible; no traces of eloquence, or common sense appear in them." Hume's
opinions of Vane's writings may well be placed on a
par with his opinions of the writings of Sidney and
Locke, which he calls "compositions the most despicable for style and matter." Criticism upon such
opinions which have found their way into grave histories is idle. It is delightful, however, to find at the
present day these opinions fast becoming obsolete, and
the prejudices of the past wearing away under the enlightened judgments of men of no less penetrating and
more liberal minds, than those of some of the historians mentioned. The writings which to Hume were
absolutely unintelligible, and in which he could find
no traces of eloquence or even common sense, are thus
spoken of by that accomplished scholar and statesman,
Sir James Mackintosh:

"Sir Henry Vane was one of the most profound
minds that ever existed; not inferior perhaps to Bacon.
His works, which are theological, are extremely rare,
and display astonishing powers. They are remarkable as containing the first direct assertion of liberty
of conscience."

The man whom Clarendon found nothing but a religious fanatic, full of rare dissimulation and all mysterious artifices, receives from the pen of our own historian, Bancroft, its beautiful and just tribute:

"A man of the purest mind; a statesman of spot-
less integrity; whose name the progress of intelligence
and liberty will erase from the rubric of fanatics and

traitors; and insert high among the aspirants after truth and the martys for liberty." Such indeed was Vane. Such did he appear to the best and purest men of his own time—to Roger Williams the pioneer of religious liberty in the wilderness of America—to Sidney and to Bradshaw, the devoted champions of civil freedom in his own country—to his friend John Milton, who knew him well, and offered him the homage of his genius in words so well known.

> " Vane, young in years but in sage counsels old,
> Than whom a better senator ne'er held
> The helm of Rome when gowns not arms repelled
> The fierce Epirot and th' African bold," &c.

The name of Sir Henry Vane is connected with the history of our own country. He was one of the earliest governors of the colony of Massachusets. Unable to enjoy liberty of conscience in England, he turned his eye upon that band of hardy pioneers who had made their homes in the wilderness of America, and, against the remonstrances of his father and friends, he embarked upon the ocean, to share the perils and hardships of the pilgrims in the new world. At the age of twenty-four, and only a year after his arrival in the colony, he was elected governor of Massachusetts. His brief but stormy administration, was conducted with a firmness and wisdom beyond his years, and withal in a spirit of liberality which proves him as a statesman to have been far in advance of his age. He returned to England in the year 1637. Events were fast ripening for that formidable convulsion which subsequently shook the kingdom—the contest between the principles of absolute monarchy and popular liberty. He returned to take part in it. He came to enrol himself among the people—to fight for those high principles of civil and religious freedom which he had professed in the new world, and to prove the sincerity of the actions of his whole life by a martyr's heroism upon the scaffold.

Vane was elected a member of the ever memorable Long Parliament, having been also a member of the Parliament which immediately preceded it. He at once took a prominent stand in the ranks of its illustrious popular leaders. Among these, after the death of Pym and Hampden, Vane, though still a young man—but little more than thirty years of age—stood confessedly the ablest and first. In 1643 he concluded his celebrated negotiation with the Scotch commissioners. Clarendon, after mentioning the name of Vane as one of the English commissioners, says—" the others need not be named, since *he was all* in any business where others were joined with him." He co-operated, as we have seen, with Cromwell in procuring the re-organization of the army. He was one of the commissioners to treat with the king at the Isle of Wight, and in almost every other great public measure of the time, the name of Sir Harry Vane prominently appears. But when Cromwell's soldiers under Col. Pride " purged" a portion of the recusant Presbyterian majority out of the Parliament, Vane, though an Independent, refused t

share in such a sad triumph, or sanction so gross an
outrage against the people's representatives. He immediately absented himself from Parliament, and did
not re-appear until after the trial and death of the
king, a proceeding which, with Sidney, he entirely
disapproved, being in favor of the wiser and more
politic course—the deposing, and not the death of the
monarch. But Vane cordially and faithfully, and
energetically supported the new government and the
commonwealth. He took his seat in the executive
council, of which Bradshaw was president. His commanding talents and experience at once placed him in
a prominent and leading position. He was at the head
of the naval department when the war with Holland
came on. The disadvantageous terms under which
England entered into the war, and its successful issue,
have been spoken of in the extract already quoted from
Sidney. Much of that success is undoubtedly due to
the genius and statesmanship of Vane, although
Cromwell when he arose to the supreme power maintained the superiority of the Commonwealth ; and the
successful soldier has thus appropriated to himself a
fame which more justly belongs to the less pretending
statesman.

Vane's noble stand against Cromwell's usurpation,
his efforts to pass the bill for a popular representation,
and his courageous conduct on the day of the dissolution of the Long Parliament, have been already spoken
of. Like Sidney he refused to accept office or employment under the Protector, and remained in private

life until the re-assembling of the Long Parliament.
So bitter were Cromwell's feelings against him, that he
caused him to be arrested and imprisoned on the publication of one of his ablest works, " A Healing Question," addressed to Cromwell, wherein he urges the
Protector to establish the public liberties by a FUNDA-
MENTAL CONSTITUTION and a popular representation.

On the Restoration, Vane was excepted from the
general amnesty, but not until the king had pledge l
the Commons that sentence of death should not be
passed upon him. The pledge was shamelessly violated. Vane, after suffering imprisonment nearly two
years, was aaraigned and tried for high treason. He
conducted his defence with the most consummate
ability and manly courage. It was every way glorious. He fearlessly and proudly justified his political sentiments and his whole public career, in the face
of a tyrannical government and an abject court. He
had defended the liberties of Englishmen against the formidable power of Charles I.; he had boldly faced Oliver
Cromwell in his march to arbitrary power; he had
denounced with scorn and contempt the feeble Richard
in his own Parliament; it was not for such a man to
purchase favor, or even life, by an abandonment of principle, or a truckling sycophancy to the restored monarch.
Vane contended with great force of argument that
he had acted under the authority of a Parliament of
the people, which could commit no treason, and that
Charles II. being out of possession and not *de facto*
king, no treason could be committed against him.

For several days he baffled his judges and the crown lawyers ; but Clarendon and Charles had resolved that Vane, as a man of " mischievous activity" must die.* He was condemned contrary to law,† and sentenced to be executed. He walked with " a serene, a calm, and almost a divine composure" to the scaffold. His last thoughts rested upon the " cause" which was so often on his lips, and for which he so cheerfully laid down his life. " I bless the Lord I have not deserted the righteous CAUSE for which I suffer," he was heard to say. For a moment he prayed upon the scaffold that God would enable his servant who was about to suffer " to glorify thee in the discharge of *his duty to thee and to his country* ;" then stretching out his hands the executioner at a blow severed his head from his body.

The theory of government and political principles entertained by Vane, have been freely indicated in this work. They may be briefly summed up in these three leading ideas, which formed the basis of a bill he reported to Parliament for establishing the government on the foundation of a democratic constitution.

1st. That a *fundamental constitution*, limiting the powers of government, ought first to be established.

---

* After the trial the king wrote to Clarendon, reminding him that Vane on his trial, had been " so insolent as to justify all he had done." " If he was given new occasion to be hanged," remarked the faithless monarch, " certainly he is too dangerous a man to let live, *if we can honestly put him out of the way.*"

† The highest authorities on the criminal law, Hale, Hawkins, Foster agree in this.

2d. That by this constitution monarchy should be declared destructive to the people's liberties.

3d. That magistrates should have no power to ex- ercise compulsion in matters of faith and worship.

In these elementary propositions is contained Vane's whole political creed. They assert the cardinal truths which lie at the foundation of our own institutions.

It is impossible not to be struck with his elevated conceptions of religious freedom, or to admire his ceaseless and noble efforts in its behalf. Freedom of intellect and freedom of worship he regarded even more, if possible, than political liberty, as the inalien- able right of mankind. For this faith of his life he was always ready to sacrifice himself. From the commencement of his public career to his last hour on the scaffold, he continued to assert and defend it. Never, to the time of his death, did he cease to be the consistent and fearless champion of universal tolera- tion. He plead alike for Biddle and the gifted Mrs. Hutchinson. Over Jew as well as Gentile—over hea- then as well as Christian, he was willing the state should throw the broad ægis of its protection. He heard unmoved the fiery denunciations of the pious, though somewhat narrow-minded Baxter; he listened with calmness to reproof from his friends, when they gently chided him for giving expression to what they were pleased to consider as latitudinarian and dan- gerous doctrines. But the reproof died away and the denunciations fell harmless at his feet, as he met them with the noble reply that he dared not exclude "even the heathen from his charity, since in doing that he might shut out those whom Christ, the great head of the Church, might possibly at the final day acknowledge and welcome as his own."

In popular estimation the names of Pym and Hampden, as the champions of English liberty, entirely eclipse that of Sir Harry Vane. In our view, standing upon the vantage ground of the nineteenth century, and in the midst of a more extended and successful development of democratic government than the world has yet seen, we should say this was but another of those errors which history has imposed upon mankind. Neither Hampden nor Pym comprehended in its full extent, the whole theory of popular liberty. Their effort was to destroy arbitrary power, to reform certain gross abuses, and to secure the independence of Parliament. They wished, however, to preserve, not to destroy, the constitution as it existed, and the monarchy ; they fought not against the king's *person* but his *prerogative.* Vane's views went much further than this. Inferior in intellect to neither Pym nor Hampden, as a statesman he was superior to both. He comprehended the theory of democratic liberty and progress as we understand it on this side of the Atlantic ; and he proposed during his public career and boldly advocated its cardinal principles, such as free religious as well as civil liberty, the separation of church and state, popular representation, and equal suffrage, the responsibility of the executive, and a WRITTEN CONSTITUTION.. While Pym and Hampden, the devoted champions of English constitutional liberty against arbitrary power, are justly entitled to the gratitude of their countrymen, Vane deserves the admiration as well as the gratitude of posterity and the world, as the statesman whose far-reaching intellect, in an age of intolerance in religion and absolutism in government, comprehended the full truth of the democratic principle, and stood forth the unflinching champion of the civil and religious liberties of the people.*

* In the foregoing reflections on Vane and Cromwell, the author has freely extracted from two magazine articles written by him and heretofore published.

CHAPTER III.

THE connection of Col. Sidney with the army and the Long Parliament, brought him into close and intimate relations with the leading republican statesmen of the Commonwealth. In the last chapter we have incidently glanced at the characters and public actions of two men of that period, most eminent for ability and influence—Cromwell and Vane—whose histories intimately blend with that of Sidney. The subject is sufficiently inviting to tempt a further digression, and to induce us to notice briefly two or three others of Sidney's contemporaries, in and out of Parliament, who

so ably upheld the fortunes of the English Commonwealth.

Among these there is none whose character stands
out so bold and striking, in its stern and almost severe
distinctness of outline, as does that of John Bradshaw.
The mention of the name at once brings before us a
vivid and distinct conception of the chief judge who
sat on the tribunal which condemned Charles Stuart
as a traitor. We imagine a man of a grave and majestic presence, as he has been described, seated on his
crimson velvet chair in Westminster Hall, surrounded
by his seventy associate judges, dressed in a loose robe
of scarlet, his massive forehead partially concealed by a
high-crowned, broad-brimmed beaver, lined with plated
steel,* his austere and inflexible features betraying no
shadow of emotion, and his deep and thoughtful eye
fixed full upon the royal criminal arraigned before
him.

Bradshaw was educated a lawyer at Gray's Inns,
and for many years before entering public life, enjoyed
an extensive practice. Though not a member of the
Long Parliament, he early entered into the views of
the popular party, and sided with the Parliament in
all its measures against the king. He was the kinsman of John Milton by the mother's side. The poet,
whose political and religious sympaties, as well as his
kindred blood, brought him into the most intimate
relations with Bradshaw, has left a sketch of his
character, in the second defence *pro populo Anglicano*,

---

* The hat worn by Bradshaw on the trial, is still preserved at Oxford.

so truthful, and so well justified by all that we know of his life and opinions, that we cannot refrain from presenting the passage. " Being of a distinguished family, he devoted the early part of his life to the study of the laws of his country. Hence he became an able and an eloquent pleader, and subsequently discharged all the duties of an uncorrupt judge. In temper neither gloomy nor severe, but gentle and placid, he exercised in his own house the rights of hospitality in an exemplary manner, and proved himself on all occasions a faithful and unfailing friend. Ever eager to acknowledge merit, he assisted the deserving to the utmost of his power. Forward at all times to publish the talents and worth of others, he was always silent respecting his own. No one more ready to forgive, he was yet impressive and terrible when it fell to his lot to pour shame on the enemies of his country. If the cause of the oppressed was to be defended, if the favor or the violence of the great was to be withstood, it was impossible, in that case, to find an advocate more intrepid or more eloquent, whom no threats, no terrors, and no rewards could seduce from the plain path of rectitude." Such indeed was Bradshaw. Possessed of such attributes of character—of an integrity and a purity of life against which no enemy has dared to breathe a whisper—of an impressive and majestic appearance—of a singularly resolute and determined mind, and a clear, cool, discriminating judgment, he was precisely the man to preside in the high court of justice convened to try the king. Bradshaw did not shink from the duty. While nearly half the commissioners appointed refused or neglected to attend the sittings of the court, Bradshaw was present from day to day, and as president arraigned the king, main-tained the authority and jurisdiction of the court throughout, against his objections, and finally passed sentence upon him as a " tyrant, traitor, and public enemy." Perhaps a tribunal more imposing than this ".High Court of Justice" never assembled. All its proceedings were dignified and impressive; nor could they fail to be so, while John Bradshaw presided over its deliberations. His deportment, at times, seems to be marked with almost too great a degree of austerity and sternness, but this was the unavoidable result of the singular position in which he was placed—a posi-tion that would have embarrassed a man of less decision of character and greatness of mind, than Bradshaw. When, in a full and firm voice, he had pronounced sentence on Charles, not as a king, but as a prisoner at the bar of his peers, the condemned monarch earnestly desired to be heard. Bradshaw in-terrupted him with the words—" Sir, you are not to be heard after sentence." Again Charles strove to speak, but was again silenced by the stern mandate—" Guards, withdraw your prisoner." Once more, in accents of deep emotion, he asked to be heard as a favor, and not a right; but the stern monasyllable from the lips of the president, " Hold!" was the only an-swer to the prayer, and the king was almost forcibly carried out of the hall.

Bradshaw was appointed president in the new executive council, where he met with Oliver Cromwell as his colleague. We have seen that up to this time Cromwell had acted consistently with the commonwealth's-men. He had been upon terms of friendship, and even confidence, not only with Bradshaw, but with Vane, Milton, Marten and Sidney. It was not until after the battle of Worcester, that Bradshaw began to suspect the sincerity of Cromwell.* That suspicion once confirmed, no one displayed a firmer courage in opposing the designs of the lord-general, or battled more manfully to sustain the Commonwealth. With Vane, and the republicans of the Commonwealth, he had borne an influential and prominent part in that successful administration which followed the first three years of the new government, himself, in many respects, the first man in England in station and honor, receiving, as president of the council, foreign ambas-

---

* A letter of Bradshaw to Cromwell about the date of the battle of Worcester, is preserved, which indicates, on the part of the writer, the utmost confidence in the lord-general. A deep, religious tone pervades this letter, like those of all the Puritans, but it is staid and sober, like the character of Bradshaw, whose well-balanced mind never was carried away by the exaggerated enthusiasm of the period. It commences as follows:—" My Lord—By the hands of this trusty bearer, accept, I pray you, of this paper-remembrance and salutation of him who, both upon the publique and his owne private account, is very much your debtor, and with other your poore friends here, prayes for and adores the manifestation of God's gracious presence with you in all your weighty affaires, which as they are undertaken in zeal to God's glory and his people's good will, through contynuance of the same dyvine presence and mercy, be crowned with answerable successe."

5

sadors, and representing the executive government of
the Commonwealth. With Vane and the republicans
he stood manfully to the last, and manfully fell with
the Commonwealth in the hour when Cromwell tram-
pled under his feet the liberties of his country. Bradshaw was president of the council on the day when
the lord-general dissolved the Parliament. None but
a man of his iron nerve and indomitable resolution,
could have sustained himself as he did on that occasion. Cromwell having returned from Whitehall,
appeared before the council, backed by his guards,
and addressed them as follows :

" Gentlemen, if you are met here as private persons,
you shall not be disturbed ; but if as a council of state,
this is no place for you ; and since you cannot but
know what was done in the morning, so take notice
that the Parliament is dissolved." The eye of Bradshaw, which had not quailed before the gaze of Charles
Stuart, calmly encountered the troubled glance of the
dictator ; the tongue which had not faltered to pronounce sentence upon his sovereign as a tyrant, traitor,
and public enemy, answered firmly : " Sir, we have
heard what you did at the House in the morning, and
before many hours all England will hear it ; but, sir,
you are mistaken to say that the Parliament is dissolved, for no power under heaven can dissolve them
but themselves ; therefore take you notice of that."
It was the last protest of the Commonwealth against
a lawless military usurpation. Bradshaw and his fel-
lows arose, and in silence withdrew.

In the first Parliament summoned by Cromwell after he had assumed the office of Protector, Bradshaw was returned as a member. A formidable opposition was at once manifested, for the republicans had elected a large number of delegates, among whom were Scot and Sir Arthur Hazelrig. On the first day of the session, the partizans of the Protector nominated Lenthal for speaker; the opposition presented Bradshaw, but finding themselves in a minority, did not press his election. On the very next day, Bradshaw arose and boldly moved to debate the question whether the House should approve the system of government devised by the Protector, and proclaimed by his military cabal. A fierce discussion ensued, which lasted several days. Cromwell, in alarm, stationed a guard of soldiers around the doors of the House, and summoned the members to meet him in the Painted Chamber. Here, after a long and angry discourse, he informed them that he should require each member to sign an engagement to be " *faithful to the Lord Protector and the Commonwealth, and not to consent to an alteration of the government, as it was settled in* ONE PERSON *and a Parliament.*" On their return to the House, the members found the guard still stationed round the doors, and a parchment containing the pledge lying for the signatures of such only as were to be admitted to their seats. Bradshaw, with Scot, Hazelrig, and about an hundred others, indignantly turned his back upon the scene, and retired from a

Parliament which was again ruled by Cromwell's soldiers.

This Parliament being brought to an untimely termination, and a new one afterwards summoned, the republicans again appeared in the field; but Cromwell now resolved on energetic measures to prevent the ablest and most influential from obtaining seats. Bradshaw, on some pretence, was arrested, and deprived of his office of chief justice of Chester, which he had so ably filled. Vane, Ludlow, and Marten were imprisoned. Yet among those elected were Scot, Hazelrig, and other decided republicans. These, the Protector resolved to exclude, and accordingly, upon the assembling of Parliament, they found the doors again closed upon them by the military. Thus were the people of England, through their representatives, denied a voice in the councils of the nation; and thus Bradshaw and his friends were finally excluded from all participation in the government.

On the assembling of the Parliament summoned by the Protector Richard, in January, 1659, Bradshaw once more took his seat as a member. It is unnecessary to say that he zealously co-operated with Vane, Scot, and his other republican associates, whose formidable opposition soon brought the new Protector's government to a close. The Long Parliament was revived; the old council of state re-instated; and Bradshaw again took his seat in it as president. But his career was about to close. Death soon removed him from the scene of his labors. He died during this year, and the honors of a burial in Westminster Abbey, accompanied with the most imposing obsequies, testified at once the general grief of a large portion of the nation, and its respect for his memory. He died tranquilly in his bed, asserting with almost his latest breath, that if the king were to be again tried and condemned, his would be the first voice to assent to the justice of the act. He was denied the glorious martyrdom which awaited some of his associates; the closing eyes of the stern republican were not doomed to rest upon the disgusting orgies which ushered in the Restoration. But the malice of his enemies pursued him beyond the grave. That sacred precinct itself was no barrier to the vindictive wrath of the vengeful royalists. His tomb was ruthlessly violated, and his bones, with those of the dead Cromwell and Ireton, were hung on gibbets and in chains at Tyburn. His head was dissevered and placed on the top of Westminster Hall. "What counsel would dare to speak for him," exclaimed the solicitor-general on the trial of Vane, "in such a manifest case of treason, unless he should call down the heads of his fellow traitors BRADSHAW and COKE* from the top of Westminster Hall." Such was the miserable vengeance which royalty, in the hour of its triumph, did not blush to inflict on the memory of the dead, as well as on the living champions of popular liberty.

* Coke acted as solicitor-general on the trial of the king, and was executed after the Restoration. His head, with Bradshaw's, was placed on the top of Westminster Hall.

JOHN MILTON was the kinsman and friend of Bradshaw; a humbler actor in the great battle for popular
freedom, but a no less ardent and devoted champion
of its sacred cause.   The religious character of Milton,
grave and serious without austerity, humble and devout, with no touch of cant, intolerance, or fanaticism,
was the counterpart of Bradshaw's.   His temper was
more gentle and serene, his will less imperious, his
manners more bland and insinuating, and his private
life equally pure and irreproachable.   His father, a
London scrivener, educated him for the Church, but
the puritanic notions of young Milton could not suffer
him to "accommodate his conscience" to the slavish
hierarchy of Laud.   His motives for refusing to enter
the Church are explained in his " Reasons for Church
Government," and furnish the key to his after unre-
lenting and bitter warfare with Episcopacy.   He was
destined of a child, he says, by his parents and friends
to the Church, " till coming to some maturity of years
and perceiving what tyranny had invaded the Church,
that he who would take orders must subscribe slave
and take an oath withal, which, unless he took with a
conscience that would retch, he must either straight
perjure or split his faith ; I thought it better to prefer a
blameless silence before the sacred office of speaking,
bought and begun with servitude and forswearing."
Milton left college to pursue his favorite studies of the
Greek and Roman classics, and occasionally to employ
his pen in those beautiful pieces of miscellaneous
poetry, which of themselves, are enough to render his

name immortal. His Comus, and his L'Allegro and Penseroso were written before he was twenty-seven years of age. When the civil troubles in England commenced, Milton, whose speculative opinions from the first strongly inclined to republicanism, was travelling on the Continent. Abandoning his intention of visiting Sicily and Greece, he returned home to share the labors and the fortunes of his friends who were battling for freedom. "I esteemed it dishonorable," he writes, "for me to be lingering abroad, even for the improvement of my mind, while my fellow citizens were contending for their liberty at home."

Milton, in London, entered with zeal and ardor into the work of defending, with his pen, the doctrines of intellectual and moral freedom, of civil and religious liberty, which were so thoroughly interwoven into his mental constitution, as to become the controlling faith of his life. His theatre of action and usefulness was neither in the camp nor the senate, but upon the broad field of political and theological controversy which the press then laid open to the intellect of the age. In 1643, at the age of thirty-five, Milton married Mary Powel, the daughter of a jovial country gentleman and zealous royalist. The serious manners and austere household of the Puritan, ill suited the gay and lively temper of the lady, and after a month of little happiness, as it may be imagined, to either party, she left his roof and returned again to her father. This matrimonial disagreement, was the practical argument, doubtless, which led his mind to

adopt those firm and unalterable opinions respecting
the lawfulness of divorce on the ground of disagreement and incompatibility of temper, which he never
surrendered, and which prompted him to compose and
publish his " Doctrine and Discipline of Divorce," and
other writings, wherein he ably sustained his peculiar
views.   His wife, however, again returned to him ;-
expressed penitence for her desertion, and was received
with kindness and affection.   She lived with him to
the day of her death, and left him three daughters.
Milton was afterwards twice married.

It is no part of our design in this brief sketch to
notice Milton's poetic compositions, or any of his volu-
minous and most neglected prose writings, except
simply to allude to the latter for the purpose of illustrating his political opinions, and the nature of the
services rendered by him to the popular cause. We
cannot pass by the *Areopagitica*, published in 1644,
when the Presbyterian majority, then in power, refused
to abolish the laws restraining the liberty of the press.
This noble defence of the liberty of unlicensed print-
ing, has justly been pronounced " a precious manual
of freedom, an arsenal of immortal weapons for the
defence of man's highest prerogative, intellectual
liberty."*   The same eloquent pen has traced in truthful lines the character of the poet, as it appeared in
vivid colors to the mind, whose benignity and great-

* Dr Channing.   Remarks on the Character and Writings of Milton,
vol. 1, p. 28.

ness our countrymen have not yet learned sufficiently to venerate.

"We see Milton's greatness of mind in his fervent and constant attachment to liberty. Freedom, in all its forms and branches, was dear to him; but especially freedom of thought and speech, of conscience and worship, freedom to speak, profess, and propagate truth. The liberty of ordinary politicians, which protects men's outward rights, and removes restraints from the pursuit of property and outward good, fell very short of that for which Milton lived and was ready to die. The tyranny which he hated most, was that which broke the intellectual and moral power of the community. The worst feature of the institutions which he assailed was, that they fettered the mind." In these elevated views of freedom, it is impossible not to admire the beautiful consistency and harmony existing between the views of Milton and those of his noble coadjutors in the cause in which he engaged, Sidney, Vane, and Marten.

The trial and execution of the king found no more decided advocate than Milton, not even Bradshaw himself. He justified it in a tract entitled the "Tenure of Kings and Magistrates," on the very title page of which he asserts the right to put "a tyrant or wicked king" to death, after due conviction of guilt, thus striking at the root of the king's objection to the competency and jurisdiction of the tribunal which condemned him.

Milton was a scholar of the most extensive and

varied learning. His attainments were now put in requisition by the new government, which appointed him secretary to the council for foreign tongues, an office which the zeal and patriotism of the poet did not suffer him to decline. Whitelocke in his Memoirs casually mentions the humble labors of Milton in this station, with a self-complacency which in our day may well provoke a smile. The foreign secretary to the council, he says, "*one Milton, a blind man,* was engaged in translating a treaty with Sweden." Strange to notice the singular changes wrought by time! The Lord Commissioner Bulstrode Whitelocke, ambassador to Sweden, eminent in his day alike as a jurist, a civilian, and a diplomatist, could look down with contempt at the obscure foreign secretary, and would have smiled at the presumption that imagined a name so humble was destined to be transmitted to posterity with a lustre equal to his own. And yet, among the many millions of civilized men in both hemispheres the very name of Whitelocke, is almost forgotten, while that of the great poet is repeated, from the palace to the meanest hovel, with reverence and admiration! The immortal epic of "Milton, the blind man," like the wonderful poem of that other blind man,

"Of Scio's rocky isle"—

the honor of whose birthplace was disputed by seven cities—was a work for all ages and all time, and has rendered its author's name immortal.

During his secretaryship Milton rendered valuable

services to the Commonwealth by his vigorous and energetic pen. The *Ikon Basiliké*, published by the royalists immediately after the king's death, and by some attributed to the pen of the king himself, produced a profound impression among the people. An answer from Milton's pen, entitled *Iconoclastes*, immediately appeared, in which the popular cause is sustained with convincing argument and triumphant success. This is considered one of the ablest of his political essays. Soon after appeared another royalist publication, *Defensio Regis*, by Salmasius; filled with the most bitter invective, and even scurrilous personalties, against the leaders of the popular party, and particularly against Milton himself. The secretary undertook to reply, and commenced his famous *Defensio pro Populo Anglicano*, a work of unanswerable power, kindled into a noble and lofty eloquence by the intense earnestness and glowing zeal of the writer, and by the greatness of the theme he discusses. If his ardor carried him beyond the bounds of propriety, if he indulged in too violent invective, and suffered himself to be betrayed into discreditable personal acrimony, it may be attributed to the nature of the controversy, to the grossly offensive challenge he had received, and to the excited temper and spirit which grew out of the times, and characterized all such disquisitions. Apart from these blemishes, the effort was a tribute fit for genius to lay upon the altar of liberty. When first appointed to his place, he had not yet become entirely blind—though intense study and literary labor had greatly impaired his sight.. His physicians distincly warned him that the consequence of this exertion would be the utter loss of sight.   Milton persisted.   His was not the same courage which nerves the soldier to meet death at the cannon's mouth; but it was a courage of a higher and nobler description, a serene, a self-sacrificing, an almost sublime heroism, which can only exist with true magnanimity of soul From his "Defence of the People of England," Milton arose blind.   The faith which sustained him through his labors, and the calm satisfaction with which, through his sore affliction, he was enabled to look back upon them, are beautifully expressed in that touching sonnet to his friend Cyriac Skinner—the spontaneous outburst of a heart whose warmest aspirations were for liberty.

> "Cyriac, this three years' day, these eyes, though clear,
>   To outward view, of blemish or of spot,
>   Bereft of light, their seeing have forgot;
>   Nor to their idle orbs doth sight appear
> Of sun, or moon, or star, throughout the year,
>   Or man or woman.   Yet I argue not
>   Against Heaven's hand or will, nor bate a jot
>   Of heart or hope, but still bear up and steer
> Right onward.   What supports me, doth thou ask?
>   The conscience, friend, to have lost them overplied
>   In liberty's defence; my noble task,
> Of which all Europe rings from side to side.
>   This thought might lead me through the world's vain mask,
>   Content, though blind, had I no better guide."

Milton acquired a high reputation both at home and abroad by this production.   The Parliament, as a recompense for his services, voted him a thousand pounds; it also granted him an allowance to maintain a table for the purpose of entertaining foreign ambassadors, and eminent literary strangers, on their arrival in England, which allowance was afterwards continued under Cromwell's government. Notwithstanding his loss of sight, his pen was employed with unwearied assiduity in the service of the Commonwealth. A year or two afterwards he published a second defence of the English people against an attack similar to that of Salmasius. From this paper the extract already quoted respecting Bradshaw is taken.

On Cromwell's rise to the supreme power, Milton continued in his office. His course, in this respect, has been censured, perhaps justly; yet it should be remembered that while the lofty independence of Vane, and the inflexible spirit of Sidney, scorned to accept favor or place under him whom they justly regarded as an usurper, the less pretending and humble sphere which Milton had filled might well appear to him the path of his present duty. Yet, in his place under the Protector, he sacrificed none of his independence or freedom of thought and action. The sonnet addressed by him to Cromwell, is too well known to be here repeated. In his second defence he addresses him in the language of friendly and frank admonition. "Recollect that thou thyself can'st not be free unless we are so; for it is fitly so provided in the nature of things, that he who conquers another's liberty in the very act loses his own; he becomes, and justly, the foremost slave."

The suffering of the Vaudois in the valleys of Piedmont deeply enlisted the sympathy of Milton, as indeed of the whole English people, and called from him the noble lines commencing:

> "Avenge, O Lord! thy slaughtered saints, whose bones
> Lie scattered on the Alpine mountains cold."

Milton himself conducted the negotiations which Cromwell carried on with the French ambassador; and so resolute was the Protector that he refused to sign the French treaty with Mazarin, until he had received satisfactory assurance that the interference of France had procured a general amnesty to the suffering Vaudois, and had restored these persecuted Christians to their ancient privileges.

It does not appear that Milton ever fell under the displeasure of Cromwell. His name is found among the five secretaries who formed part of the magnificent procession which followed the dead body of the Protector to Westminster Abbey. Ever true to his republican sentiments, he vigorously opposed the Restoration. On the occurrence of that event, it was to be expected that the author of " Iconoclastes" and the " Defences of the People," would be excluded from the general amnesty; but, strangely enough, his name was not found in the act. He was, however, arrested in the place where he had taken refuge, but was released, it is said, by the friendly interference of Sir William

Davenant, to whom he had been of service on an occasion of similar danger. Reduced to poverty, Milton now retired to a humble and obscure residence in London, married his third wife, and, separated entirely from the excitement and asperities of political controversies, applied himself to literary pursuits during the remainder of his life, which closed in 1674, in the sixty-sixth year of his age. During the first years of his retirement, his mind was engrossed with the composition of that sublime poem which has immortalized his name. Milton doubtless wrote it with the consciousness that posterity alone was to appreciate its merits. A small and unpretending volume, entitled " Paradise Lost," on which the publisher had ventured to advance five pounds, first appeared in 1667. The wits of Buckingham Palace and Whitehall sneered at the book, if indeed they met with it at all, and the men of letters as well as the courtiers of that and the succeeding reign, turned with affected disgust from the writings of an author who had penned the answer to Salmasius. The noblest genius can never soar above the combined influence of political animosity and a corrupt taste ; and it is not therefore strange that for many years the Paradise Lost should have found no place in English literature. The work of the despised republican, whose memory was assailed with the same rancorous ferocity which assailed the memory of his dead kinsman, whose head graced the top of Westminster Hall—of the man whose political writings, with Buchanan's and Baxter's, the University of

Oxford ordered to be publicly burned, was at that day undeserving even of criticism. No wonder is it that the Paradise Lost was so long treated with neglect, in an age when wits and men of letters would turn aside from the brilliant satire of Dryden, to gloat over the ribald jests of Rochester and the licentious comedy of Wycherly. The prejudice extended even beyond that better era which marked the downfall of the house of Stuart; and it was not till a succeeding reign, that the cultivated mind and refined taste of an Addison drew Milton from his obscurity, and placed him on the eminence he now occupies, by the side of Homer, of Virgil, and of Dante—foremost among the greatest poetic geniuses of antiquity or of modern times.

HENRY MARTEN, or as he is more familiarly called, Harry Marten,* was one of the most active and decided of the republican statesmen of that day. Not only was he a statesman and a man of genius, but a scholar and a wit. Although his character is not wholly without blemish, yet there is much in it to respect and admire. His errors and failings, for the most part, were those into which he was betrayed by an impulsive temper and a convivial disposition. Marten was, in taste and by nature, a cavalier; and doubtless he

---

* So Marten styled himself. On his trial he denied that his name was in the act excepting him from pardon. The clerk, on producing the act, read the name " Henry Marten," to which he replied—" Henry Marten? my name is not so; it is Harry Marten." The Court overruled his objection.

would have been so by association, had not his republican theories and his enthusiastic notions of liberty led him from the first day of his public life to go hand in hand with those who went farthest in the popular cause. He had no feeling in common with the religious austerity of the Puritans, and yet with the Puritans he labored zealously in the common cause. His vivacity, his-joyous, mercurial disposition, his fondness for conviviality, and the elegant luxuries of a society that Puritanism did not tolerate, made him the very antipode of such men as Cromwell, Vane, and Bradshaw; and yet these men were not only his intimate political associates, but his friends; whose strict manners and stern morality Marten could respect and esteem, while they in turn could pass by in silence, or complacently listen to, the witty and sometimes reckless sallies which fell from the lips of one whose fidelity to the popular cause had been so thoroughly tried, and whose genius and eloquence had rendered such signal services to the Commonwealth. Marten, says Aubrey, was " as far from a Puritan as light from darkness." Bishop Burnet says of him that he never entered into matters of religion; that he "was all his life a most violent enemy of monarchy, but all that he moved for was upon Greek and Roman principles." Upon this view of his character, sustained as it is by Mr. Hume, who classes him with Challoner, Harrington and those whom he calls *the Deists* of the Revolution, or as Cromwell styled them, the "heathen," Marten and his associates have been likened to the Girondins in the French Convention, who deified liberty, and whose imaginations, glowing with the inspiration kindled by the study of antiquity, saw arising upon the ruins of feudalism their own ideal republic. Marten's gaiety of temper and brilliancy of conversation are noticed by one of his inveterate enemies, old Anthony Wood, whose pen very rarely indulged in anything respecting him but abuse. We quote a passage, the latter part of which, perhaps, may be a calumny:

" He was a man of good natural parts, a boon familiar, witty and quick with repartees ; was exceedingly happy in apt instances, pertinent and very biting, so that his company being esteemed incomparable by many, would have been acceptable to the greatest persons, only he would be drunk too soon, and so put an end to all the mirth for the present."

One or two specimens of Marten's repartee and "apt instances" may be given, as we find them in the pages of an entertaining modern writer,* collected from various sources. In drawing the remonstrances of the army which changed the monarchy to a commonwealth, Marten used the expression "RESTORED to its ancient government of commonwealth." A member arose to reprimand him for asserting the antiquity of the Commonwealth. Marten whimsically replied—" There was a text which had often troubled his spirit, concerning the man who was blind from his mother's womb, but

* Forster. Statesmen of the Commonwealth. Life of Marten.

at length whose sight was *restored* to the sight which
he should have had."

On another occasion Cromwell, in the heat of some
debate, called his old friend " Sir Harry Marten."
The wit arose, and bowing very gravely, replied—" I
thank *your majesty*, I always thought when you were
king, that I should be *knighted.*"

A Puritan member, offended at some light remark
dropped by Marten, suggested that it would be well to
have a motion to expel " all profane and unsanctified
persons." To this Marten replied, in a serious tone,
that he should move " that all fools might be put out
likewise, and then the House might probably be found
thin enough."

His pleasantry did not desert him in the darkest
and most trying hour of his life. In the petition for
a reprieve, which he presented on being condemned to
death with the regicides, he observes that he had surrendered himself upon the king's " declaration of Breda,"
and that since " he had never obeyed any royal proclamation before this, he hoped that he should not be
hanged for taking the king's word now."

The father of Marten, the most eminent civilian of
his day, had left him a large fortune, which, says
Anthony Wood, "his ungodly son, Harry, squandered
away." A large share of it, however, it should have
been added, was squandered in the service of the public, he having contributed to the Parliament on one
occasion the sum of £3000. Becoming embarrassed
in his circumstances, he presented a petition praying

the settlement of his arrears as colonel in the army, but it was not very speedily acted upon. On this occasion Marten, having heard that some recent unworthy appointments had been made, remarked— " That he had seen at last the Scripture fulfilled: ' Thou hast exalted the humble and the meek : thou hast filled the empty with good things, but the rich thou hast sent empty away.' "

Marten was elected to the Long Parliament from the county of Berks, having been also a member of the Parliament which met in April of that year. His reputation for learning and ability was already established, and he soon, by his forensic talent placed himself in the foremost rank as a parliamentary debater. " His speeches," says Aubrey, " were not long, but wondrous poignant, pertinent, and witty." He had contracted friendships with the most eminent men of the day, Pym, Hampden, Fiennes, and Hyde, afterwards Lord Clarendon. It is unnecessary to say that his theoretic opinions, at this early day, were decidedly republican, though he found no proper occasion to avow them publicly. In a private interview, however, with Hyde, he did not hesitate, with that frankness and freedom of speech so natural to him, to express his disapprobation of the monarchical principle. " I do not think," he says, " one man wise enough to govern us all." The future lord-chancellor was shocked at the sentiments which had so early entered " into the hearts of some *desperate* persons," and left him without reply. So resolute was Marten's opposition to all the arbitrary measures of Charles, that on the breaking out of the civil war, he was, with Pym, Hampden, and Hollis, specially excepted from pardon in the king's proclamation. But he resolutely and steadily continued his opposition to the royalists and the royal cause, and was the very first man in England publicly to avow his preference for a republican form of government, and to declare upon the floor of the House, that "it were better one family should be destroyed than many." On being questioned to explain whom he meant, Marten boldly answered, "The king and his children!" For this he was expelled the House and committed to the Tower, although his friend Pym, while he disapproved the language, endeavored in vain to extenuate it. Marten was a prisoner only two weeks, but he did not resume his seat in the House until a year and a half afterwards. From that time to the period of Cromwell's usurpation of the government, his name is intimately blended with every great public measure of the day, and is found inseparably associated with the names of Vane, Sidney, Scot, Bradshaw, and St. John. The political views of Marten were those entertained in common by these illustrious men, and the great measures of public policy they advocated found in him a ready and most efficient supporter. Perhaps in his speculative views of social progress and political equality, in his theory of a pure republican government and institutions, he may have gone beyond the more sober views of some of his associates, and have

sympathised too deeply with the speculations of **Harrington**, the author of the "Oceana," or of Neville,*
the author of the "Plato Redivivus;" but in all *his actions* Marten was the wise and practical statesman,
and the firm, steady, and consistent friend of free institutions.   In his views of a full and ample religious
toleration, he went beyond some even of the most liberal of the Independents.   There was no fetter to the
intellect and conscience, no restriction upon creed or
race, that he was not willing to remove; and to his lasting honor be it said, that he was the first to propose a
repeal of the statute against the Jews, who for three
hundred and fifty years in England had been a proscribed and persecuted race.   A higher and more
honorable mention still is made of him as a legislator,
that when mercy was to be shown, or an act of liberal
or kind-hearted justice done, Henry Marten was sure
to be found not wanting.

If he trusted too far to the good faith and sincerity
of Cromwell, he was the first to acknowledge his
error.   If he made a mistake in countenancing the
military outrage of Col. Pride against the Presbyterian majority in the Parliament, he amply atoned for
it by his noble conduct on the day of the dissolution
by Cromwell, when with Vane and Sidney, he indignantly turned his back on the usurper, and abandoned
him forever.   Nor did Marten ever recognize his government; and though subsequently imprisoned, he

* These also are classed by Hume with Sidney and Marten among the
Deists of the Revolution.

firmly refused to acknowledge his power or yield to his authority.

On the trial of the king, Marten was a member of the commission, and, with the exception of Cromwell, the most active and influential member of the high court of justice. During the whole of the prior proceedings, no one contributed so much toward preparing the way for the Commonwealth. He was upon the committee to prepare charges against the king; he was a member of the executive government, and concerted all the measures, with Ireton and others, for altering the regal insignia into the symbols of a republic. To Cromwell's question what answer they should give the king, when he asked them by what authority he was to be tried, Marten replied—"In the name of the Commons and Parliament assembled, and all the good people of England." Marten sat through the whole of the trial, and was one of the fifty-nine commissioners who signed their names to the death-warrant. On this occasion a scene is recorded between Cromwell and Marten, which certainly exhibits an unbecoming levity of character on the part of both, at such a time, and in the execution of so stern a duty. Cromwell, having signed his name, laughingly marked Marten's face with the pen, which Marten, in the same spirit, returned. It was charged against Marten at his trial, as an evidence of malice, that this was done " merrily and in great sport." " That does not imply malice," the prisoner quietly replied.

Marten was elected a member of the executive

council in the new Commonwealth ; and certainly no one exhibited greater ability in setting in motion the new machinery of the government. He introduced a bill for the sale of the royal property, including the king's lands, regalia, furniture, jewelry, and paintings, and assisted in organizing the courts of justice under the new order of things. At the re-assembling of the Long Parliament on the abdication of Richard Cromwell, Marten re-appeared upon the scene, and made his last stand for a commonwealth against the designs of the traitor General Monk. At the restoration, he was excepted, as to life and property, out of the act of indemnity and oblivion ; and in October, 1660, was brought to trial, at the Old Bailey, before the thirty-six commissioners appointed to try the regicides. Among these commissioners sat Marten's old friend Hyde, now lord-chancellor, eager to shed the blood of the colleague by whose side, twenty years before, he had sat in the Long Parliament. Sir Anthony Ashley Cooper, formerly an active Parliament man, afterwards one of the godly members of the "Barebone Parliament," now a zealous royalist, sat by the side of the double traitor, General Monk, Duke of Albemarle, who had fought for and against the king. It is humiliating to find also on that judgment seat, Hollis, who, with the prisoner at the bar, had been excepted by name from the general pardon proclaimed by Charles ; and even the Earl of Manchester, under whose victorious banner Cromwell and Sidney had fought at Marston Moor. The defence of Marten on his trial was dignified, but mild and conciliatory. He regretted the blood shed in the civil war, and the death of the king, but justified his conduct on the ground that he acted on what he supposed a lawful authority. As to King Charles II., he avowed his willingness to pay him obedience so long as the representative body supported him. The mildness of his defence, however, availed him nothing on his trial ; he was convicted, and sentenced to be executed. The sentence would, undoubtedly, have been carried into effect, had not the numerous friends of Marten, who, in palmier days, shared his conviviality and enjoyed the charms of his society, made great interest for him in the House of Lords. He had not hurled defiance at his judges on the trial, as did some of the regicides, and since his conviction he had manifested a submission that the court mistook for penitence. His sentence was accordingly commuted to *imprisonment for life.* He lingered twenty years, and died in prison. Toward the close of his life, the old man was asked whether if the deed were to be done again, he would sign the warrant for the execution of Charles I. With a firm voice he answered, " Yes." The poet Southey, *before* he became the laureate of George IV., wrote an inscription for the apartment in which Marten was confined, containing the following noble lines :

> " Dos't thou ask *his crime ?*
> He had rebelled against a king, and sat
> In judgment on him—for his ardent mind
> Shaped goodliest plans of happiness on earth,

And peace and liberty. Wild dreams!
But such as Plato loved; such as with holy zeal
Our Milton worshipped. Blest hopes! Awhile
From man withheld even to the latter days,
When Christ shall come and all things be fulfilled."

A different fate was that of Marten's heroic friend
and colleague, THOMAS SCOT. It is impossible to conceive of a man of greater nerve, and of a more inflexible courage, physical or moral, than Scot. He was a
member of the Long Parliament, an ardent and enthusiastic republican, the friend of Sidney, Vane, Marten,
and Bradshaw. He sat in the high court of justice as
one of the commissioners to try the king. In the new
government, Scot's well-known integrity and great devotion to the public interest, were such as to cause
him to be selected, with Edmund Ludlow and three
others, to choose the new council of state. With
Bradshaw he took his seat as a member of Oliver
Cromwell's Parliament, where, with the same energy
that had marked his efforts for the popular cause in the
Long Parliament, he assailed the arbitrary measures of
the Protector. Portions of Scot's speeches in Oliver's
Parliaments, and in the Parliament of the Protector
Richard, yet remain. They prove that he was a man
of undoubted ability, gifted with a nervous and lofty
eloquence, and unquestionably one of the most accomplished debaters of the day. His mind was impulsive
and ardent. Sometimes his ardor betrayed him into a
too impassioned declamation. A tone of fierce defiance,
of fiery sarcasm, breathes through his sentences ; but

withal there is a dignity, and often a startling majesty of expression in his language, which must have arrested the attention of every hearer. "Shall I," he exclaimed in a speech against Cromwell's House of Lords, "shall I, that sat in a Parliament which brought a king to the bar and the block, not speak my mind freely here?" And again—"The lords would not join in the trial of the king. We must lay things bare and naked. We were either to lay all that blood of ten years' war upon ourselves or upon some other object. We called the king of England to our bar and arraigned him. He was, for his obstinacy and guilt, condemned and executed; and so let all the enemies of God perish!"

"I am not ashamed of the title," he exclaims a few days after, referring to the title given the House by Cromwell's quasi "lords." "It is not enough that they christen themselves, but they christen you—that you are 'Commons.' I am not ashamed of the title, it being the greatest honor under heaven to serve the people in the meanest capacity in this house, *all power being originally in the people.*"

No one act of his whole life, did Scot more boldly and proudly justify, everywhere, and on all occasions, than the condemnation of Charles Stuart. In Richard Cromwell's Parliament, while battling by the side of Vane, against the resolution which recognized the "undoubted right" of the Protector, and striving to bring back the government to the simple form of a republic, as it had existed before the usurpation of

Oliver. He thus vindicated his motives and his con .
duct on the trial of the king: " It was impossible to
continue him alive. I wish all had heard the grounds
of our resolutions in that particular. I would have
had all our consultings *in foro* as anything else was.
It was resorted to as the last refuge. The representatives, in their aggregate body, *have power to alter or
change any government*, being thus conducted by
Providence. The question was—whose was that
blood that was shed? It could not be ours. Was it
not the king's by keeping delinquents from punishment and raising armies? The vindictive justice
must have his sacrifice somewhere. The king was
called to a bar below to answer for that blood. WE
DID NOT ASSASSINATE, OR DO IT IN A CORNER. WE DID
IT IN THE FACE OF GOD AND OF ALL MEN."

And subsequently, in another speech in the same
Parliament, Scot delivered this impassioned exclamation—" I would be content it should be set on my
monument—if it were my last act I own it—I WAS
ONE OF THE KING'S JUDGES! I hope it shall not be said
of us as of the Romans once—*O homines ad servitu-
tem parati !*"

But the hope of the indomitable republican was
doomed to disappointment. A few brief months revealed to him the disheartening truth that the English
people, like the degenerate Romans, were already prepared for slavery. Scot re-assembled with his intrepid
associates in the Long Parliament; and during the
brief period of the restoration of the Commonwealth,

endeavored to counteract the popular revulsion which was rapidly bearing the nation onward to monarchy. When Monk had marched his army upon London, when the restoration of the monarchy was resolved on, and the Long Parliament was about finally to dissolve, many of the Presbyterian members desired to exculpate themselves, and make their peace with the returning royalists, by passing a resolution denouncing the "horrid murder" of the late king. One weak-spirited member arose to protest that he had neither hand nor heart in that affair. Then Scot stood up—his spirit unconquered and unyielding, amid the wreck of all the hopes he had cherished for freedom—and with a stern, moral courage, that may well be called heroic, fearlessly avowed his participation in the deed: "Though I know not where to hide my head at this time, yet I dare not refuse to own, that not only my hand, but my heart also, was in it!" They were the last words he uttered in Parliament. With his fellow "regicides," he was dragged to the bar of the Old Bailey, and arraigned for high treason. The heroism of his defence was worthy the intrepidity of his whole public career. With proud exultation he justified his conduct on the principle he had always avowed, that with the people rested the sovereign power to alter or change their government, and to bring their rulers to account; and far from craving or expecting mercy, he hurled an almost fierce defiance at his judges and the royal authority. Nor did he shrink from avowing on the scaffold his unalterable devotion to the cause for which he suffered. He blessed God " that of his free grace he had engaged him in a cause, not to be repented of—I say in A CAUSE not to be repented of——." Here the sheriff interfered, and the sentence died away on the lips of the martyred regicide !

It would be pursuing this digression too far should we notice, in detail, all the eminent contemporaries of Sidney, who united with him in establishing and sustaining the Commonwealth. We must therefore pass over the names of such men as BLAKE, the illustrious admiral, whose flag never declined the challenge of an enemy ; of FAIRFAX, the resolute and able commander-in-chief of the armies of the Parliament ; of LUDLOW, the frank-hearted and valiant soldier, and the honest and consistent republican ; of Cromwell's kinsman, OLIVER ST. JOHN, lord chief justice of England, decidedly one of the ablest statesmen of the age, who, though he subsequently adhered to the Protector's government, yet with Vane, Marten, and Bradshaw, rendered the noblest service to the popular cause. One name, however, stands out too prominent and illustrious on the annals of that period, to be passed over in silence—it is the name of HENRY IRETON, the splendor of whose talents gave promise of the most noble services, and whose premature fate has been universally regretted by all who sympathize with the popular cause.

IRETON was bred to the bar. It is remarkable that the great mass of the legal profession, and the most learned and able members of that profession, adhered to the Parliament and the cause of the people ;

although some of them, such as Maynard, Glyn, and Cooper, subsequently suffered themselves to be made the tools of royalty. Among the eminent lawyers who sustained the popular side during either the common wealth or the protectoral government, (besides the names just mentioned,) were Sir Matthew Hale, Selden, Whitelocke, St. John, Rolle, Aske, Coke, Bradshaw, and Nicholas.

Having joined the parliamentary army, Ireton soon acquired the entire confidence of Cromwell, whose daughter Bridget he married. On the remodelling of the army, and the appointment of Fairfax, general-in-chief, with Cromwell as his lieutenant and general of the horse, Ireton was named one of the twenty-six colonels. More fortunate than Sidney, who received his appointment at the same time, Ireton was enabled at once to take the field under Cromwell, and joining the army of Fairfax, participated in the decisive battle of Naseby. Cromwell's faculty in the discrimination of character was no less remarkable than Napoleon's. No one more thoroughly understood or justly appreciated the great qualities of Ireton and the superiority of his genius. Indeed, if he had a confidant in the world—if there was one man to whom, without reserve, the inner workings of that incomprehensible mind were laid open—that man was Ireton. There was no person in the army, or out of the army, on whose judgment and counsels the lord general so firmly relied, as upon his able and accomplished son-in-law. In the great battle of Naseby, though Fairfax

was nominally commander-in-chief, Cromwell was in
reality the master spirit, and made the principal arrangements for the fight. At his instance Fairfax
conferred on Ireton, upon the field, the rank of com-
missary-general, and entrusted to him the important
command of the left wing of the army. Cromwell
himself held the right, and Fairfax and Skippon com
manded the centre. The conduct of Ireton upon that
day was the conduct not only of an able and skillful
commander, but of a hero. He was placed in the
hottest part of the battle, to face the charge of Rupert
and his cavalry ; nor had Cromwell over-estimated the
indomitable courage of the lion-hearted soldier. His
command, it is true, yielded before that terrible charge,
which never, save by Cromwell, was successfully resisted, but Ireton, with desperate valor rallied it
again and again to the contest. It was not till
he was carried a prisoner, wounded and insensible, from the field, that the left wing was finally
routed. But the day was not lost while Cromwell's
Ironsides remained unbroken. The great general, by
one of those rapid and overwhelming movements which
so often turned the scale of battle, retrieved the fortune of the day, rescued the wounded Ireton from the
hands of the enemy, and routed the whole royal army
with great slaughter. The star of Charles' fortune
went down on that field of blood forever !

Ireton's conduct in war was, on all occasions, equal
to his gallantry at Naseby fight. In the expedition
against Ireland, Cromwell chose him his second in

command, and at the close of the campaign left him
in the government of that kingdom. Here Ireton displayed his usual ability, both in the field and in the
administration of the government. Even Hume is
forced to admit his great capacity, and his " strict
execution of justice in that unlimited command which
he possessed in Ireland." The same historian, while
he sneers at what he calls the facility with which
Ireton was able " to graft the soldier on the lawyer,
the statesman on the saint," renders to his memory
the somewhat equivocal tribute of saying that " *it was
believed by many* that he was animated by a sincere
and passionate love of liberty, and never could have
been induced, by any motive to submit to the smallest
appearance of regal government." Hume does not
state whether he shared in this belief; but we
think it evident that he little appreciated or sympathized with that Roman integrity and virtue, that stern
and inflexible devotion to republican principle, which so
elevate the character of Ireton in the eyes of mankind.

The genius of Ireton, though it shone with resplen-
dent lustre on the field, was far better adapted to the
pursuits of the civilian, or the statesman, than to
those of the soldier. Before Cromwell found him en-
rolled as a " captain in Col. Thornhaugh's regiment,"
and while yet a young man at the bar, he had projected various legal and constitutional reforms, of an
original and striking character. But at the commencement of the civil wars, he laid aside the toga for the

cuirass; and with the same readiness, he quitted the field for the floor of Parliament.

The singular influence he possessed over Cromwell, has been noticed.* While Ireton lived, and shared the lord-general's counsels, the latter remained true and steadfast to the cause of the Commonwealth. Ireton was the connecting link which bound Cromwell to the republicans. It appears, however, that just before his death, he began to suspect the ambitious designs of the lord-general. Mrs. Hutchinson states that Ireton had actually determined to return to England, in order to divert Cromwell from his destructive course. Who shall say what different phase might have been given to the great struggle for English liberty, had not death untimely ended the career of one of its noblest champions !

Ireton was elected to Parliament during the same year with Sidney. One cannot help imagining that kindred political sentiments served to cement a friendship between two young men of characters in many respects so similar. It is impossible to speak here of the many, and varied, and eminent services rendered by Ireton to the cause, during his legislative career. It may be mentioned, however, that he was one of the most determined and resolute of those who urged on the trial of the king ; a proceeding whose stern justice

---

* Whitelocke says of him—"Cromwell had a great opinion of him, and no man could prevail so much or order him so far, as Ireton could. He was stout in the field, and wary and prudent in his counsel, and exceedingly forward as to the business of a commonwealth."

—whatever may be thought of its expediency—we have the less reason to doubt, from the very fact of its being advocated by one of a mind so pure, and a character so disinterested. With Marten, he was on the most important committees for effecting the necessary change in government. With Cromwell and Bradshaw, he was on the judgment seat that sent his sovereign to the block. Indeed, Bishop Burnet shields Cromwell, and throws upon Ireton the chief responsibility. " Ireton was the person," he says, " that drove it on ; for Cromwell was all the while in some suspense about it. Ireton had the principles and the temper of a Cassius ; he stuck at nothing that might have turned England to a Commonwealth." The same Roman virtue and resolution, who can doubt, would have stuck at nothing to have prevented that Commonwealth, once established, from being overthrown, even though its betrayer had been the friend in whom Ireton had trusted. One instance of the disinterested nature of Ireton's patriotism, is preserved by Ludlow, and may be here related. The Parliament, after the battle of Worcester, voted pensions and estates to several who had made pecuniary sacrifices in its cause, and among others, an estate of two thousand a year to Ireton. Alone, of all, he refused to take it, saying to the Parliament, in reply, that " they had many just debts which he desired they would pay, before they made any such presents." Soon after this he died suddenly in Ireland, of the plague, in the prime of life, aged about forty years. His death was a melancholy affliction to Cromwell, who both admired and loved him.   His dead body, at the instance of the lord-general, was brought from Ireland, and laid, with magnificent funeral ceremonies, at the public charge, in Westminster Abbey, among the tombs of kings, there to remain, till the saturnalia of the Restoration, when his sepulchre was violated, and his bones hung up by the side of Cromwell and Bradshaw, upon a gibbet at Tyburn—the three malefactors, whose names were, of all others, most odious and detestable to the royalists.

After the dissolution of the Long Parliament, Sidney remained in retirement at Penshurst.   Like Vane and Marten, he refused to sanction the legality of Cromwell's government, by accepting any office.   At the close of the war between Holland and England, in 1654, he went over a second time to the Hague. Through Beverningk, the Dutch ambassador, whom he had known in London, he became acquainted with many of the celebrated men of that country, and among others, with that truly great and virtuous statesman, JOHN DE WITT.   De Witt was, at that time, Grand Pensionary of Holland.   Though yet a young man, three years the junior of Sidney, he had acquired a reputation famous throughout Europe—a reputation which a subsequent brilliant career exalted, and which has become, deservedly, the most illustrious in the political annals of his country.   He was the son of a burgomaster of Dort.   From his father he inherited republican principles, and hostility to the

House of Orange. On the death of the Prince of Orange, in 1650, De Witt, then just entering upon public life, firmly and successfully opposed the project of raising the infant son of the Prince of Orange to the stadtholdership. By his ability and eloquence, he maintained the influence of Holland in the Councils of the United Provinces, and secured to his country the blessings of free and popular institutions.

Though he had zealously labored to avert the calamity of a war with England, yet, when that war came on, he exhausted the resources of a mind singularly fertile in invention, to crown the arms of his country with triumph, and to bring the contest to a successful close. It is a fact worthy of remark, that the two ablest statesmen in Europe—Sir Harry Vane, in England, and John De Witt, in the United Provinces—were at the head of the foreign departments of the two republics during this unnatural war. The contest was carried on upon the ocean; but with De Witt in her cabinet, and Van Tromp and De Ruyter in command of her fleets, Holland was not yet destined to lose the trident of the seas. Through the influence of De Witt, whose abilities had raised him to the office of Grand Pensionary, the war, so ably conducted on the part of the States, was brought to a close. Holland returned to the peaceful pursuits of her commerce and industry; her republican institutions seemed based upon the most enduring foundations; she was preparing to inscribe in her annals a

glorious chapter, with which the name of this, her noblest son, was destined to be forever associated.

It was at this period that Sidney first met De Witt. The intercourse of two such minds, is a fact worthy of note in the history of both. The speculative thoughts which the one meditated in his closet, were precisely the thoughts which the other was laboring practically to apply in his sphere of public duty. They were men who could appreciate and understand each other. Sidney's was a character which De Witt could not fail to admire and esteem ; to the English republican, the Dutch minister doubtless appeared such as years afterwards Mr. Fox described him—" the wisest, the best, and most truly patriotic minister that ever appeared upon the stage."

Such, indeed, was John De Witt—the melancholy catastrophe of whose death almost demonstrates the discouraging maxim that republics are ungrateful. For twenty years he served his country with a conscientious rectitude, and an ardor of patriotism that has never been excelled. The profound genius of the man we can estimate only by the great deeds he achieved. During the second war with England, which he again labored unsuccessfully to avert, he was the soul of those stupendous exertions which pervaded every branch of the Dutch marine. He crowded the harbors and whitened the seas with the fleets of the republic. Defeat itself seemed only to endow him with new energy, and develope in him new resources. The waves had scarcely closed over the shattered r mains of one armament, ere another sprang up, as if by magic, to supply its place. Rupert and Monk had scarcely borne back to England the news of a triumph over the enemy, ere the startled citizens of London heard the thunder of De Ruyter's cannon from the Thames. His comprehensive mind took in at a glance, the broadest principles and the minutest details of government. His abilities made him master of every branch of the public service. When occasion required, he took command of the fleet in person, and by the novelty and value of his inventions,* and the improvements he introduced, in this new sphere of action, proved that his genius was not only original and profound, but universal. His magnanimity was displayed in accepting the tuition of the young Prince of Orange, a trust which he executed with scrupulous fidelity and care. The wisdom and discernment of the prince, still a mere boy, was no less remarkable, in consenting to receive instructions from one who, though the first statesman of his country, he might regard, as in some sort, his hereditary enemy. It is not too much to say that the philosophical and enlightened instructions of De Witt, and above all the example of his exalted virtues and patriotism, contributed much to the formation of the character of a king, to whose wisdom and ability England is so largely indebted for the liberty she this day enjoys.

The fate of this wise and virtuous republican magistrate, has been truly characterized as one of the most completely discouraging examples which history

* The invention of chain-shot is ascribed to De Witt.

affords to the lovers of liberty. After more than twenty years of public service, he was driven from the station he had filled, by one of those sudden revulsions of public feeling which is engendered by despair, at a moment of fearful danger to his country, when the most powerful nations in Europe were leagued for her destruction, and when such services and such fidelity as his, were most needed. Visiting his brother privately in prison, the popular wrath fell upon the head of the devoted minister. The furious mob dragged the illustrious victims from the place of their retreat, and literally tore them in pieces. Such was the inglorious martyrdom of De Witt; a sacrifice to the insane fury of the populace, whom he had so long and so faithfully served—immolated by a blinded democracy at the very shrine which his own hands had consecrated to liberty.

On his return from the Hague in 1654, Sidney again retired to Penshurst, and, except for an occasional excursion to London, or a visit to his relative, the Earl of Northumberland, at his seat in Sussex, he rarely left his retreat. He devoted much of his time to literary pursuits, and to those dignified and philosophical speculations upon history and political ethics, which were so congenial to his taste. An *Essay on Love*, found among his papers, is supposed to have been written during this period. His *Commonplace Book*, preserved in the library at Penshurst, is said to exhibit a copious store of materials collected from the political history of all civilized nations, illustrative of every branch of policy and government. It is thought that the materials for his great work, the *Discourses on Government*, were, at this early period, collected and partially arranged, and that the imperfect papers produced at his trial, a part of the same design, were also written during his residence at Penshurst.*

Constant to the principles he had adopted, Sidney still refused to acknowledge the Protector's government. Though his friends Bradshaw and Scot did not hesitate to appear among the ranks of the opposition in Cromwell's Parliament, he himself embraced other views of duty, and continued to regard an entire seclusion from public affairs as the course most consistent with his own sense of propriety. His eldest brother, Philip, Lord Lisle, adhered to the Protector, and was one of his warmest partisans. Lisle had been summoned by Cromwell as a member of the " Barebone Parliament," and so highly did he acquire the lord-general's confidence, that on the installation of the protectoral government, he was named the first upon the Council of State. He seems to have taken great umbrage at the contempt and disgust which Sidney manifested toward the Protector and his government. On one occasion Sidney, to relieve the dulness which reigned at Penshurst, and to amuse his lordship's household, managed to get up a lay, which, either by accident or design, reflected severely upon the Protector. The indignation of his brother could no longer be restrained. In a letter to the

* Meadley's Memoirs, p. 57.

Earl of Leicester, under date of June 17th, 1656, he thus expresses himself :—

" In my poor opinion, the business of your lordship's house hath passed somewhat unluckily, and that it had been better used to do a seasonable courtesy to the Lord Protector, than to have had such a play acted in it, of public affront, which doth much entertain the town. I have been in some places where they told me they were exceedingly pleased with the gallant relation of *the chief actor* in it, and that by applauding him they put him several times upon it."

The play is thought to have been Shakspeare's *Julius Cæsar*, Sidney,—" the chief actor,"—sustaining the part of Marcus Brutus. The dissatisfaction of his brother was increased by the suspicion that Algernon was the favorite son of his father. The old earl, on all occasions, manifested towards him an affection and confidence which awakened the keen jealousy of the eldest son and heir. In the same letter, Lisle does not pretend to conceal his spleen and mortification, and even indulges in some very unworthy reflections on his brother :—

" I have my constant sorrow to see that your lordship never omits an opportunity to reproach me ; and in earnest I think, laying all other matters aside, this, which hath appeared most eminently upon this occasion, is very extraordinary, that *the youngest son* should so domineer in the house, that not only in regard to this matter, which I have spoken of, but at all times, I am uncertain whether I can have the liberty to look into it or not; for it seems it is not his chamber, but the great rooms of the house, and perhaps the whole, he commands, and upon this occasion, I may most properly say it, that *his extremest vanity and want of judgment* are so known that there will be some wonder at it."

Sidney was recalled from his retirement by the downfall of the protectoral government, and the summoning together on the 7th of May, 1659, of the members of that Parliament which Cromwell had dissolved. Here he met his old associates, Vane, Marten, Scot, and the other chiefs of the republican party. Sidney co-operated with them in their first act, the passage of a resolution to secure the liberty and property of the people, and to administer the government without "a single person, kingship, or a House of Lords." The forms of the Commonwealth were once more revived; the republic was for a brief season re-established; the statesmen of the revolution were again at the helm. Sidney took his place in the Executive Council of the government. He remained in it, however, but a brief period. Within a month after the Parliament assembled, he was called to a new sphere of duty, and to the performance of other and no less responsible services in behalf of the Commonwealth. He accepted the trust, and resigned his seat in the Council and House. His legislative career closed forever.

It is unnecessary to trace the counter revolution

which overthrew the Commonwealth and brought in
the king. That the Parliament was decrepid and
powerless ; that it had outlived the public sentiment
which had formerly sustained it ; that the people were
wearied with these frequent changes in the government ; that a strong re-action had taken place in the
public mind in favor of royalty, is evident from the
events which so rapidly followed. The golden moment had gone by when the Republic might have
been established. The soul of the Commonwealth lay
entombed in the grave of Cromwell. Monk marched
his army from Scotland to the city of London. He
found the republican party broken, discordant, and
aimless. The noblest of them, in the front rank of
whom stood VANE, made a stout resistance ; but resistance was idle. Monk, at the head of his army,
acted the dictator, as Cromwell had done. He declared
for a " free Parliament." All London, we are told,
was wild with joy ; the streets blazed with bonfires ;
the gutters ran with ale. The king was invited back
" to enjoy his own again," and raised without conditions to the throne. In a moment of enthusiastic
loyalty and blind folly, the people of England surrendered, unreservedly, to Charles II., the liberties
which the swords of the Puritans had wrung from the
reluctant hands of his father.

CHAPTER IV.

HAVING accepted the mission conferred on him by
Parliament, Sidney at once entered on the discharge

of its duties. In conjunction with Whitelocke and Sir Robert Honeywood, who were appointed to act with him, he was charged to mediate a peace between the kings of Denmark and Sweden. Whitelocke was unwilling to undertake the service, by reason, as he alleged, of his old age and infirmities, but really, as it seems, out of jealousy. He had been sent by Cromwell sole ambassador to the Queen of Sweden, and he could not brook the thought of acting a subordinate part at the same court. "I well knew," he observes in his Memoirs, "*the overruling temper and height of Col. Sidney.*" Whitelocke thereupon declined the appointment, and Thomas Boone, a merchant of London, was named one of the commissioners in his stead. It appears manifest, however, that Sidney had the chief control of the negotiations, and that he derived very little aid from the counsels of his associates.

This mission was one of much importance to both England and Holland, as a peace between their allies, Denmark and Sweden, would secure to both nations the free navigation of the Sound. Accordingly the States General united with England in the appointment of plenipotentiaries to negotiate a peace. The English commissioners set out early in July, 1659, and arrived at Elsineur on the 21st of the same month. Admiral Montagu, afterwards Earl of Sandwich, was then in command of the English fleet lying in the Sound. The officers of the several ships, who had been apprised of the change of government, had sent in their adhesion to the Commonwealth; but Mon-

tagu was secretly attached to the interests of Charles
II., and was even then preparing to return to England with his whole fleet, to favor the royal cause.
He had an interview at Elsineur with Sidney, who
soon fathomed his intentions, and immediately apprised the Parliament. Six additional frigates were
ordered to be equipped, under the command of Lawson,
to prevent the attempt, and to oppose any invasion by
the cavaliers from Flanders. But, as it proved, it was
not from this point that the real danger to the republic was to arise. It lay less obvious and nearer home.
Traitorous friends, and not foreign enemies, were to
destroy the fabric which the statesmen of the Commonwealth had reared, and lay the liberties of England once more at the footstool of her kings.

In the prompt execution of this mission, Sidney
repaired from Copenhagen to Stockholm. He was
eminently successful. In this new field—the field of
diplomacy—his fertile genius appeared as well adapted to advance the honor of his country, as it had
proved to be in the senate and on the field. Having
completed the negotiations, as he subsequently with
truth expressed it, " to the advantage of all Europe,
and the honor of this nation," he was ready to return
to his own country, according to the permission given
him and his colleague by the council of state ; but, in
the mean time, the restoration of the king had been
effected, and Sidney, not knowing what construction
would be put upon his conduct by the restored government, wisely concluded for the present to remain be-

yond seas. Some of his letters to his father, about this period, have been preserved, and strikingly exhibit the steadiness of his temper, and his high-toned sense of duty and honor. In one of these, written before the news of the restoration of the king had reached him, though in view of that event which was then pretty certain to take place, he says : " If I do not receive new orders, I shall return speedily home, and shall then follow that way which your lordship shall command and my best friends advise, as far as I can, *without breaking the rules of honor or conscience*, which I am sure will never be expected from me by your lordship, nor those whose opinions I consider. Whilst I am here I serve England, and will, with as much care and diligence as I can, endeavor to advance its interests, and follow the orders of those that govern it. I reserve the determination of other points to counsels upon the peace."

In another letter, dated at Stockholm, June 16th, 1660, as appears after the object of his mission had been accomplished, referring to the restoration of the monarchy he says :—

" We could not think it at all reasonable to leave the work in which we were employed, when we saw a certainty of accomplishing it within a short time, unless we had received a positive command.   *   *   *   *   I am here alone. My colleague intended to make the same journey, but the gout confined him to his bed. I look upon all the powers granted unto us as extinguished by the coming in of the king, and do not take upon me to do anything, as a public minister, except it be giving notice unto the crowns of Sweden and Denmark, of the restitution of the ancient government of England, and the proclaiming of the king. Upon this occasion I accept of a public audience which is here offered unto me; I should have avoided it upon all other occasions."

The progress of this negotiation is accurately detailed by Sidney in his several letters to his father. At first it was attended with many difficulties and delays, and the Council of State even gave the Commissioners leave to return home, if they thought proper, before it was accomplished. This, however, they did not do, but dispatched one of their number, Mr. Boone, to England, during the year. Sidney writes, that he himself desired that place, but that " the princes with whom we are to treat, and our fellow-mediating ministers did not consent."

In a letter under date of the 23d of June, 1660, he congratulates his father upon his having resumed his former place in the House of Peers. The object of his mission had then been accomplished, and regarding his powers as extinct, he was preparing to retire from Sweden.. In relation to the peace he had just concluded, and his reception at the court of Sweden, he remarks :—

" The conclusion of what has been managed by my colleagues and me, must be left to such person as the king shall please to employ in it. God be thanked, he will find little difficulty ; if he can but write his name, he will be able enough for anything that remains to be done. 1 have been received here as I desired; if I would have had more ceremony, the State would have allowed it to me; but esteeming my powers extinct by the king's restitution, I did avoid all things of that kind that could be decently omitted. I find this crown exceedingly well satisfied with the peace that is made, and resolved to perform exactly and handsomely, all that was agreed."

In respect to his own equivocal relations with the English government, he adds :—

"'I am uncertain how my actions or person will be looked upon at home. I hope I shall be able to give a good account of all that I have done here, and for *other things* I must take my fortune with the rest of my companions. The Council, in their last letter to my colleague and me, said, that for the future, we must expect orders from the king, unless we did resolve to return home according to the liberty formerly granted us. We embraced that concession, and the peace being made for which we were sent, resolve to return, *unless we have some commands from his Majesty.* If we receive any such, they shall be obeyed; nothing else shall, by our consent, retard our return."

But Sidney waited in vain for any commands from his majesty, or, indeed, any recognition of his character as a public minister. He had been too deeply engaged in the revolution, was too prominent and marked an object, to receive anything but enmity

and persecution at the hands of the government of
Charles II. It is true he came within the general
act of amnesty, afterwards passed, which excepted
alone the " regicides," as they were called, and a few
others ; but he lay, for years after, under the ban of
the government, and his return into England, if not
absolutely prohibited, it was more than intimated,
would be a matter of personal peril and danger. To
a mind like Sidney's, expatriation and banishment
appeared the heaviest misfortunes that could befal
him. He loved his country with a sincere and ardent
affection. Even in her fall it was his country still,
and he longed to return once more to her shores. It
is not remarkable, therefore, that we find some of his
letters, about this period, expressing much solicitude
as to his return, and the probability that he might
find sufficient favor with the government to suffer
him, at least, to place his foot once more upon the
soil of England. In one of his letters from Stockholm, he says :—

" I do not at all know in what condition I am
there, (in England,) not what effect I shall find of General Monk's expression of kindness toward me, and
his remembrance of the ancient friendship that was
between us ; but the Lord Fleetwood's letters to the
Senate, and private persons here, mention discourses
that he makes much to my advantage."

June 27th, 1660, a day or two before leaving Sweden, he writes :—

" The news I have from England is punctual and

certain enough ; but my friends are so short in what relates particularly unto myself that I can make no judgment at all upon what they say. Perhaps the truth is, they can say nothing to my advantage and leave me to guess at the rest by public things."

In the same letter he speaks of a report that his father is to be sent governor into Ireland, adding, that if the report be true, " I should not be content to stay here, believing that if I am capable of doing service in any place in the world it is there, where I have some knowledge of persons, places, and business, *but how likely my service is to be accepted I cannot at all judge.*"

From Copenhagen, on the 14th of July, he again wrote to his father a long letter, filled mainly with matters relating to his public business, which was now closed. The conviction he before expressed that he did not feel at all assured that new orders would be sent to him, was now rendered a certainty, and he was preparing to leave Denmark, as he had left Sweden, where, his public mission being closed, he did not choose to reside as a private person. His course was directed to Hamburgh and Holland. Previous to leaving Copenhagen, he wrote once more to the Earl of Leicester a brief letter, expressing some impatience that he had not received any directions in respect to his future course. " I do not yet very well know in what place I shall stay until I hear further from England. I did hope that upon such occasions as those that have of late befallen me, your lordship would have been pleased to have sent me some commands and advices how to dispose of myself, more particularly than by such an one as I had sent over with letters."

His father's answer at length came—a cold and unwelcome answer—confirming the resolution he had already formed, not to return to England. The old earl in his letter is somewhat querulous and pettish. He excuses his neglect as a correspondent, by saying, "Disuse in writing hath made it weary to me. Age makes it hard, and the weakness of sight and hand makes it almost impossible." He then chides his son for his neglect :—"After you had left me sick, solitary, and sad at Penshurst, and that you had resolved to undertake the employment, wherein you have lately been, you neither came to give a farewell, nor did so much as send one to me, but only writ a wrangling letter or two about money," &c.

The sum of the letter seems to be, that his lordship thinks it unfit, and, perhaps as yet, *unsafe* for his son to come into England. The reason he assigns is, that he had heard Sidney was likely to be excepted out of the act of pardon and oblivion; he knew not, he says, what his son had done or said, but he has in several ways heard that there is as ill an opinion of him as of any, even of those that condemned the late king. He had spoken, he further says, in his behalf, to the General, (Monk,) who was then, of course, high in favor with the king, and had "intended to speak with somebody else, you may guess whom

I mean,"—this probably refers to the king himself—
" but since that, I have heard such things of you, that
in the doubtfulness only of their being true, no man
will open his mouth for you." These reports which
had thus reached the Earl of Leicester's ears, and
were whispered in the court of Charles II., were
some of them true. They were, no doubt, one of the
causes of the inveterate enmity so long cherished
against Sidney by that monarch. Highlyprejudicial to
his character in that court, to us they appear nothing
more than the free and bold thoughts of a mind which
the deeply cherished principles of liberty. We shall
give these reports, which so shocked the old earl, in
his own quaint language.

"It is said that the University of Copenhagen
brought their album unto you, desiring you to write
something therein, and that you did *scribere in albo*
these words :—

> ——Manus hæc inimica tyrannis
> Ense petit placidam sub libertate quietem.*

It is also said that a minister who hath married a
lady Laurence, here at Chelsea, but now dwelling at
Copenhagen, being there in company with you, said—
' I think you were none of the late king's judges, nor

---

* In Lord Molesworth's preface to his account of Denmark, it is said
that these words were written by Sidney in the book of mottoes in the
king's library, according to the liberty allowed to all noble strangers,
and that the French ambassador had the assurance to tear out the leaf
containing the passage, considering it a libel on the French government
and also upon that of Denmark, the establishing of which France was
then favoring.

guilty of his death,' meaning our king; 'Guilty,' said you, ' *do you call that guilt? why it was the justest and bravest action that ever was done in England or anywhere else,*' with other words to the same effect. It is said also that you having heard of a design to seize upon you, or cause you to be taken prisoner, you took notice of it to the King of Denmark himself, and said—' I hear there is a design to seize upon me ; but who is it that hath that design ? *Est ce notre bandit ?*' by which you were understood to mean the king. Besides this, it is reported that you have been heard to say many scornful and contemptuous things of the king's person and family, which, unless you can justify yourself, *will hardly be forgiven or forgotten,* for such personal offences make deeper impressions than public actions either of war or of treaty."

The earl was undoubtedly right. Such offences as these were neither to be forgotten nor forgiven. They exhibited the high spirit and lofty independence of character of Algernon Sidney too plainly for him to expect either favor or clemency from the vengeful government of Charles II. and Clarendon. It was penitence for the past, a time-serving sycophancy, a total, abject submission, a complete sacrifice of opinions and independence, that was demanded as the condition of pardon. The proud and lofty mind of Sidney could not bend to this imperious demand; he refused to submit to the humiliation, and scorned the infamous condition of royal clemency. On the very day his father was penning the letter, from which the foregoing extracts are made, Sidney wrote to him from Hamburgh, assuring him that he had abandoned, for the present, all thoughts of returning home. His proud and unbending spirit seems to breathe through every sentence he pens. There is an earnest sincerity, a high-toned and manly sentiment, a deep, and stern, and resolute determination, pervading the language in which he contemptuously spurns the condition of pardon offered him, and which elevate even our highest conceptions of his character.

"I know myself to be in a condition that for all circumstances, is as ill as outward things can make it : this is my only consolation, that when I call to remembrance, as exactly as I can, all my actions relating to our civil distempers, I cannot find one that I can look upon as a breach of the rules of justice and honor. This is my strength, and I thank God by this I enjoy very serene thoughts. If I lose this, *by vile and unworthy submissions, acknowledgment of errors, asking pardon, or the like, I shall, from that moment, be the miserablest man alive, and the scorn of all men.* I know the titles that are given me of fierce, violent, seditious, mutinous, turbulent, and many others of the like nature ; but God that gives me inward peace in my outward troubles, doth know that I do in my heart choose an innocent, quiet retirement, before any place unto which I could hope to raise myself by those actions which they condemn, and did never put myself upon any of them, but when I could not enjoy the one, or thought the other my duty. If I could write and talk like Col. Hutchinson, or Sir Gilbert Pickering, I believe I might be quiet; contempt might procure my safety ; *but I had rather be a vaga-bond all my life than buy my own country at so dear a rate.*   *   *   *   *   *

It will be thought a strange extravagance for one that esteemed it no dishonor *to make himself equal unto a great many mean people, and below some of them, to make war upon the king,* and is ashamed to submit unto the king, now he is encompassed with all the nobles of the land, and in the height of his glory, so that none are so happy as those that can first cast themselves at his feet. I have enough to answer all this in my own mind ; I cannot help it if I judge amiss. I did not make myself, nor can I help the defects of my own creation. I walk in the light God hath given me ; if it be dim or uncertain, I must bear the penalty of my errors. I hope to do it with patience, and that no burden shall be very grievous to me except sin and shame. God keep me from those evils, and in all things else dispose of me according to his pleasure."

In respect to the offences charged against him by the earl, Sidney subsequently writing from Augsburgh, explains :—

" That which I am reported to have written in the book at Copenhagen, IS TRUE ; and having never heard that any sort of men were so worthy the objects of

enmity as those I mentioned, *I did never in the least,
scruple avowing myself to be an enemy unto them.*"

As to his reported remark to the minister in relation
to the execution of the king :—

" I do not know that he ever asked me any such
question. If he had, I should have given him such
an answer as his folly and ill-manners would have
deserved ; but that which is reported is not in my
style ; I never said it. Yet, that your lordship
may not think I say this in compliance with the time,
I do avow, that since I came into Denmark I have
many times SO JUSTIFIED THAT ACT, as people did believe I had a hand in it ; and *never did disavow it,*
unless it were to the king of Sweden and Grand
Maître of Denmark, who asked me privately."

In this letter Sidney mentions his having seen the
act of indemnity. He expected, he said, to have been
excepted by this act from pardon, especially when he
heard how Vane and Hazelrig were dealt with. He
hoped as little favor from the king as any man in
England. But although, he remarks, there was not
a clause in the act of indemnity which could trouble
him, he did not value its protection a straw.

That Sidney thoroughly understood the cause of
the animosity of the king and court against him, and
knew precisely upon what terms of abject and unqual-
ified submission his pardon might be obtained, is evident from his next letter dated at Augsburgh, on the
26th of September. In it he says :—

" The cause and root of all the bitterness against

me, is from my stiff adherence to the party they hate. I do not wonder at it; the reason is sufficient, but that which the king cannot avow without contradicting the very grounds upon which he doth promise to govern."

But the same letter discloses more fully than ever, his iron will, and his unconquerable resolution. He is determined never to sacrifice a principle, never to renounce an opinion, never, in short, to yield up his independence of thought, to confess his past life a falsehood, or, with a pusillanimous spirit, seek for *pardon* at the foot of a throne he scorns and despises. He does believe, he says, that his peace may be made, but not by the means proposed.

" The king doth not give any testimony of desiring to destroy *all* that were against him, but he will have *all to submit, to recant, to renounce, and ask pardon.* I find this and other things are expected from me. I can do the *first*, cheerfully and willingly, as he is acknowledged by the Parliament; *nothing of the others.*"

And thus Sidney submitted to exile. " These reasons," he says, "have persuaded me to content myself with a temporary exile as the least evil that is within my power of choosing." And never did Algernon Sidney prove recreant to the rule he laid down in this spirited and noble letter. Years after, though he *submitted* to the ruling powers, and returned to his native country, as he at this time declared himself willing to do, yet he did not *recant, renounce, or ask the pardon*, that was expected of him. To the last, he maintained that stern self-reliance, and independence of character, which never suffered him to sacrifice a principle to an expediency, and which led him to prefer a life of exile in a foreign land, to one of dishonor and humiliation in his own country.

In his apology, he says, he could not for some time comprehend why he was treated with such asperity and harshness when others who had been his companions and had given more just cause of hatred against them than he had done, were received into favor or suffered to live quietly, but that at length a person who well understood the temper of the court, explained the mystery by letting him know that " *he was distinguished from the rest, because it was known that he could not be corrupted.*"

The conduct of the king's government at the restoration in the trial of the regicides and others, has already been alluded to in the sketches of Sidney's cotemporaries and is of itself sufficient to show that it was not so much the punishment of past offences which was aimed at, as of present political opinions. Some of these trials are among the most disgraceful proceedings to be found in the annals of English criminal jurisprudence. Among these, the execution of Scrope, one of the king's judges, and of Sir Henry Vane, have a precedence of infamy, because of their being in direct violation of the solemn pledge of the government. Scrope had come in upon the king's proclamation of pardon to such of the regicides as should surrender themselves within fourteen days. In the very face of this solemn guaranty, he was tried, condemned and executed, because, in private conversation he had not acknowledged that he was *convinced of his guilt in condemning the king*. The case of Vane was, if possible, still more infamously unjust. With Lambert and Sir Arthur Hazelrigge, he had been excepted out of the act of pardon, but only on the solemn pledge of the king to the House of Commons that his life should be spared. This pledge with Lambert and Hazelrigge was kept. They were both *penitent* and entirely submissive. Hazelrigge, in particular, before the king's return, had bargained with General Monk, for his life and estate, by surrendering his command. The lives of these two were therefore spared, and they were condemned to imprisonment. But Vane stood fast to his principles, and with indomitable courage and firmness, defended himself on his trial. It was the pleasure of the king and his chancellor that Vane should die, notwithstanding the royal word had passed to the contrary; and to the disgrace of the nation he was condemned by an English court, on the verdict of an English jury, and died on the scaffold. His devotion to the " old cause," his opinions and principles, not his offences, constituted the crime for which he was condemned.

Mr. Hume has glossed over this part of Charles's administration, and with an evident bias in favor of the crown, which even his air of dignified impartiality

cannot conceal, would make these executions appear
to be the just and merited punishment of past treason,
and even from their *small number*, distinguished not
only for their justice, but for what he calls an ".unex-
ampled lenity." He mentions the names of the six of
the king's judges thus dealt with—Harrison, Scot,
Carew, Clement, Jones, and Scrope ; the rest he says,
"by an unexampled lenity were reprieved, and they were
dispersed into several prisons." Of these judges, nine-
teen had surrendered themselves on the king's proclamation, relying on the promised pardon; the remainder,
including all who were executed, except Scrope, had
been captured in their flight. It is true, Hume does
not undertake to justify the executions of Scrope and
Vane ; neither on the other hand, does he condemn
them. As for the rest, including the enthusiast, Hugh
Peters, and Coke the lawyer, who appeared for the people on the king's trial, we are given to understand
their deaths were the deserved reward of past crimes.
Such historical opinions, under the sanction of Hume's
authority, have long passed current in our country as
well as in England ; but the time has come when they
ought at least to be doubted, if not repudiated. The
same argument would justify the execution of every
man who had sided with the Parliament during the
civil war. The head of Monk should have rolled from
the scaffold, and the infamous Ashley Cooper should
have incurred the still more severe sentence which the
common law pronounced in cases of high treason.
According to the same argument, it was through th

magnanimity and mercy, not the justice of the king,
that Milton was spared, and a grateful posterity is
indebted alone to the " unexampled lenity" of Charles
Stuart for the Paradise Lost. If the theory be true,
that these executions were not a bloody vengeance, inflicted for present opinions as well as past offences,
but just, and discriminating, and necessary punish-
ments, why should Lambert and Hazelrigge have received more favor than Vane, or why should the case
of Marten have been made to differ from those of Harrison and Scot? Lambert was no less guilty than
Vane, but he was penitent, and his life was spared;
while Vane faced his judges with intrepidity, boldly
justified his conduct, recanted no opinion of his life,
and was sent to the block. Marten upon his trial, as
we have seen, did not exhibit the same bold and daunt-
less front, and though equally *guilty*, his punishment
was commuted to imprisonment. Harrison* and Scot

---

* Hume sneers at the conduct of Harrison upon his trial, and asks—
" Can any one without concern for human blindness and ignorance, consider the demeanor of General Harrison who was first brought to his
trial ?"

For one, we doubt if any can arise from perusing Mr. Hume's own
account of his demeanor on the occasion referred to, with other sentiments than respect for Harrison's sincerity and admiration of his fortitude and intrepidity. The account is as follows:

" With great courage and elevation of sentiment, he told the court
that the pretended crime of which he stood accused, was *not a deed performed in a corner;* the sound of it had gone forth to most nations; and
in the singular and marvellous account of it had chiefly appeared the
sovereign power of Heaven; that he himself, agitated by doubts, had
often, with passionate tears, offered up his addresses to the Divine Majesty, and earnestly sought for light and conviction: he had still received

did not flinch from their principles, or quail before their judges. They neither asked nor expected, perhaps did not desire mercy, and Harrison and Scot were condemned to die.

This digression will serve to show more clearly the position of Sidney with respect to the restored government, and the secret of the vindictive persecution which subsequently pursued him. It will be remembered that he was not one of the king's judges, or in any way connected with his death. He was not

assurances of a heavenly sanction, and returned from those devout supplications with more serene tranquillity and satisfaction; that all the nations of the earth were, in the eyes of their Creator, less than a drop of water in the bucket, nor were their erroneous judgments aught but darkness, compared with divine illuminations; that these frequent illapses of the Divine Spirit, he could not suspect to be interested illusions, since he was conscious that for no temporal advantage would he offer injury to the poorest man or woman that trod upon the earth; that all the allurements of ambition, all the terrors of imprisonment, had not been able, during the usurpation of Cromwell, to shake his steady resolution, or bend him to a compliance with that deceitful tyrant, and when invited by him to sit on the right hand of the throne, when offered riches, and splendor, and dominion, he had disdainfully rejected all temptations; and neglecting the tears of his friends and family, had still, through every danger, held fast his principles and his integrity."

Harrison was, doubtless, not only a fanatic, but the wildest of visionaries in his views of government; yet, no more earnest or sincere man lived in those times. He opposed the usurpation of Cromwell, but he did not share the enlightened opinions of Vane and Sidney. He was one of those zealots who expected the coming of the fifth monarchy, the reign of the saints upon earth. In the novel of Woodstock, Sir Walter Scott, with inimitable skill, laying hold of these striking traits in the character of this distinguished soldier, has produced a picture, which, though exaggerated, and too highly colored, is yet, like all the creations of his master hand, easily mistaken for the original.

excepted by name out of the general act of pardon, and therefore did not come literally within the law, and was not justly liable to any prosecution for his past conduct. Yet his father and his friends advised him, and doubtless with truth, that his return to England would be perilous. The act of amnesty, under a capricious and tyrannical government, so easily violated in other cases, would have been no protection unless at such a sacrifice of principle and independence as they well knew a spirit like Sidney's could never brook. So too he himself viewed it, as will be seen by the following extract from a letter to his father, written from Rome on the 19th of November, 1660.

"I think the counsel given me by all my friends to keep out of England for a while, doth too clearly appear to have been good by the usage which my companions have already received, and perhaps will be yet further verified by what they will find. Nothing doth seem more certain to me than that I must either have procured my safety *by such means as Sir Arthur Hazelrigge is said to have used,* or run the fortune of some others who have showed themselves more resolute. I hope my being here will, in a short time, show that the place was not ill-chosen, and that besides the liberty and quiet which is generally granted to all persons here, I may be admitted into that company the knowledge of which, will very much recompense my journey. I was extremely unwilling to stay in Hamburgh, or any place in Germany, finding myself too apt to fall into too deep melancholy if I have neither business nor company to divert me; and I have such an aversion to the conversation and entertainments of that country, that if I stayed in it, I must have lived as a hermit, though in a populous city. I am here, well enough at ease, and believe I may continue so; unless somebody from the court of England doth think it worth their pains to disturb me, I see nothing likely to arise here to trouble me."

Such, then, was the position of Sidney; a wanderer and an exile, though not in terms proscribed by the law. The fate of his associates, under the fraudulent promises of the government, admonished him of what would probably be his own, if he once placed himself within the power of his enemies. His past conduct he knew was less reprehensible than that of many who had risen to favor at home, but his present opinions he also knew were such as would find no favor there. He had been no less guilty than Sir Henry Vane, if such actions as his could be called guilt. He sympathized fully in the devoted and noble principles of that great republican statesman, with whom he had been on terms of intimate friendship. He had all his moral courage, and fortitude, and firmness of purpose. This was well known at the court of Charles, and, besides, it was known that Col. Sidney was a man who *could not be corrupted.* His colleague, Sir Robert Honeywood, had returned from Denmark to England, and the king had been graciously pleased to admit him into his presence. Some which common misfortune had but served to cement ; and the intelligence could not fail to furnish new food for the slanders which were circulated against him at Whitehall, and to place still farther off the period of his return to his native country. Sidney, at his departure, presented Ludlow a pair of pistols of Italian workmanship, as a token of his friendship ; and proceeding to Berne, rendered some good offices to the exiles, with the magistrates of that place.

Soon after this, Sidney, persecuted on every side, and almost entirely deprived of the means of subsistance, attempted to enter into some foreign employment, and with this view undertook to make arrangement to serve in Hungary as a volunteer. He wrote to his father with the view of proposing to the English government, through the Earl of Sunderland, his nephew, to engage in the service of the emperor a body of troops raised from among his old associates. But the government not only discountenanced but thwarted his designs, and the project seems to have been abandoned.

In 1665, war again broke out between Holland and England. De Witt was then at the head of affairs in the Dutch Republic ; and his liberal sentiments, known to be thoroughly in accordance with those of the English republicans, were such as to give encouragement to the exiles, many of whom looked forward to the success of Holland as the prelude to the restoration of the Commonwealth. Among these was Col. Sidney, who repaired to the Hague with the view of urging the Dutch government to attempt the invasion of England—a design then, doubtless, premature, but which, after more than twenty years of misgovernment, was successfully brought about by William of Orange. De Witt, however, gave little countenance to the proposed invasion. He doubted not only its policy but its practicability; and jealous of the liberties and prosperity of his own country, he did not choose to hazard these by any such enterprize, which, however it might enlist his sympathies, presented so doubtful an issue. When France united with the States' General, the project of an invasion was renewed, and both Sidney and Ludlow were invited to Paris. Ludlow, however, seems to have suspected the sincerity of the proposal, and refused to leave his retreat; but Sidney, after a conference with the French resident at Mentz, repaired to Paris, where he submitted to the court his proposals for exciting an insurrection in England. The French government offered him twenty thousand crowns, with a promise of all necessary assistance when there should be a more certain prospect of success. Sidney, considering this entirely inadequate to the accomplishment of the object in view, declined it; and here the negotiations ended. The treaty of Breda, in 1667, put an end to all these designs; the cause of the exiles was abandoned; Louis XIV. resorted to diplomacy, intrigue, and bribery, to maintain his ascendency in England, and the hope of the restoration of the Commonwealth vanished forever.

friends of Sidney argued well for him, from this reception of his colleague, and even pressed him to return; intimating a prospect of his being employed in the service of the government. The answer of Sidney is strikingly characteristic of his lofty and independent spirit; such an answer as is worthy the pen of the man who, in his character and actions, strove to emulate the stern virtues and heroic constancy of Brutus. It gives a correct view of the sentiments he then entertained toward the government of England, and is otherwise of peculiar interest as opening to us a clearer and broader insight into his character :—

"SIR—I am sorry I cannot, in all things, conform myself to the advices of my friends. If theirs had any joint concernment with mine, I should willingly submit my interest to theirs; but when I alone am interested, and they only advice me to come over as soon as the act of indemnity is passed, because they think it is best for me, I cannot wholly lay aside my own judgment and choice. I confess we are naturally inclined to delight in our own country, and I have a particular love to mine. I hope I have given some testimony of it. I think that being exiled from it is a great evil, and would redeem myself from it with the loss of a great deal of my blood. But when that country of mine, which used to be esteemed a paradise, is now like to be made a stage of injury; the liberty which we hoped to establish oppressed; luxury and lewdness set up in its height instead of piety, virtue, sobriety and modesty, which we hoped God, by our hands, would have introduced; the best men of our nation made a prey to the worst; the Parliament, court, and the army corrupted; the people enslaved; all things vendible; no man safe but by such evil and infamous means as flattery and bribery; *what joy can I have in my own country in this condition?* Is it a pleasure to see that all I love in the world is sold and destroyed? Shall I renounce all my old principles, learn the vile court arts, and make my peace by bribing some of them? Shall their corruption and vice be my safety? Ah! no; better is a life among strangers than in my own country upon such conditions. Whilst I live I will endeavor to preserve my liberty, or at least not to consent to the destroying of it. *I hope I shall die in the same principles in which I have lived, and will live no longer than they can preserve me.* I have in my life been guilty of many follies, but, as I think, of no meanness. I will not blot and defile that which is past, by endeavoring to provide for the future. I have ever had in my mind, that when God should cast me into such a condition as that I cannot save my life, but by doing an indecent thing, *he shows me the time is come when I should resign it.* When I cannot live in my own country, but by such means as are worse than dying in it, I think he shows me I ought to keep myself out of it. Let them please themselves with making the king glorious, who think a whole people may justly be sacrificed for the interest and pleasure of one man and a few of his followers; let them rejoice in their subtlety, who, by betraying the former powers, have gained the favor of this, and not only preserved, but advanced themselves in these dangerous changes.* Nevertheless, perhaps, they may find the king's glory is their shame, his plenty the people's misery, and that the gaining of an office, or a little money, is a poor reward for destroying a nation, which, if it were preserved in liberty and virtue, would truly be the most glorious in the world; and that others may find they have with much pains purchased their own shame and misery, a dear price paid for that which is not worth keeping, nor the life that is accompanied with it. The honor of English parliaments has ever been in making the nation glorious and happy, not in selling and destroying the interests of it to gratify the lusts of one man.

"Miserable nation! that from so great a height of glory is

---

* Reference is here undoubtedly made to Ashley Cooper, now Earl of Shaftesbury, and other commonwealth's men, who, like him, were high in favor with the king. Perhaps, also, he means his old friend, General Monk, then Duke of Albemarle.

fallen into the most despicable condition in the world, of having all its good depending upon the breadth and will of the vilest persons in it! Cheated and sold by them they trusted! infamous traffic, equal almost in guilt to that of Judas! In all preceding ages Parliaments have been the palaces of our liberty, the sure defenders of the oppressed; they who formerly could bridle kings and keep the balance equal between them and the people, are now become instruments of all our oppressions, and a sword in his hand to destroy us, they themselves, led by a few interested persons who are willing to buy offices for themselves by the misery of the whole nation, and the blood of the most worthy and eminent persons in it. Detestable bribes, worse than the oaths now in fashion in this mercenary court! I mean to owe neither my life nor liberty to any such means. When the innocence of my life and actions will not protect me, I will stay away until the storm be passed over. *In short where Vane, Lambert, Hazelrigge cannot live in safety, I cannot live at all.* If I had been in England, I should have expected a lodgment with them; *or though they may be the first, as being more eminent than I, I must expect to follow their example in suffering, as I have been their companion in acting.* I am most in amaze at the mistaken informations that were sent to me by my friends, full of expectations of favors and employments. Who can think that they who imprison *them* would employ *me*, or suffer me to live when they are put to death? If I might live and be employed, can it be expected that I should serve a government that seeks such detestable ways of establishing itself? Ah! no; I have not learnt to make my own peace by persecuting and betraying my brethren more eminent and worthy than myself. I must live by just means, and serve to just ends, or not at all. After such a manifestation of the ways by which it is intended the king shall govern, I should have renounced any place of favor into which the kindness and industry of my friends might have advanced me, when I found those that were better than I were, only fit to be destroyed. I had formerly some jealousies; the fraudulent proclamation for indemnity increased them; the imprisoning of those three men, and turning out of all the officers of the army, contrary to promise, confirmed my resolution not to return. To conclude, the tide is not to be diverted, nor the oppressed delivered; but God in his time will have mercy on his people. He will save and defend them, and avenge the blood of those who shall now perish, upon the heads of those who, in their pride, think nothing is able to oppose them. Happy are those whom God shall make instruments of his justice in so blessed a work! *If I can live to see that day, I shall be ripe for the grave, and able to say with joy, 'Lord now lettest thou thy servant depart in peace.'* Farewell. My thoughts as to king and state depending upon their actions, no man shall be a more faithful servant to him than I, if he make the good and prosperity of his people his glory; *none more his enemy if he dothe the contrary.* To my particular friends I shall be constant in all occasions, and to you a most affectionate servant."

It is not necessary to make the least apology for the introduction of this admirable letter, long as it is, in this place entire. It opens to us the innermost thoughts of Sidney, and gives us a truer insight into his character than any narrative of his actions that could be related. The reader will not fail to be struck with the singleness of purpose, and the determined energy which is breathed in every line of it. Sidney had adopted his political principles with deliberation, and with the honest sincerity of a thorough conviction of their truth. Not for an instant did he temporise with them. The thought of the possibility of change of these principles does not seem to have occurred to him; between their sacrifice, and banishment, he did not suffer himself a moment to hesitate. This letter is without a date; it is uncertain when it was written. From the evidence it bears upon its face, we may infer some time after the act of indemnity, so called, was passed by the Parliament, and before the trial of Vane and others. His views upon taking employment under the government, it will be observed, are entirely changed. In June, 1660, as we have seen, he wrote to his father, hinting that he would be willing to serve in Ireland ;—this was before Charles II. had so cruelly deceived the hopes of the nation. Now, however, he says, he should "have renounced any place or favor," into which he might have been advanced, after such "a manifestation of the ways by which it is intended the king shall govern." The letter is further interesting as containing his own reasons for remaining out of England. He formerly had "some jealousies" (suspicions) of the good faith of the king, in his declaration at Breda, proclaiming a general amnesty. These suspicions were increased by "the fraudulent proclamation for indemnity," by imprisoning "those three men," (Vane, Lambert, and Hazelrigge,) and "turning out all the officers of the army, *contrary to promise.*" From these indications of bad faith, on the part of the king and Parliament, towards others, Sidney judged rightly, that though he himself was not excepted out of the act of pardon, by name, yet there was no safety in England for him or protection from the wrath of his bitter and revengeful enemies.

CHAPTER V.

In July, 1660, Sidney having finished his mission, took his leave of the Capital of Denmark, for Hamburgh, where he awaited further orders from his father. Here he had several interviews with the celebrated and eccentric Christina, Queen of Sweden, who had some years before resigned her crown. From

Hamburgh, he travelled through a portion of Holland and Germany, and the following month we find him, by the date of a long letter, written to his father, in Frankfort on the Main. The Earl of Leicester had advised him not to go to Italy for the present, but to remain at Hamburgh. Yet Sidney, with his characteristic independence of disposition, had resolved otherwise, and accordingly we find him, in November of the same year, at Rome.

An extract from his first letter from Rome has already been given, in which he informs his father of his arrival there, and apologizes for neglecting the paternal advice. He found himself at Hamburgh " too apt to fall too deep into melancholy," &c. In short, he was uncomfortable at Hamburgh, or at any place in Germany, and he resolved to visit the imperial city, now that all present hopes of his return to England were abandoned. He remained at Rome during the winter, and for some time after travelled in other parts of Italy. Various letters have been preserved in the collection to which reference has been made, written during this period, some of them dated at Rome, others at Frascati.

His manner of life in Italy was simple, retired, and unobtrusive. He neither courted nor shunned observation. He did not seek notoriety, but yet as a noble and distinguished stranger, every access to the society of all in Rome, who were remarkable for learning, or talents, were open to him. He became acquainted with many of the distinguished cardinals of that city;

8

"some of them," he says, "the most extraordinary persons I ever met with, others equal with the rest of the world. With some, I pretend only the performance of a civility and desire only a little knowledge of them; with others, I seek a straighter conversation, and by frequent visits endeavor to gain it." In a long letter to the earl, dated from Rome, he sketches the characters of the twelve principal cardinals, in a manner, as he says, that may be relied on for truth, "without any bias." The reader may be curious to know how close an observer of character Sidney was, and with what degree of fidelity he traced it; we therefore subjoin one of these sketches of a very distinguished and learned man of that day in Rome— the Cardinal Pellavicini :—

"Italy hath not a finer wit than Pellavicini, nor hath any convent a monk of a stricter life. It is said that sixpence a day serves him in meat; his bread and wine are furnished from the palace. Women never trouble his thoughts; they are unknown to him. He hath constantly refused great church livings; and being lately pressed by the pope, who favors him very much, to receive one of great value, he answered—'Your Holiness can add nothing to the favor of giving me this hat, but by employing me in such things as may be for your service, and bear testimony of my gratitude, I want nothing else.' He makes good his words, receiving not above three or four thousand crowns a year to keep up the state of a cardinal, having had nothing before he came to it. He labors incessantly in those knotty businesses that require much pains and yield no profit. This humor defends him from having rivals in his pretences. He hath showed it to be possible for the same man to be excellent in the *Belle Lettres* and the most deep and abstruse sciences. I do not think he hath so well joined the theory and practice of business. The extreme acuteness of his wit, renders him admirable in the one, and fills his head with notions too nice and high for the other. Besides this he hath lived more among books and papers than men. He ever aims at perfection, and frames ideas in his fancy not always proportionable to worldly business, sometimes forgetting that the counsels as well as the sermons of men are ever defective, and that in human affairs, governors and ministers are not so much to seek what is exactly good as what is least evil, or least evil of those things which he hath power to accomplish. He is most meek and humble in his behaviour, easy and gentle in treating of his own concernments; but in spiritual and ecclesiastical affairs, his zeal renders him sharp and violent. These qualities show him to be an excellent cardinal, but would render him an ill pope, at least in the opinion of the courtiers, who will not endure to be overlooked by so sharp a sight master, nor reformed by such a bitter enemy to corruption and looseness. His severity beginning with himself, it is not hoped he will spare others."

The residence of Sidney in Italy, as in other places during his long exile, and his wanderings through Europe, were humiliated, if not embittered, by straightened resources and pecuniary difficulties. The Earl of Leicester does not appear to have dealt him out from his ample means with a very lavish hand. His own fortune was almost entirely wasted by the unhappy issue of the revolution, and, with the exception of what he might realize from his own industry, he looked solely to the pittance he received from his father, to support those decent external circumstances which became his rank and name. Fortunately, he says, living was cheap in Rome. "The prices of all things necessary to life are much increased since I was here the first time, *but temperance is in fashion;*

everybody lives upon little, so that the burden is not great upon strangers. Five shillings a day serves me and two men very well in meat, drink, and firing."

Notwithstanding these moderate wants of Sidney, the supplies came very slowly. Occasionally his private affairs are briefly mentioned in his letters of this period, and once or twice he even uses the language of reproach at the parsimony of his relative. Thus in his letter to his father from Rome, of December 29th, 1660, he says :—

" If there be no difference in living but he that hath bread hath enough, I have some hopes of finding a provision for a longer time than I mentioned. If there be no reason for allowing me any assistance out of the family, as long as there is a possibility of my living without it, I have discharged you. If those helps are only to be given to those who have neither spirit nor industry in anything to help themselves, I pretend to deserve none. Or if supplies are only the rewards of importunity, or given to avoid the trouble of being solicited, I think I shall for ever free you from that reason. And as I have *for some years run through greater straits than I believe any man of my condition hath done in England since I was born* without ever complaining, I shall with silence suffer what fortune soever doth remain unto me. I confess I thought another conclusion might reasonably have been made upon what I have said, but I leave that to your lordship's judgment and conscience. If you are satisfied with yourself, you shall not receive any trouble from

" Your lordship's etc.,

"ALG. SIDNEY."

Another letter, dated just before he left Rome, May 2d, 1661, is written almost in a tone of despondency. He is afflicted, he says, with one of his ordinary fits of the headache ; and is evidently in the lowest possible state of spirits, so much so, that he declares his only hope is, that God will put an end to his troubles or his life. Some of the heaviest of these troubles appear to be his pecuniary embarrassments, and these must have been of great magnitude, if we judge from his own statement. "The misfortunes in which I was fallen by the destruction of our party did not shake me. The cheats and thefts of servants were too ordinary to trouble me. I suffered my mother's legacy to be drawn from me upon which I might have subsisted a good while. I was not very much surprised to find myself betrayed and robbed of all that with which I had trusted Lady Strangford, but I confess that I am sorely troubled to find that Sir J. Temple is going into Ireland," &c., &c. Sidney then mentions the difficulties he had heard concerning certain mortgages and real estate, and adds: "And by all these means together I find myself destitute of all help at home, and exposed to all those troubles, inconveniences, and mischiefs unto which they are exposed who have nothing to subsist upon in a place far from home, where no assistance can possibly be expected, *and where I am known to be a man of quality*, which makes all low and mean ways of living shameful and detestable." To a proud and sensitive mind like that of Sidney such embarrassments must have been galling in the extreme, and we can readily appreciate the feeling that stung him into these expressions of impatience in his correspondence with a relative, on whose kindness and assistance he had such strong claims.

But to turn to more agreeable matters. From Rome he went to Frascati, where we find him courting solitude and seclusion—a student of books as he had been, in the imperial city, a student of men. He had fixed his residence at the villa of Belvidere, one of the finest in Italy, a short distance from Frascati, from whence his letters are dated. A nephew of the late Pope, the Prince of Pamphili; had given him very convenient apartments in the palace with the use of a rare library and beautiful gardens. Here Sidney passed his time, for a brief season, in all the elegant tranquillity of a refined and philosophic mind.*

In his first letter to his father from Frascati, under date of June 7th, 1661, he dwells with evident satisfaction upon the comforts of his new residence, and also describes his studies and pursuits :—

"Whilst everybody at Rome is panting and gasping for life in the heat, which they say this year is much greater than ordinary, I enjoy so fresh an air as to have no reason to complain of the sun. Here are wells and fountains in the greatest perfection, and though my natural delight in solitude is very much increased this year, I cannot desire to be more alone than I am and hope to continue. My conversation is with birds, trees, and books; in these last months that I have had no business at all, I have applied myself to study a little more than I have done formerly; and though one who begins at my age, cannot hope to make any considerable progress that way, I find so much satisfaction in it, that for the future I shall very unwillingly (though I had the opportunity) put myself

*Brief Memoirs by Richard Chase Sidney.

into any way of living that shall deprive me of that entertainment. Whatever hath been formerly the object of my thoughts and desires, I have now intention of seeking very little more than quietness and retirement."

The villa of Belvidere of which Sidney thus speaks, was half a mile from Frascati. From the glowing descriptions he gives, it must have been a place of rare and enchanting beauty, and finely adapted to that life of quiet and contemplative retirement which he was now courting. In his very next letter to his father he again speaks of the beauties of his retreat, and the nature of his present pursuits :—

"Nature, art, and treasure, can hardly make a place more pleasant than this. The description of it would look more like poetry than truth. A Spanish lady coming not long since to see this house, seated in a large plain, out of the middle of a rock, and a river brought to the top of the mountain, ingeniously desired those that were present not to pronounce the name of our Saviour, lest it should dissolve this beautiful enchantment. We have passed the solstice, and I have not yet had occasion to complain of heat, which in Rome is very excessive, and hath filled the town with sickness, especially that part of it where I lived. Here is what I look for, health, quiet, and solitude. I am with some eagerness fallen to reading, and find so much satisfaction in it, that though I every morning see the sun rise, I never go abroad until six or seven o'clock at night; *yet cannot I be so sure of my temper as to know how long this manner of life will please me.*"

Sidney then speaks of the hapless condition to which he is reduced by the late misfortunes which had befallen his party, and his country. His language, though desponding, still gives evidence that he possesses the same firm and unbending spirit in adversity :

"I cannot but rejoice a little to find that when I wander as a vagabond through the world, forsaken of my friends, poor, and known only to be a broken limb of a shipwrecked faction, I yet find humanity and civility from those who are in the height of fortune and reputation. But I do also well know, I am in a strange land, how far those civilities do extend, and that they are too airy to feed or clothe a man. I cannot so unite my thoughts unto one object, as absolutely to forbid the memory of such things as these are to enter into them; but I go as far as I can, and since I cannot forget what is passed, nor be absolutely insensible of what is present, I defend myself reasonably well from increasing or anticipating evils by foresight. The power of foreseeing is a happy quality unto those who prosper, and can ever propose to themselves something of greater felicity than they enjoy; but a most desperate mischief unto them who, by foreseeing can discover nothing that is not worse than the evils they do already feel. *He that is naked, alone, and without help in the open sea, is less unhappy in the night when he may hope the land is near, than in the day time when he sees it not, and that there is no posibility of safety.*"

Sidney was now living, as he himself expressed it, " a hermit in a palace." He had left Rome, (where his virtues and noble conduct had procured him the respect and friendship of the most distinguished of the nobility, clergy, and learned men of the day,) " to avoid the necessity," as he says in the letter above quoted from, " of making and receiving visits" among so large a circle of acquaintances. In his " Apology" he states one of his reasons for making Rome his retreat; it was in order that the most malicious of his enemies should not pretend that he

practiced anything against the government, since
Rome "was certainly an ill scene to act anything
that was displeasing with it." But, he further remarks, he soon found out his mistake, and that " no
inoffensiveness of behavior could preserve me against
the malice of those who sought to destroy me ; and
was defended from *such as there designed to assas-*
sinate me only by the charity of strangers." His
change of residence from Rome to Frascati, and his
withdrawal into a profound seclusion, he hoped would
be attended with better results, and that if not entirely forgotten at home, he would at least not be
molested with the officious notice and slanders of
those who desired to effect his ruin. In his last letter,
dated from Frascati, July 24th, 1661, he says on this
subject :—

"I intend this half burial as a preparative to an
entire one, and shall not be much troubled though I
find, if upon the knowledge of my manner of life,
they who the last year at Whitehall did exercise their
tongues upon me as *a very unruly headed man,* do so
far change their opinion of me on the sudden as to
believe me so dull and lazy as to be fit for nothing.
When *that opinion* is well settled, I may hope to live
quietly in England, and then shall think it a seasonable time to return."

But many years were destined to elapse before
such an opinion was formed of him at the court
of Charles II. as could induce the government to
suffer his return. The sentiments he was known to

entertain, united with genius, courage, and intrepidity, made him a man who could not be the friend, and was sure to prove the formidable enemy of the government. He was therefore honored with unceasing hostility and persecution. No where was he safe. Vengeance was forever on his path, and the stealthy step of the assassin continually pursued him. It seems well established that the government, on more than one occasion, attempted to resort to the base and detestable means of secret assassination, in order to get rid of one who was regarded by it as a dangerous enemy. Not only at Rome, but also in Flanders and Holland, Sidney says in his " Apology," the same dangers surrounded him, and that even when he withdrew into the remotest parts of Germany, one Andrew White, and some others were sent to murder him. This latter circumstance is also related in the memoirs of Ludlow, who states that it was in the year 1665, upon the breaking out of the war between England and the United Provinces. Col. Sidney was then at Augsburgh, and ten ruffians were despatched by authority of the king's government to assassinate him ; it is added that they might have accomplished their infamous purpose, if he had not before their arrival retired from that city into Holland, being called thither on some matters of business.

How long Sidney remained in his retreat at the villa of Belvidere is not known. His last letter from Frascati, and indeed the last which has been preserved,

Sidney now retired into the south of France and buried himself in obscurity. The very place of his retreat was unknown. It appears, however, that he kept up an occasional correspondence with the celebrated diplomatist, Sir William Temple, son of his old friend, Sir John Temple, who resided as ambassador at the Hague, after the downfall of De Witt and the accession of the Prince of Orange to the government. In this retirement, where he remained for nearly ten years, it is supposed that he completed, if he did not actually digest, and write the whole of his celebrated *Discourses on Government*. Mr. Meadley observes that, "no other portion of his life afforded adequate leisure for the important task, as his work is evidently the result of much reading and reflection combined with a very accurate knowledge of the human character as developed by the practice of mankind." He occasionally, too, visited Paris where his high character and capacity were known and respected by the courtiers of Louis XIV. An anecdote is related of Sidney, in one of these visits, which is strikingly illustrative of his spirit and moral courage He was the owner of a fine English horse with which, one day, he joined a chase in the retinue of the king. Observing the fine movements and spirit of the animal, the king resolved to have him, and sent a messenger to Sidney requesting him to deliver the horse and name his own price, of course not anticipating a refusal. To the surprise of Louis, the English exile declined the proposal; whereupon the king, determining to take no denial, gave orders to tender the money and seize the horse. On hearing this, Sidney drew a pistol and shot it, saying, " that his horse was born a free creature, had served a free man, and should not be mastered by a king of slaves."

The period of Sidney's exile at length drew to a close. After an absence of seventeen years, the Earl of Leicester, now having reached the advanced age of eighty-two, and every day rapidly failing in health and strength, desired once more before he died, to see his favorite son. The Earl of Sunderland was then an influential member of the royal councils. Henry Saville, the younger brother to the Marquis of Halifax, was ambassador to France. By their joint influence, but principally by that of Saville, Sidney obtained permission to return to England. In a letter to Saville, dated at Paris, November, 14th, 1682,— the date of which, as published in the collection of his letters, is evidently a mistake, it being in the year 1676 he inquires of Saville respecting his success in the " business you were pleased to speak of," referring, of course, to the negotiations for his return. The same year, Dec. 18th, he acknowledges to Saville the receipt of three letters. Sidney was then at Nerac, and in these letters from the ambassador, he was informed of his liberty to return to England. His gratitude to the friend who had thus served him, is sincere and frankly expressed :

" My obligation unto you is the same, and I so far acknowledge it to be the greatest that I have in a long

time received from any man, as not to value the leave
you have obtained for me to return into my country
after so long an absence, at a lower rate than the sav-
ing of my life. You having proceeded thus far, I will
without any scruple *put myself entirely upon the
king's word*, and desire you only to obtain a passport,
signifying it, and that his majesty is pleased to send
for me, so as the officers of the ports and other places
may not stop me, as they will be apt to do as soon as
they know my name, if I have not that for my protection."

In the same letter, after stating in confidence to
his friend that he has no other business in England,
except such as concerns his person and family, he declares his intention, if the king is not satisfied with
his remaining there, to return to France after the end
of three months.

That this was Sidney's intention, is also evident
from a letter written by him, after his return, from
Leicester House, London, to one Benjamin Purly, a
merchant at Rotterdam, in which he says :—

" I can give you no other account of my return
than that my desire of being and rendering some service unto my old father, persuaded me to ask leave to
come over. And living in a world subject to all manner of changes, easily received a grant of that which I
could not formerly have obtained. But my father
being dead within six weeks after my arrival, I have
no other business here than to clear some small
contests that are grown between one of my brothers

and me, concerning that which he hath left me, and if it please God to give success unto my endeavors in composing them, I shall have nothing relating unto this world, so much at heart as the desire of returning from hence, *without one thought of ever retiring*, and carrying with me that which may be sufficient to purchase a convenient habitation in Gascony, not far from Bordeaux, where I may in quiet finish those days that God hath appointed for me."

It has been represented by Hume, and some other writers, that Col. Sidney asked from Charles II. a *pardon*, and that, having obtained it, he treacherously acted against the government. But the charge is utterly untenable ; Sidney neither asked nor accepted a pardon, as appears manifest from the letters to Saville and Furly, just quoted as well as from his other letters to his father, and his known independence and firmness of character. This charge was made against him, after his trial and execution, by Dr. Sprat, who wrote the history of the Rye-house Plot, by command of Charles and James, and was rewarded for his services by being soon after created bishop of Rochester. Subsequent writers have made the same statement on the authority of Dr. Sprat, the falsehood of which is apparent from the letters already alluded to, as well as from the fact mentioned by a friendly biographer,* that nothing was said on the subject at his trial by Jeffreys, or the other law officers of the crown, who would undoubtedly have availed themselves of the cir-

* Richard Chase Sidney. Brief Mem. of Algernon Sidney.

cumstance to have influenced the jury against him.
Nor does the Duke of York, in his letters to the Prince
of Orange in 1683, take any notice of his *pardon*.
These facts seem conclusively to refute the idea that
he had asked or received any *pardon* from the government.

Having obtained the king's passport, and relying,
as he says, " entirely upon the king's word"—a pledge
which in Vane's case had been so shamefully violated
Sidney returned to England in the Autumn of 1667.
His father died soon after his arrival, and on the 13th
of November of the same year, at Penshurst, he gave
a discharge to the Earl's executors for the legacy bequeathed to him, amounting only to five thousand one
hundred pounds. His return into France, however,
was prevented by his elder brother, Lord Lisle, now
Earl of Leicester, questioning his title to some property, which he had received from his father. This
led to a long and vexatious suit in chancery, which
detained him in England. The suit terminated favorably, and his claims were finally established ; but in
the meantime Sidney became involved in that unfortunate combination of public events which finally led
him to the scaffold.

CHAPTER VI.

SIDNEY's continued residence in England, occasioned,
as we have seen, by the suit in which he had become
so unexpectedly involved, was permitted by the
government, not as a matter of favor to him, but,
most probably, out of consideration to his connections
and friends, such as Sunderland, Halifax, and Sir
William Temple, the most influential and ablest
statesmen in the councils of Charles II. He did not,
however, remain long in his native country before the

lively interest he had always felt in its public affairs manifested itself in open and decided action. Hume says that Sidney joined the popular party, when the factions arising from the Popish plot began to run high; and that, full of those ideas of liberty which he had imbibed from the great examples of antiquity, he was even willing to seek a second time, through all the horrors of civil war, for his adored republic. The statement would have been nearer the truth had it been that Sidney always belonged to the popular party; and if he now "joined it," in the sense, perhaps, intended by the historian, it was not to seek a republican government, through all the horrors of civil war, but to carry out consistently and firmly the political principles which his whole life illustrated.

We shall assume that the reader is familiar with the leading features of the political history of this period, and will not attempt, therefore, to do more than to mention, in a general manner, that train of public events connected with Sidney's career, which eventually led to his execution. The long Parliament which Charles II. had summoned, composed principally of servile and devoted royalists, had now been in existence during a period of nearly eighteen years. The inglorious and every way despicable administration of the king, had brought the country into disgrace and contempt. A greater contrast it is scarcely possible to conceive than between the England under the rule of the Protector, and that same

England under the government of Charles II., at one time assisted by the counsels of the intolerant Clarendon ; at another, under the guidance of his contemptible " *Cabal*." Charles was known to be a pensioner of Louis XIV., receiving that monarch's money without scruple, and furthering the policy of Barillon, the intriguing minister of the French king. But besides the effeminacy and shameful profligacy of the king, and his truckling subserviency to a foreign monarch, the tendency of his whole policy, so far as it could be said that he had a policy, under his ministers, particularly the *Cabal*, and the Earl of Danby, had been to enslave his subjects, to destroy the liberties of his country, and to make himself absolute master of his people.

At this period, when the Parliament was urging the king into a war with France, a favorite design of Charles' seems to have been to raise and keep on foot a standing army, which experience has always shown to be the most formidable instrument of tyrants. Sidney, whose knowledge of the danger of a standing army in Cromwell's time, had given him just views on this subject, earnestly deprecated this projected war with France, and did not hesitate to declare to his friends that it was " a juggle, since the two courts being in entire confidence, nothing more was intended by this show of warfare than to raise an army and afterwards to keep it for training and modelling beyond sea." The war, however, was popular in England : the Parliament voted the king supplies, and in a few weeks an army of twenty thousand men was equipped, ready for action, and an alliance between England, Holland, Spain, and the Emperor, projected. This alarmed Louis XIV., whose address and diplomacy, however, soon succeeded in warding off the threatened danger, and in renewing with his brother of England, those amicable relations, no less advantageous to the one, than disgraceful and ignominious to the other. That Sidney's suspicions as to the object and design of the war on the part of Charles were correct, may be reasonably inferred from the fact, that Louis as usual resorted to the purse in order to detach the King of England from the coalition, and offered him large sums of money if he would consent to allow France to make an advantageous peace with the allies. The bait was too tempting for the king to refuse; but there was one article of the negotiation, we are told, which displeased, as well as surprised him; Louis required that he should never keep above eight thousand regular troops in England. "'Odd's fish!" exclaimed the king, breaking out into his usual exclamation, "Does my brother of France think to serve me thus? Are all his promises to make me *absolute master of my people* come to this? Or does he think *that* a thing to be done with eight thousand men?" A more despicable example of the monarch of a great nation, trafficking in the honor, and bargaining away the interests and liberties of his country for inglorious ease, pleasure, and gold, it is difficult to find in history.

It was this opposition to the contemplated war with France—the jealousy of entrusting the King of England and his brother the Duke of York with an army, for fear that it might be brought to subvert what was left of the constitution and liberties of the country, which first drew upon Sidney the calumny that he was a pensioner of France. Though the jealousy was shared by many of the most eminent of the opposition, or country party as it was then termed, with whose liberal sentiments Col. Sidney sympathized, yet he seems to have been the first to encounter the charge. It originated, however, from no very elevated source —the Earl of Shaftesbury. Sidney and the earl had a violent quarrel. Shaftesbury asserted that Sidney was a French pensioner, and a spy of the Earl of Sunderland. Of a temper that could ill brook such an insult in silence, Sidney at once sent a message by his friend Hampden demanding an explanation. That the explanation was satisfactory, may be inferred from Sidney's well known courage and pride of character. Between him and Shaftesbury all intercourse thereafter ceased.

The malice of his enemies has left upon Sidney's memory but this one dishonorable charge—the charge of being a pensioner of France—which, dying with Shaftesbury in 1682, was nearly a century afterwards revived. Sir John Dalrymple, in his "Memoirs of Great Britain and Ireland," which appeared in 1773, has published certain papers, obtained from the public archives in France, tending to show that Sidney actually received the money of Louis XIV. for the purpose of furthering the designs of that monarch in England, and of preventing the war against France. It will be proper here briefly to examine the origin and ground of this serious accusation.

The papers published by Dalrymple, purport to be extracts from the despatches of Barillon, the ambassador of Louis in England, from which it appears that Barillon had carried on his intrigues with Lords Russell and Hollis, the Duke of Buckingham, Hampden, Sidney, and others of the opposition, all of whom, except Russell and Hollis had received *presents*, either from Barillon himself or his agents. It appears from the papers, that Sidney, on two occasions, had taken sums of five hundred guineas each. Thus authenticated, the charge has been credited by other and subsequent writers, among whom we regret to find Mr. Macauley, who, while he recognizes the claim of Sidney " to be called a hero, a philosopher, and a patriot," sees no reason to discredit the evidence on which he stands accused. Mr. Macauley, in speaking of these *pensioners* says—" It would be unjust to impute to them the extreme wickedness of taking bribes to injure their country. On the contrary, they meant to serve her; but it is impossible to deny that they were mean and indelicate enough to let a foreign prince pay them for serving her;" and, on the authority of Sir John Dalrymple's disclosures alone, he thinks that even the virtue and pride of Algernon Sidney were not proof against the temptation.

9

It is impossible to dissent from an authority so eminent and so liberal as this accomplished author, without
distrusting the correctness of our own conclusions.
But in this case, the charge is one so repugnant to
every idea we have been able to form of the character
of Sidney, so utterly at variance with the whole tenor
of his life, so inconsistent with every sentiment to be
found in his written discourses, or his private correspondence, that it seems, notwithstanding Mr. Macauley's indorsement, to bear its own refutation on its
face. The source of his authority—the one isolated,
naked relation contained in the despatch of Barillon,
as published by Dalrymple—is as open to our own investigation as to his, and, upon an examination of it,
the inference seems irresistible that the evidence is
entirely insufficient to fasten such an unworthy suspicion upon such a man as Sidney. It may be mentioned
that besides other writers of less note, one of the most
eminent of living British statesmen, Lord John Russell,
on a full examination of the charge, pronounces it a
calumny. In the life of his noble ancestor, Lord William Russell, the co-patriot and fellow martyr with
Sidney, he carefully investigates and conclusively refutes the dishonorable accusation. His opinion on this
subject is briefly summed up in the following passage :
" No one of common sense, I imagine, can believe that
he took the money for himself His character is one
of heroic pride and generosity. His declining to sit in
judgment on the king; his extolling the sentence
when Charles II. was restored; his shooting a horse

for which Louis XIV. offered him a large sum, that he might not submit to the will of a despot, are all traits of a spirit as noble as it is uncommon. With a soul above meanness, a station above poverty, and a temper of philosophy above covetousness, what man will be envious enough to think that he was a pensioner of France."

The accuracy of the copies of these despatches published by Dalrymple has been doubted.* Admitting, however, for the sake of the argument their genuineness, they seem to bear upon their face, in connexion with the known circumstances under which they were written, evidence of their falsehood. Barillon was undoubtedly deceived himself, or he wilfully deceived his sovereign ; the latter supposition being the most probable. No doubt there were some members of the parliament, as well as Charles himself, who received French gold,— and Barillon was Louis' disbursing agent. He came over to England in not very affluent circumstances,

---

* Of Sir John Dalrymple's book, Lord Russell says: " At first one is inclined to believe that his taste for bombast led to numerous errors; but when it appears, as I think it does in the following pages, that there is not a single member of the whig party of any note whom he has not traduced by false allegations, it is difficult to acquit him of intentional misrepresentation."

It should be mentioned that the accuracy of Dalrymple's copies which he took in France, rests solely upon his own evidence. Lord Russell, while engaged in collecting the materials for his work, was very naturally desirous of inspecting personally these records, and for that purpose made an application to the French government through its minister in London, the Count de Caraman. The request was, however, refused, the ambassador assuring him that it was entirely contrary to the regulations of the office, and citing him a precedent to that effect.

and returned after the Revolution loaded with riches. The diplomatic agents of the French king were permitted, if not authorized, to pay themselves out of the money entrusted to their care. That all the money of which Barillon pretended to give an account to his master, actually passed out of his hands, is not at all probable, judging from his sudden acquisition of wealth, as well as from his known character for intrigue and double-dealing. He doubtless deceived Louis and put the money into his own pocket ;* and the question is, therefore, which supposition is the most rational, the venality of Barillon, or the corruption of Sidney ? Certainly the ambassador has nothing the advantage on the score of character.

It is to be observed, too, that at the period of the alleged receipt of these presents from Barillon, Sidney had been but a short time in England, was under the ban of the government, entirely devoid of political influence of any kind, and was really not worth the purchasing, particularly by so shrewd a bargainer as Barillon ; yet his was exactly the name for that wily ambassador to use in his dispatches to Louis to cover up his peculations. The French king had known Sid-

---

* Lord Russell inclines to the other opinion. Although he more than doubts the integrity of Barillon, yet from the fact that the money was not personally disbursed by him, but was made to pass through the hands of a few corrupt tools of the minister, he arrives at the conclusion that Barillon was imposed upon. "It seems most probable, upon the whole," he says, "that Barillon was persuaded he was buying the first speakers in parliament, and ruling the decisions of the House of Commons, whilst in fact he was only paying a few skillful intriguers."

ney, and was well acquainted with his determination and energy of character during his long residence in France, and Barillon could well conceive that his master would sanction this part of his accounts for money expended in gaining over such a man, especially when accompanied with the falsehood that Sidney was really a man of political influence and that he had been of "great service to him on many occasions." The ambassador seems very willing indeed to disburse a larger amount of money on that account and he intimates to Louis, that by "*a little more being given*," he believed that Sidney might be easily gained over to his majesty's service. We think these dispatches carry their own refutation with them, and that the mean imputation they cast upon the character of Sidney, sustained as it is only on Barillon's *secret* communication to the French court, is undeserving a notice in history. It should be added, too, that the whole amount of this secret service money claimed to have been disbursed by Barillon was only sixteen thousand pounds in three years, and that the recipients were twenty or more, among whom were the Duke of Buckingham and other members of parliament of the greatest influence, who certainly, one would think, were not to be purchased for a song.* It

* Lord John Russell on this point very justly observes : "It is remarkable that of the twenty persons mentioned in Barillon's last and longest list, not above half were in parliament, and almost all of these were leaders. Now, if any one or two obtained money from Barillon for persons to whom they did not distribute it, or if Barillon himself embezzled the money, the names which would naturally appear in his

does not seem very probable that the shrewd Frenchman would actually have wasted a thousand guineas
on the proscribed Sidney, when members of parliament and votes were to be had, as he pretends, at a
less price.

That Sidney entertained a contempt for the charac-
acter and pretensions of Barillon, and that any intercourse he may have had with him, so far from being
of a confidential nature, was merely tolerated and not
courted is evident from Sidney's correspondence of
that period with Saville, the English Ambassador in
Paris.   In a letter under date of July 10th, 1679,* he
contemptuously mentions the French minister :—

" You know Monsieur de Barillon governs us, if he
be not mistaken ; but he seems to be not so much
pleased with that, as to find his *embonpoint* increased
by the moistness of our air, by frequently clapping his
hands upon his thighs, showing the delight he hath in
the sharpness of the sound that testifies the plumpness
and hardness of his flesh ; and certainly if this climate
did not nourish him better than any other, the hairs of
his nose and nails of his fingers could not grow so fast
as to furnish enough of the one to pull out, and of the

list would be those of the speakers of the greatest reputation.   But if
the transactions were real, it is much more probable that he should have
been able to buy the lower and more obscure members of parliament,
than those whose fame stood highest for ability and integrity."—*Life of
Lord William Russell*, vol i., p. 199.

* One of Barillon's charges of money against Sidney, is of the date
of December 14th, 1679 ; the other of December 5th, 1680.

other to cut off, in all companies, which being done, he pricks his ears with as good a grace as my Lord La!'"

The pretended war with France, the raising of an army which the king refused to disband, and the long series of arbitrary measures which the government of Charles was enabled, by a servile Parliament, gradually to adopt, at length awakened the minds, and aroused the spirits of the English nation. During the seventeen years of the present Parliament there had been many vacancies among its members, mainly occasioned by death. These had been filled up in nearly every instance by members opposed to the court. And the country party, or, as it was at this period, first styled, in derision by its opponents, the *whigs*, were soon in a situation to control its deliberations and to thwart the royal designs.

The famous Popish Plot at this time broke out. It was quickly seized upon by Shaftesbury, and some of the more unscrupulous leaders of the whigs, and soon became a most formidable political engine. The hatred against popery at that time, and for years after, was a common sentiment with both political parties in England. It was believed, and, doubtless, with some truth, as the next reign sadly illustrated, that the establishment of popery was dangerous to the liberties and constitution of the nation; and accordingly, ever since the Reformation, with the single exception of the reign of Queen Mary, Parliament had enacted and continued the severest, and, in some cases, the most intolerant laws against the Papists

and their religion.   Even the liberal principles of the
republicans, and the tolerance of the Protector's government itself, were not broad enough to take in the proscribed jesuit and the devotee of Rome.   Sidney, when
advocating the noblest principles of civil and religious
liberty, and conceding to all men as a natural right,
freedom of conscience and worship, still seemed to
make the same discrimination.   In his " Apology," he
says, he never failed to sustain the doctrines he avows
"against corrupt principles, arbitrary power, and *popery*."   The reason which influenced his mind, and the
minds of others of the leading men of that age, was
not one of narrow sectarian prejudice, but it was the
comprehensive and conclusive reason, confirmed by
past experience, that popery was absolutely inconsistent with freedom, and that its establishment must
inevitably lead to the building up of despotism on the
ruins of the English constitution.   Popery, to Sidney,
was in itself tyranny, and he opposed it with the
same motives and views that he did the usurpation of
Cromwell and the despotism of Charles II.

It is not surprising that Sidney should have been a
believer in the reality of the " Popish Plot," and the
existence of a conspiracy, on the part of the jesuits,
to kill the king, and to elevate his brother, the Duke
of York, a papist, to the throne.   The belief was almost unanimous all over England, though the plot
was sustained by no better testimony than that of the
infamous and perjured Titus Oates and his associates.
The king himself professed to believe it, and if we are

to credit the testimony of the poet Dryden, no willing witness certainly against the Duke of York, or in favor of the whigs, there was at the bottom of all this absurdity something of reality. In his Absalom and Achitophel, he says :—

" Some truth there was, though mix't and brewed with lies."

Be this as it may, the Popish Plot served its turn, and contributed more than anything else to rouse the minds of the English nation against the succession of the Duke of York and even against the government over which the Duke was suspected of having too much influence. The king finding his Parliament refractory, and, in the language of Hume, " treading fast in the steps of the last Long Parliament," at length ventured to dissolve it, which was done in January, 1679.

A new Parliament was at once summoned. The friends of liberal principles throughout all England were aroused. A spirited and angry contest succeeded for members, such as had never yet been known since the foundation of the monarchy. The court engaged openly and warmly in this contest, and endeavored to influence the elections. Sidney offered himself as a candidate for the borough of Guildford, in Surry. The celebrated William Penn, then an active opponent of the arbitrary measures of the government, was one of his most ardent partizans. Penn appeared on the hustings to encourage his friends in the support of Sidney. He was rudely interrupted by an officer of the crown, who unlawfully attempted to administer an oath to him, which neither the conscience nor the pride of the sturdy Quaker would suffer him to take. Penn was compelled to leave the court, and with many of his friends was prevented from voting. Other irregularities, equally gross, were practised, by means of which the opponent of Sidney was returned to the house. Penn subsequently wrote to Sidney, urging him to resist the outrage, and to present his claims in a petition to the House of Commons, which he did. The petition was referred to the committee of privileges and elections, but the matter was not acted upon, owing, probably, to the dissolution of the Parliament soon after.

Notwithstanding the efforts of the court, the new Parliament was more unmanageable than the old one. A decisive majority of its members were hostile to the Duke of York, and determined upon passing a bill to exclude him from the throne. The bill was introduced into the House of Commons, and passed that body. Its provisions were severe and highly penal, and exhibit very favorably the resolute spirit which actuated this Parliament. Sidney, in the correspondence which he kept up with his friend Saville, at Paris, speaks of the introduction and provisions of this bill, in a letter under date of May 19th, 1679:

" The severe bill against the Duke of York was read on Thursday last, and is appointed to be read again to-morrow. It recites the Pope's pretensions to power over kings, particularly in England; the immorality of the Roman religion; incompatibility of those who profess it with English Protestants; their perpetual plots against the government; sedulity in seducing the duke, and a multitude of other things of like nature in the preamble; *asserts the power of Parliament to dispose of the succession,* as best conducive to the good of the kingdom, which had been often exercised in debarring those that were nearest in blood, but never with so much reason as now. Wherefore it doth enact, 'that the duke should be, and was thereby, excluded;' declares him attainted of high treason, if he landed in England before or after the king's death; forbids commerce or correspondence with him under the same penalty of high treason."

This bill passed the House of Commons by a majority of seventy-nine, but was not brought to a vote in the House of Lords, the Parliament being soon after dissolved. By its provisions the succession was fixed in the next heir of the Duke of York, who was the Princess Mary, married to the Prince of Orange. The whigs, however, were divided in their views of the succession. A portion of them, and those who went farthest in support of liberal principles, favored James, Duke of Monmouth, a natural son of the king by Lucy Walters, a beautiful Welch girl, whom Charles had met in his exile at the Hague, and had made his mistress, but to whom it was now pretended he had been secretly married. To Sidney, the exclusion of the Duke of York at first seems to have been a matter of entire indifference. The firmness and consistency of his principles admitted no temporizing with monarchy. The free institutions toward which he looked, and that civil liberty for which he had struggled, were not to be attained merely by a change of rulers. He frankly declared it was indifferent to him whether James, Duke of York, or James, Duke of Monmouth, succeeded to the throne. It was, however, suggested to him, " that a prince with a defective title would be sure to govern well, considering himself at the mercy of the hereditary claimant, if, by neglecting the interests, he should lose the affections of the people." This suggestion was not lost upon him. Sidney thenceforth labored to avert the fearful despotism which subsequently overtook England, in the accession to the throne of the bigoted and blood-thirsty tyrant James II.

As between the Prince of Orange and Monmouth, Sidney's views during the agitation of the exclusion bill, were frankly expressed to Saville :—

" The first hath plainly the most plausible title by his mother and his wife ; but besides the opinion of the influence it is believed the Duke of York would have over him, it is feared that the Commonwealth party in Holland would be so frighted with that, as to cast itself absolutely in the hands of the king of France, who might, thereby, have a fair occasion of ruining both England and Holland. I need not tell you the reasons *against* Monmouth ; but the strongest I hear alleged *for* him are, that whosoever is opposed to York, will have a good party ; and all Scotland, which is every day likely to be in arms, doth certainly favor him, and may, probably, be of as much importance in the troubles that are now likely to fall upon us as they were in the beginning of the last."

It will be seen from this that Sidney was not a partizan of York, of Monmouth, or of the Prince of Orange, and really favored the pretensions of neither. Yet he deprecated the succession of the Duke of York as the greatest calamity that could befal his country. Monmouth he believed to be the most eligible candidate to concentrate public opinion, and the whole strength of the friends of liberty, in opposition to the Duke ; and as a choice of evils, he therefore looked to Monmouth rather than the Prince of Orange, as the rival of James. But there is no evidence that Sidney favored monarchy even with the prospect of raising Monmouth to the throne, or, as we shall presently see, that such was the design of any conference he may have had with Russell, Hampden, and Essex, upon which the charge of treason was based against him.

At this period, Charles being embarrassed by the importunities of the popular party, and having failed in his attempts to govern by his ministry, as a last resort availed himself of the counsels and well known abilities of Sidney's old friend and correspondent, Sir William Temple. By the advice of Temple, the king consented to appoint a privy council of thirty members, by whose assistance he was to carry on the government. Many eminent members of the country party were appointed, and, among others, the Lords Russell and Essex. Shaftesbury, then at the height of his popularity, was named president. Of this council four members were charged with the chief authority, and formed a sort of privy council or cabinet; these were Temple and Essex, and Sidney's relatives, Halifax and Sunderland.

The expedient, however, proved unsuccessful. Charles broke his pledged word to take no important step without the advice of his council. Alarmed at the progress of the exclusion bill, and the bold tone of the leaders of the opposition, he first prorogued, and then dissolved the Parliament, not only without the advice, but without the knowledge of his council. The dissatisfaction occasioned by the first of these steps is thus noticed by Sidney in a letter of June 2d, 1679, to Saville:

"No man will avow having been the king's counsellor in this business; and some wonder that his majesty, having promised, in constituting the privy council, that he would in all things follow their advices next unto those of the Parliament, should so suddenly prorogue that great council without so much as asking the other. This fills men's minds with many ill humors; the Parliament men go down discontented, and are likely, by their reports, to add unto the discontents of the counties which are already very great; and the fears from the Papists at home, and their friends abroad, being added thereunto, they begin to look more than formerly into the means of pr·

serving themselves. Some, that know matters better than I do, must tell you whether we shall have the same Parliament at the end of the prorogation, or a new one, or none at all; but I think this or another will be found necessary; and if this be dissolved, *another will be chosen of less inclination to favor the court.*"

Sidney's prediction was abundantly verified. A new Parliament was summoned early in the following year, and a large majority of the opposition were returned to the House of Commons. Sidney was again a candidate, this time from the borough of Bramber in Sussex, and again was he zealously sustained by the influence of his friend William Penn. Sir John Fagg and Sir John Temple also warmly aided at the polls. The feeling of the electors was strongly enlisted in his behalf, and his friends confidently predicted his success. The court once more interfered by means of Sir John Pelham, who exerted all his influence in favor of Sidney's younger brother Henry, then on a mission in Holland. The polls closed with a double return. Sidney thought himself duly elected, and claimed his seat in the House. Still, when the Parliament met, in October, 1680, after repeated prorogations, his election was declared void.

While the question was still undecided, and indeed soon after the election, Sidney wrote to Saville expressing his doubt as to the result:

" I am not able to give so much as a guess whether the Parliament shall sit the 26th of January or not, there being a double return ; and nothing can be assured until the question arising thereupon be determined ; unless it be that as *I and my principles are out of fashion, my inclination going one way, my friendship and alliance with those that are like to give occasion for the greatest contests, drawing another*, I shall be equally disliked and suspected by both parties, and thereby become the most inconsiderable member of the House."

He alludes here, doubtless, to his intercourse and family connexion- with such men as Sunderland, and Saville's brother, Halifax, with whose principles he was widely at variance. Halifax, by his genius and eloquence in the House of Lords, subsequently defeated the Exclusion bill in that same Parliament, and thus rendered the most vital service to a cause which the sterner principles of Sidney never permitted him to favor, and to a government which he despised. Sidney well observed in this letter, that he and his principles were out of fashion ; he might have added, that he had become an object of suspicion and enmity to the government, and that his presuming to aspire to a seat in Parliament was considered as an act of the highest effrontery. It is quite apparent that long before his arrest the government had resolved on his ruin, and that a decent pretext only was wanted to accomplish it. Even his most trivial actions were laid hold of and magnified into crimes. For no greater offence than looking from a balcony in London, at a warm contest between the court and people in the election of sheriff, he was indicted for a riot. It was attempted to involve him in a pretended conspiracy of the *non-conformist* to murder the king and exclude the royal family. Sidney, on this occasion, appeared before the king in person, and proved to the natural good sense of Charles, that there neither was nor could be anything of that nature. The principal informer of the " Meal Tub Plot," in which it was designed to involve Sidney, was the vagabond Dangerfield. This man, however, when summoned to the bar of the House, seemed all at once to change sides, and instead of implicating the Presbyterians, to throw the odium upon the Papists. Sidney mentions in a letter to Saville, that Dangerfield declared positively, at the bar of the Commons, "that the Duke of York had offered him a great sum of money to kill the king. He also said that the Lord Privy Seal Peterborough, and Sir Robert Payton were contrivers of the ' Meal Tub Plot.' "

The judgment of Charles seems to have been superior to all these clumsy contrivances, and he never appears to have seriously feared assassination. There was good sense, as well as wit, in the remark he playfully made to his brother, the Duke of York : " Believe me, James, nobody will kill *me* to make *you* king." A plan for his assassination, and perhaps the only one ever seriously entertained, was concerted during the Commonwealth, long before Charles came to the throne, and Sidney himself was the means of preventing its execution. It was no idle boast of his, therefore, when he said, " I think I did once save his majesty's life." How the obligation was repaid will presently be seen.

The new Parliament was found still more refractory, and even revolutionary, than the old. The discontent of the nation at the arbitrary government of Charles, and particularly at the possibility of a Popish successor in the person of his brother James, whose principles were as odious as his conduct was tyrannical, manifested itself in the most determined opposition. Parties seemed to be preparing for a struggle similar to that which twenty years before convulsed the nation. Within a week after the assembling of Parliament the Exclusion bill was again introduced. The chiefs of the popular party—Sidney's friends, Sir William Jones, Russell, and Hampden—rallied in support of it. It passed the Commons by a great majority. When the bill came to the House of Lords, it received the powerful support of Shaftesbury, Sunderland, and Essex; the debate was spun out till a late hour of the night in presence of the king; Halifax opposed the bill, and brought all his consummate ability and his masterly eloquence to the aid of the court, and with the most triumphant success; on the final vote, the bill was rejected by a considerable majority. The disappointment of the popular party was keen and deep. It manifested itself in open resentment. The House of Commons refused to vote subsidies for the king. Charles, driven almost to despair, humbly begged of them a-supply, alleging as a pretext, that it was necessary to meet the danger which threatened Tangier. The house replied that it was better that Tangier fell into the hands of the King of Fez, than serve to discipline Papist troops. The spirit of John Hampden seemed to animate his grandson, who boldly avowed in his place, that "the Duke of York is Admiral of Tangier, and therefore we prefer that Tangier be abandoned." Alarmed at the determined temper exhibited in the Parliament, the king resolved to dissolve it; yet, at the very moment of its dissolution, the House was engaged in passing some spirited resolutions and acts, which proved that it was fully determined never to abandon the position it had assumed.

CHAPTER VII.

New Parliament summoned at Oxford—Differs with the King, and is dissolved—Proclamation of the King—Pamphlet of Sidney in reply—Prosecution of College—Shaftesbury— His character—His connection with the popular party—His quarrel with Sidney—Lord Howard and the Duke of Monmouth—Sidney introduced to the duke by a fraud of Howard—Sidney's intercourse with Monmouth, Russel, Essex, and Hampden—Nature of the conferences between the patriots—Council of six—Sidney's connection with it—The Rye-house plot—The conspirators betrayed to the government—Rumors of Sidney's connection with it—Arrest of the conspirators—Sidney arrested—His conduct before the council—Committed to the Tower—Is waited upon by a committee to be examined—Refuses to answer questions—Efforts to obtain evidence against him—Arrest of Lord Howard—He turns king's evidence—Trial and execution of Lord Russell—His life and character—Death of Essex—The court resolves to bring Sidney to trial—Hampden tried for a misdemeanor and convicted—Preparations for the trial of Sidney—Difficulties in the way of his conviction.

THE implacable and narrow-minded James counselled his brother to adopt severe and arbitrary measures. Immediately after the dissolution he wrote to him : " The moment is come to be truly king, or to perish ; 'no more Parliaments ;' it is to France you must have recourse for subsidies." Charles, however, for once disregarded the advice, and summoned a new Parliament at Oxford. Notwithstanding the efforts of the court, most of the popular members were returned, and the same speaker was elected. Thousands of citizens followed the London deputies to Oxford, armed, and bearing ribbons on their hats, with the device, " *no slavery*," " *no popery*." The king took a firm attitude on opening the Parliament, but declared his attachment to the religion and constitution of the state. The Commons replied, reiterating their demand that the bill excluding the Duke of York should be accepted as the first condition of a truce between them and the throne. A session of a few brief and stormy days satisfied the king that this Parliament was, if possible, still more rebellious and unmanageable than the last; he hastily dissolved it, and retired with his whole retinue to London.

It was on this occasion, in March 1681, that Charles issued a proclamation justifying his conduct, and assigning reasons for dissolving the last two Parliaments. To this declaration a spirited answer appeared, entitled " A Just and Modest Vindication of the Proceedings of the two last Parliaments." The answer was from the pen of Sidney, revised and corrected by Sir William Jones. Bishop Burnet says of this pamphlet that for " spirit and true judgment, it was the best written paper of the times." Sidney charges the Duke of York with advising the dissolution of the Parliament; with being at the head of the popish faction; with favoring the designs of Louis

XIV., by encouraging traitors and pensioners; with endeavoring to reign without Parliaments, and introduce the popish religion ; with betraying the secrets of state to Barillon, the French ambassador, who knew of the intended dissolution of Parliament three days before it was known to the peers at Oxford, by which means the time of dissolving the Parliament was known sooner in Paris than in London ; and he observes—" Good God ! to what a condition is this kingdom reduced, when the ministers and agents of the only prince in the world who can have designs against us, or of whom we ought to be afraid, are not only made acquainted with the most secret passages of state, but are made our chief ministers, too, and have the principal conduct of our affairs. And let the world judge if the Commons had not reason for their vote, when they declared those eminent persons who manage things at this rate, to be enemies to the king and kingdom, and promoters of the French interests."

This paper, able though it was, and convincing, had but little effect. Indeed a strong reaction seemed to have taken place, and the dissolution of the Parliament at Oxford, and the manifesto of the king, all at once, and most unaccountably, turned to the profit of the court. The strength of the exclusionists was divided, if not broken, and the resolute front which Charles showed his opponents, seemed to indicate that he had taken the duke's advice, and like his father was resolved to attempt to carry on the government without Parliaments.

Emboldened by success, the court party strove to retaliate with a heavy hand upon their enemies. A noisy whig, named College, was arrested as a conspirator against the life of the king ; but a London grand jury, being summoned by whig sheriffs, refused to indict him. College was then removed to Oxford, where he was indicted, tried, convicted, and executed. The next object of the vengeance of the court was a more formidable enemy—the celebrated, and infamous as celebrated, Earl of Shaftesbury. The earl was arrested and committed to the tower, but a London grand jury again stood resolutely, and this time successfully, between the throne and its intended victim.

This veteran politician was one of the most singular characters of the period in which he lived, and, as his history is somewhat connected with that of Sidney and his friends, we may interrupt the narrative a moment to glance at it. Gifted with a brilliant but versatile mind—devoured with a fierce ambition—a consummate but most unscrupulous politician, utterly devoid of principle and moral feeling, Sir Anthony Ashley Cooper was emphatically the Talleyrand of his age. The pen of the poet Dryden has admirably sketched the character of this celebrated statesman, under the name of *Achitophel*, in a satire that will last as long as the English language is spoken :

> " Of these the false Achitophel was first,
> A name to all succeeding ages cursed.
> For close designs and crooked counsels fit ;

Sagacious, bold, and turbulent of wit;
Restless, unfixt in principles and place,
In power unpleased, impatient of disgrace;
A fiery soul, which working out its way,
Fretted the pigmy body to decay,
And o'er informed the tenement of clay.
A daring pilot in extremity;
Pleased with the danger when the waves went high;
He sought the storms; but for a calm unfit,
Would steer too nigh the sands to boast his wit.

    *   *   *   *   *

In friendship false, implacable in hate,
Resolved to ruin or to rule the state,
To compass this the triple bond he broke;
The pillars of the public safety shook,
And fitted Israel for a foreign yoke.
Then seized with fear, yet still affecting fame,
Usurped a patriot's all atoning name," &c.

Ashley Cooper had been deeply implicated in all the political intrigues of the day, and had figured conspicuously in the affairs of the Commonwealth under the Protector. He had alternately served and betrayed all parties, and so well-timed was his treachery upon every change of administration, that it universally redounded to his own advantage.

In early youth he had been a royalist. When the cause of the king began to wane, he turned Presbyterian and patriot, and joined the Parliament. His keen eye saw at a glance that Cromwell was the rising star; and on the dissolution of the Long Parliament, he separated himself from the republicans and adhered to the fortunes of the lord-general. With his fellow-traitor, Gen. Monk, the future Duke of Albe-

marle, he was a member of Cromwell's " Barebone
Parliament ;" and from this period his fortune may
be dated. Here he obsequiously followed the nod of
the dictator, and performed for him various important
services—among others, introducing a bill to abolish
the forms of the Commonwealth, by annulling the
engagement " to be true and faithful to the Commonwealth of England, as then established without king
or House of Lords ;" the bill was rejected only to
be renewed and carried in a subsequent Parliament
summoned by the Protector. This statesman, so unscrupulous and subtle-minded, was yet a profound
and able lawyer. He was made a member of the
celebrated commission appointed by the " Barebone
Parliament," to codify and remodel the whole body
of the English statute and common law ! Sir Ashley
Cooper was then a radical reformer, and, of course, a
most active and influential member of the commission;
but it seems to have met with no better success than
has attended the labors of a similar commission in
more modern times.* He was also an effective
instrument in the dissolution of this Parliament and
the elevation of Cromwell to the Protectorship. For
these services he was rewarded with a seat in the
council of state in the new government, and subsequently was appointed by the Protector lord chancellor
of England. It may be mentioned as one of the
most curious instances of Sir Ashley Cooper's versa-

* The author alludes to the commission to codify the laws, appointed pursuant to the new constitution of the State of New York.

tility of character and accomplishments, that he was
ready to perform any service, secular or religious,
assigned him.   Thus his name is found in connection
with those of the Presbyterian divines, Owen and
Baxter, in the commissions appointed by Cromwell's
government to examine the clergy, and to eject scan-
dalous and ignorant clergymen from the ministry!
And yet, this man who thus

"Groaned, sighed, and prayed, while godliness was gain,"

afterwards became the corrupt and facile minister of
the licentious Charles II.

No one saw with clearer perception, or keener
glance, the true nature of the reaction which followed the abdication of the Protector Richard Cromwell, and the re-assembling of the Long Parliament.
With Gen. Monk, he was among the first to turn
renegade to the Commonwealth, and the most zealous
for the Restoration.   Charles II., on coming to the
throne, rewarded these disinterested services by be-
stowing on him the title, Lord Ashley, and appointing
him a member of his first council of state.   But the
measure of Cooper's infamy was filled by his consenting to act as one of the commissioners appointed
to try the regicides, and others excepted by the act
of Parliament.   In this station he sat in judgment on
men with whom he had formerly acted, and who
were not more guilty of treason than he; and among
others, his old associates in the counsels of Cromwell,
Carew and Gen. Harrison.   Charles rewarded the

venal courtier for these and similar services, by
creating him Earl of Shaftesbury, and afterwards
raising him to the dignity of lord chancellor. It is
remarkable, says the historian Hume, that this man,
whose principles and conduct were in all other respects so exceptionable, proved an excellent chancellor ; and that all his decrees, while he possessed
that high office, were equally remarkable for justness
and for integrity. A more noble and manly tribute
is paid to this redeeming feature in Shaftesbury's
career by the same poetic pen whose keen satire we
have just quoted :—

> "Yet fame deserved no enemy can grudge,
> The statesman we abhor, but praise the judge.
> In Israel's courts ne'er sat an Abethdin
> With more discerning eyes, or hands more clean,
> Unbribed, unbought, the wretched to redress;
> Swift of despatch, and easy of access.
> Oh ! had he been content to serve the crown,
> With virtues only proper to the gown,
> Or had the rankness of the soil been freed
> From cockle that oppress'd the noble seed,
> David for him his tuneful harp had strung,
> And heaven had wanted one immortal song."

The genius and tact of Shaftesbury during the first
years of Charles' administration were thrown entirely
in favor of the court and the royal authority. In
1670, he became one of the five ministers of the king,
known by the name of the "Cabal," and in this position he applied all his energies to the service of his
master in upholding the royal prerogative, and in re-

ducing the people to subjection. A few years brought about another change. Shaftesbury, anticipating the fall of his party, betrayed the king and the court, as he had betrayed the Parliament and the Commonwealth. He arose in his place, in the House of Lords, and to the astonishment of all, vehemently opposed one of his colleagues in the Cabal, the Lord Treasurer Clifford, who had made an intemperate speech in opposition to some measure advocated by the country party, and levelled at the court, especially at the Duke of York. The king and the duke were both spectators of the debate. " What a knave of a chancellor have you there ?" said the latter as he left the House. " And you, brother," answered the king, " what a fool of a treasurer have you given me."

From this period Shaftesbury sided with the popular party, and in the language of Dryden :—

" Usurped a patriot's all atoning name."

So vehement and dreaded was his opposition to the court that the king dismissed him from his office of chancellor. In 1677, he made himself still more obnoxious by denying the legality of a Parliament assembled by the king. For this offence he was arrested and sent to the tower, where, after a year's confinement, he was released on his promised submission. On the rise of the country party, Shaftesbury again appeared upon the surface. In the council which Charles called around him on the advice of Sir William Temple, he was made president, to the unbounded joy and satisfaction of the populace. With the early fall of that council, Shaftesbury again fell, and at once entered deeply into the confidence and intrigues of the Duke of Monmouth, whom he flattered with the hopes of succeeding to the crown. The most constant passions of this able and daring man were hatred and resentment. Dryden who truly described him as the pilot

"Pleased with the danger when the waves went high,"

described him also truly as a man "implacable in hate." His hatred to the Duke of York was a passion which never deserted him. Soon after his removal by the king as President of the Council, Shaftesbury had the audacity to appear in Westminster Hall, with Lord Russell and other leaders of the popular party, and present the duke to the grand jury of Middlesex as a popish recusant. The chief justice, in alarm, suddenly dismissed the jury, but Shaftesbury accomplished his end by showing that between him, with his friends of the popular party, and the duke, all accommodation was impossible. From this time he was constantly engaged in violent opposition to the court, and in plots against the government. Committed a second time to the tower, the court, as we have seen, attempted to indict him on a charge of treason; but a whig grand jury threw out the indictment, and the prisoner was released amid the acclamations of the citizens of London. This was in 1681. Soon after the king was seized with a dangerous sickness. Shaftesbury, who had then become deeply implicated in the projects of the Duke of Monmouth, entered into a conspiracy to rise in arms in case of the king's death, and oppose the succession of the Duke of York. The king recovered. The arbitrary proceedings of the court against the city of London resulted in reducing the metropolis to submission. The whig sheriffs were turned out of office. No obstacle now remained to Shaftesbury's indictment. He lurked about the city of London in secrecy. He vainly endeavored to urge upon Lords Essex, Russell and Grey, his plan for a general insurrection to dethrone the king and to crown the Duke of Monmouth. Disappointed on all sides, disgusted with the inactivity of the chiefs of the popular party, alarmed at the impending danger of his situation, he suddenly quitted England and retired into Holland, where he soon after died in exile and obscurity.*

We have seen that Shaftesbury resolutely attempted to draw into his own plans for a conspiracy, Monmouth, Essex, Russell, and Grey, but without success. Hitherto, Sidney had kept entirely aloof from the councils of the conspirators. His personal distrust and dislike of Shaftesbury were open and unconcealed. From the time that the earl had accused him of being a spy of Sunderland to the day of Shaftesbury's volun-

---

* Lord John Russell is of the opinion that many of the charges brought against Shaftesbury were unfounded, and that much injustice has been done his character. See his reflections on Shaftesbury in the "Life of Lord William Russell."

tary banishment, he had refused to have any intercourse with him.   With Monmouth he was entirely
unacquainted.   A friend of Sidney, Lord Howard of
Escrick, a man of a worthless character and corrupt
principles, caused Sidney and Monmouth to meet, by
pretending to Sidney that the duke was desirous to
dine with him, and to Monmouth that Sidney wished
to meet him but had a delicacy in courting his acquaintance.   This fraud of Howard succeeded, and
Sidney met the Duke of Monmouth.   With the ambitious projects of the duke, Sidney had no connection
and no sympathy.   It was immaterial to him whether
Monmouth or York succeeded to the crown so far as
the question of royalty was concerned ; but York was
intimately associated with the idea of popery and
absolute power, and with Monmouth the main hope of
popular liberty seemed to rest.   Sidney, therefore, did
not hesitate, after Shaftesbury's departure, to enter
into intimate and confidential counsel with Monmouth's friends upon the best means of averting the
public dangers, and of defending the liberties and
constitutional rights of his countrymen against the in-
sidious and arbitrary measures of the court.

With Monmouth himself Sidney never was intimate.
Up to the period of his arrest, he had spoken to him,
he says, but three times in his life.   With the noble-
minded Russell, with Essex, a sincere and ardent lover
of liberty, and with Hampden, he was upon terms of
friendship.   To the councils of these men, Monmouth
after he had been released from his connection with

Shaftesbury, committed himself, and there is no evidence, certainly none worthy of credit, that anything treasonable on the part of any of them had been meditated or resolved upon, at least after the departure of Shaftesbury. That nobleman, just previous to his leaving England, had so far implicated Russell and Essex, as to procure an interview between them and two of his creatures, Rumsey and Ferguson, at the house of a wine merchant, named Shepherd; and subsequently, Shaftesbury himself met Essex and another of the conspirators at the same place, where the plan of an insurrection was discussed, and the project of surprising the king's guards mentioned. This evidence given against Russell on his trial was fatal to that nobleman, and led to his conviction. Sidney, however, was entirely unconnected with, and ignorant of the conspiracy, (if indeed it is deserving the name,) until after the soul of the intrigue, Shaftesbury, whom he so heartily despised, had left England.

What was the precise nature of the conferences between Sidney and his friends, and what was in reality the object of their meetings, it is difficult to say. The evidence rests almost exclusively on the oath of the ingrate and triator, Lord Howard, whom Sidney had so indiscreetly admitted to his confidence. Howard pretended in the testimony which he gave on Sidney's trial, (of which we shall speak more in detail hereafter) that a " council of six" was formed to conduct an " enterprise,"the nature of which he does not explain; that this council consisted of the Duke of Monmouth, the Lords Essex and Russell, Col. Sidney, Mr. Hampden and himself; that two meetings only were held at which Sidney was present—one at the house of Hampden, and the other at Lord Russell's; that at the latter meeting there seemed to be a diversity of sentiment, occasioned by a remark of Hampden as to the object and design of the " enterprise;" that at this conference the Duke spoke of raising the sum of thirty thousand pounds, and Sidney proposed a messenger, one Aaron Smith, to be sent with a letter, written, as Howard *believed*, by Lord Russell, into Scotland.* This is the substance of the direct testimony which connects Sidney with this " conpsiracy" for a general insurrection to overthrow the government and kill the king. It will be observed that the whole of Howard's statements might be taken as true, without making out a case to convict either of the so called conspirators of high treason. No plan of action was agreed upon, no design was formed, no definite object was proposed to be accomplished; the conspirators separated, having done nothing, and agreed upon nothing; Russell and Hampden to indulge their warm aspirations for the triumph of liberty under the ancient forms of the constitution; Sidney and Essex to speculate upon the practicability of a commonwealth;

* Howard also testifies that at a conference between himself, Monmouth and Sidney, which was doubtless the first interview ever had between them, at the day of the dinner, that Monmouth undertook to bring over Lord Russell, and Sidney to engage Essex and Hampden in the enterprize.

10*

and Monmouth to dream of his succession to the throne.

In the meantime a wilder and more desperate band of conspirators—the creatures of Shaftesbury—were engaged in planning what was afterwards more familiarly known as the "Rye-house Plot." Of these subordinate conspirators, the principal were Col. Rumsey, an old republican officer, West, a lawyer, Keeling, a salter, Ferguson and Rumbold. Their design was, undoubtedly, insurrection. The project of assassinating the king and the Duke of York, and of thus making way for Monmouth to the throne, was freely discussed among them; and it is said that Monmouth and Howard were not ignorant of the existence of this subordinate conspiracy and of their wild designs, though it is not pretended that the knowledge was shared by any others of the "Council of six." Rumbold had a farm called the Rye-house, on the road to Newmarket, whither the king and the duke commonly went for diversion once a year. The project was discussed among the conspirators of stopping the king's coach at this place, and of assassinating him and the duke; but it does not appear that this wicked and desperate scheme was ever fully resolved on. The whole plot, however, was soon betrayed to the government by Keiling, one of the conspirators. The secretary of state paid little regard to it, till West and Rumsey offered to purchase their worthless lives by turning king's evidence, and fully corroborated in every particular the story of Keiling. When Rumsey

surrendered himself as a witness (who, it will be remembered, had been present with Ferguson at the first
meeting at Shepherd's) the Duke of Monmouth at
once took the alarm, and retired from England. The
city was now full of rumors. Sidney's name was in
every coffee house as connected with the plot. He
was informed that the government meditated his
arrest, and on inquiring the reason, was told of the
allegations made by these men, with not one of whom
he had the slightest acquaintance. Sidney disbelieved
the report; but his informant urged upon him that an
occasion would certainly be found to arrest him, and
that if once arrested he could not possibly escape conviction from such judges and juries as the court was
determined to employ. But Sidney, conscious of his
own innocence, disregarded the admonition, and determined to remain where he was, even after he heard
that the Duke of Monmouth had retired.

West and Keiling could give no evidence against
any of the Council of six. Rumsey was, with difficulty, brought to mention the meeting at Shepherd's,
at which Russell and Essex attended. Shepherd was
arrested and confirmed the account; yet against Sidney and Hampden there was no evidence, except
vague reports, or such loose information as Rumsey
himself had gained from Monmouth and Howard, or
such statements as he chose wilfully to fabricate.
The government, however, determined to arrest all the
pretended conspirators. Monmouth had taken timely
flight, Gray escaped from his guards. Essex, Russell,

and Hampden were thrown into prison, and Howard himself was seized while attempting to conceal himself in a chimney.

On the morning of Sidney's arrest, the 26th June, 1683, he was engaged in his usual studies, and in receiving the visits of his friends. So entirely conscious was he of his own personal innocence, and so far removed did he feel himself to be from every thing that could implicate him in a plot against the king, knowing the prudence that had kept him aloof from all intercourse and conversation with those who were disaffected to the government, save the friends in whose honor he confided, that he entertained no apprehensions for his own safety. While at dinner on that day, he was arrested by an order from the Privy Council in the king's name. Soon after a second order arrived *to secure his papers.* After ransacking the house and finding nothing in any place of concealment, the officer took into his possession some manuscripts which lay upon the table, and in an open trunk beside it. Sidney was desired to put his seal on the packet after it was enclosed, but he refused, remembering, as he says, " what had passed on a similar occasion, and not knowing what might have been put in." The officer thereupon put his own seal to the package, and promised Sidney that it should not be opened except in his presence. This was the last he ever saw of the papers until their production on his trial.

On being brought before the privy council, Sidney answered some of the questions put to him "respectfully and without deceit;" but on being further pressed, he replied, that "if they had any proof against him he was ready to vindicate his conduct, but that otherwise he would not fortify their evidence." Although there was not the shadow of evidence against him beyond vague rumors and hearsay, and nothing whatever to justify his imprisonment, he was arbitrarily committed to the tower on a charge of high treason!

For some time Sidney was kept a close prisoner. His money, and other property, even to his wearing apparel, were seized. His friends were not permitted to see him, and his servants prevented from carrying him a change of linen. Even his faithful servant, Joseph Ducasse, was denied access to him, until, applying to Lord Halifax, he obtained a reluctant permission to attend and visit him. So rigorous was his confinement, that it began to affect his health, but he bore up under it with unflinching fortitude and spirit. The government was no doubt satisfied of the unlawfulness of his imprisonment, and of the weakness of its evidence; but determining to bring him to the scaffold, it employed various artifices to procure the requisite testimony. A committee of the privy council waited upon him in the tower, hoping to derive matter of accusation from his own confessions. Sidney answered haughtily, and with more than his natural acerbity of temper, that "they seemed to want evidence, and were come to draw it from his own mouth; but they should have nothing from him." It

is stated, and doubtless with truth, that the prisons
were ransacked, and threats and persuasions employed
among the prisoners to induce them to furnish evidence against him. Aaron Smith, the messenger
whom Howard alleged had been sent into Scotland by
Sidney, and who was now in custody, on being tam-
pered with by some of the agents of the government,
who desired Smith to propose his own terms for reveal-
ing testimony which might suit their purpose, frankly
replied, "that he could not say anything that would
touch a hair of Col. Sidney's head." The same poor
success met the efforts of the court in other quarters.
At length, however, a witness appeared.

The notorious Howard had been arrested on the 8th
of July. Overcome by the fear of death, the craven
wretch did not hesitate to follow the base example of
Rumsey, West, and Keiling, and to purchase his life.
by offering his evidence against the illustrious prisoners
in the tower. Some of the "Rye-house" conspirators
were convicted on the evidence of the three informers,
West, Rumsey, and Keiling, and were executed the
20th of July. The court, however, was not satisfied
with this puny vengeance, but resolved upon the
sacrifice of noble victims. Accordingly, about the
same time, Lord Russell was brought to trial. With
the aid of the testimony of Howard, before a court
and a jury entirely under the royal influence, Russell
was easily convicted and condemned. His wife,
daughter of the Earl of Southampton, threw herself
at the king's feet, and pleaded in vain for pardon.

Once condemned, such a victim was too agreeable to
the court, and particularly to the vindictive feelings
of the Duke of York, whose resolute enemy he had
always been, to expect mercy. The pardon was refused him. The touching scene in the tower—the
parting of the condemned from his devoted wife and
infant children, nearly overcame the manly fortitude
of the prisoner ; but he quickly recovered it, and as he
turned away after the last embrace, he exclaimed,
" The bitterness of death is now past." For him the
scaffold and the block had no terrors. On the 21st of
July, 1683, Russell was beheaded in Lincoln's Inn
fields. He died in the forty-second year of his age.*

* Lord Russell, whose name is so gloriously associated with that of
Sidney, was the third, and only surviving son of the Duke of Bedford,
and was heir to the most splendid fortune in the kingdom. Bishop
Burnet observes that he was a man of a slow but a sound understanding.
Even his enemies admitted the sincerity of his character, his unim-
peachable private worth, and the purity of his motives. His political
sentiments were liberal in the extreme, but, like those of Hampden, not
revolutionary. He desired to preserve the ancient forms of the monarchy, but to establish constitutional liberty on its broadest basis ; and he
therefore opposed with all the energy of his nature the Duke of York,
and zealously labored to exclude him from the throne. Russell had
represented the county of Bedford in all the parliaments of Charles II.;
and so great was his influence, and so wide-spread his popularity among
all classes of the people, that he was justly regarded as the head of the
liberal party. We have seen that he was one of the council appointed
by the king at the recommendation of Sir W. Temple. He accompanied Shaftesbury to Westminster Hall when that nobleman presented
the Duke of York to the grand jury as a Popish recusant; and a few
months after he carried up the Exclusion bill to the House of Lords at
the head of two hundred members of Parliament. The proof of treason,
on his trial, was confined to the interviews at Shepherd's and elsewhere,

On the very day of Russell's trial, Essex was found
dead, with his throat cut, in the tower. He was a
man of elevated and estimable character, whose
views of popular liberty coincided nearer with Sidney's than with those of any of his other associates.
The only remaining members of the Council of six,
who remained in the power of the king, were Sidney
and Hampden, and it was determined to bring them
to trial. The difficulty attending the procuring of evidence sufficient to convict them, was a formidable obstacle, and long delayed the proceeding. Howard was
indeed ready to swear away the lives of his other
associates, as he had done the life of Russell; but
the crown lawyers were aware that the single and
unsupported oath of such a witness was hazardous in
any criminal case, unless with a jury composed entirely of the creatures of the court. Besides, another
difficulty, almost insuperable, existed. By the statute
of treasons, under which it was proposed to indict the
prisoners, there could be no conviction unless on the

already spoken of, and the law was shamefully perverted to his destruction. Hume himself admits the proof to have been " that the insurrection had been deliberated on by the prisoner; the surprisal of the
guards deliberated, but not fully resolved upon; and that the assassination of the king had not been once mentioned or imagined by him."
The best authorities concur in the opinion that his condemnation was
illegal, and it was on this ground that his attainder was subsequently reversed by act of Parliament. Russell's nobleness of mind was exhibited to the last in his declining the generous offer of his friend Lord
Cavendish, to favor his escape by exchanging clothes; and also the proposal of the Duke of Monmouth to deliver himself up if he thought
the step would be serviceable to him. " It will be no advantage to
me," he said, " to have my friends die with me."

oaths of two concurring witnesses to some overt act. In the case of Hampden, it was found impossible to obviate this difficulty, as Howard was the only witness who could in the slightest degree implicate him. Yet, even Hampden could not entirely escape the vengeance of the court, or rather of the Duke of York. After some length of time he was tried for *a misdemeanor*, convicted on the testimony of Howard, and sentenced to pay a ruinous fine—no less than forty thousand pounds sterling. His whole fortune was insufficient for this purpose, and he was committed to prison.*

The case of Sidney in reality stood upon precisely the same ground. He was no more and no less guilty than Hampden, and there was not a particle more of legal evidence against him ; yet, nothing but his life would satiate the vengeance of his royal enemies, and it was therefore resolved to bring him to trial for high treason. We shall presently see, when we come to speak of his trial, the nature of the additional proof that was adduced against him, and the astonishing audacity of the prosecution in offering it. The chief justice of the King's Bench, who tried Lord Russell, was now dead. He had been succeeded by Sir George Jeffries, on the 29th September, 1683. The city of London had ceased to elect whig sheriffs, these officers being now selected by the court. Daniel and Dashwood, two of the most violent partisans of

* Hampden actually paid £6,000 of this fine, and was released from prison.

the king, had been appointed sheriffs of London and Middlesex by a commission under the great seal. They named Rouse and Hargrave, equally subservient tools and devoted to the service of the Crown, under-sheriffs. All things were now prepared for the sacrifice of Sidney, and the Crown lawyers at length deemed it safe to bring on the trial. Jeffries himself actually consulted with the counsel for the Crown on the means of compassing the prisoner's death, and a paper containing the result of the conference had been found on the attorney-general's table. The preliminaries, therefore, being finally arranged, on the 6th of November, after more than four months imprisonment, Sidney was informed by the lieutenant of the tower that he had received orders to bring him, the next day, by a writ of *habeas corpus* before the King's Bench, at Westminster Hall.

CHAPTER VIII.

Arraignment of Sidney—Lord Jeffries and his associates—Sidney excepts
to the indictment—His exceptions overruled—Oppressive conduct of
the Court—Sidney forced to plead to the indictment and remanded to
prison—Appears at the bar of the King's Bench for trial—Means taken
to secure his conviction—Selection and character of the jury—The
judge refuses him a challenge—Sidney demands counsel and is refused
—The trial—Oppressive and tyrannical conduct of the Court—The
evidence—Its insufficient nature—Objections of Sidney—They are
overruled by the Court—Lord Howard of Escrick—His character—
His evidence—Testimony of Foster and Atterbury—The writings of
Sidney introduced in evidence—Defence of the prisoner—His objections overruled by the Court—He introduces testimony—Impeachment
of Lord Howard—Contest with the Court—Brutal conduct of Jeffries
—Sidney's argument to the jury—Speech of the Solicitor-General—
Charge of the Judge—Verdict of the jury—Surrender of the Duke of
Monmouth after the trial—Hopes of a new trial—Petition of Sidney
to the king—Its failure—Sentence of Sidney—Scene between the prisoner and the Court—Heroic conduct of Sidney—Condemned to be
executed—Petition of Sidney to the king to commute his sentence to
banishment—Is refused—His fortitude and resolution in his last hours
—Description of his execution by the sheriff—Is beheaded—Buried at
Penshurst—Reflections upon his trial, condemnation, and execution.

ON the 7th of November, 1683, Col. Sidney was
arraigned for high treason before the King's Bench in
Westminster Hall. The infamous Sir George Jeffries,

lord chief justice, presided on the bench, assisted
by his associate justices, Wythins, Holloway, and
Walcott.

It is difficult to find in the history of any civilized
people, a character more loathsome than that of Jeffries.   In early life he had practiced at the Old
Bailey ; had afterwards become a serjeant-at-law, and
been subsequently made Recorder of London.   Nature
had endowed him with a quick and ready talent, and
some of the attributes of an able judge.   His percep-
tive powers were acute, and his intellect, when not
unsettled by strong drink, singularly clear, enabling
him at a glance to comprehend, and to carry out to
the very letter, the work that his master prepared for
him.   Yet Jeffries, notwithstanding the possession of
some legal ability, was utterly unfit and unworthy, in
character, in talents, and in habits, to occupy the
place he filled.   A violent, shameless, cruel, vindictive
man, a renegade and traitor to every principle,* the
slave of the vilest sensual passions, a debauchee
and a common drunkard, a demon incarnate, whose
hands were polluted with gold and stained with the
blood of innocence.   The imagination can scarcely
conceive a character so execrably base as that of this
corrupt and wicked judge.

Only a month or two before Sidney's trial, Charles
had rewarded Jeffries' valuable services by promoting
him to the seat he disgraced ; but Charles himself was

---

* Jeffries once passed himself off as a " Round-head."—*Macaulay's
History of England.*

at the same time sensible of his baseness. "That man," said he, "has no learning, no sense, no manners, and more impudence than ten carted streetwalkers." But the Chief Justice found a congenial spirit in the Duke of York, who, when he afterwards came to the throne, was so highly delighted with Jeffries' services, that as a peculiar mark of the royal favor, he conferred upon him a peerage, gave him a seat in the cabinet, and created him Lord Chancellor of England!

The judicial murder of Sidney was the first notable exploit of the Chief Justice after his elevation, as it was, undoubtedly, one of the most ingenious of his whole life. Other and more brutal triumphs followed him in his subsequent blood-stained career. When he had become more familiar with his position, and placed a surer reliance on the power that sustained him, he was accustomed in the fury of brutal passion, or maudlin rage, to terrify his juries into a verdict of guilty. Twice was the lady Lisle brought in by the jury acquitted of the charge preferred against her, but a third time was the jury sent out under a furious speech from the judge, and finally by threats and violence compelled to convict the victim. "Why, thou vile wretch!" he exclaimed to one of the witnesses on this trial—"Dos't thou think because thou prevaricatest with the court here, that thou cans't do so with God above, who knows thy thoughts? And it is infinite mercy that with those falsehoods of thine he does not strike thee into hell! Jesus God! there

is no conversation or human society to be kept with
such people as these are, who have no religion but
in pretence."

Feats like the conviction of the lady Lisle, however, were not achieved by Jeffries until some time
after the trial of Sidney.   He was now comparatively
a novice, and resorted to artifice and cunning to accomplish the nefarious purposes of the government;
and surely none of his achievements was performed
with more clever dexterity than this, and no man was
ever juggled out of his life more coolly, under the
falsest pretences, than Algernon Sidney.

By the side of the Chief Justice sat three men of
straw.   Wythins, like Jeffries, was a debauchee and
a drunkard ; was drunk on the bench during the proceedings, and gave Sidney the lie in open court.   Holloway and Walcott were also creatures of the court,
but said little on the trial.   They of course concurred
in all Jeffries' decisions, and Justice Holloway, at one
stage of the proceedings, insulted the prisoner with
the remark, " I think you have had a very fair trial."
Well might Sidney say of judges like these, after a
calm review of his trial, " Lest the means of destroying the best Protestants in England should fail, the
*bench must be filled by such as had been blemishes to
the bar.*"

It seems that Sidney was brought up from the
tower at an early hour in the morning, before it was
known there was any indictment against him, and
that he was detained at a tavern about an hour, until

the bill was found.   On his being brought to the bar, the attorney-general, Sir Robert Sawyer, informed the court that there was an indictment against the prisoner, and prayed he might be charged with it.   The clerk of the Crown then directed him to hold up his hand, which he did, and the indictment was read to him.   It was long, confused, and perplexed, so much so, that the ablest lawyers could give him, from recollection, but a very imperfect account of its contents. It alleged a variety of crimes, distinct in their nature, relating to different statutes, and distinguished from each other by law ; setting forth no overt act of treason precisely, no person with whom he had conspired, and fixing on the 20th of June, when he was actually a prisoner, as the medium time of his conspiring in the parish of St. Giles in the field.*

When the reading was finished, Sidney took exceptions to the indictment.   This he did in person, the law of England at that time not permitting the prisoner the benefit of counsel at his trial, unless upon the argument of some point of law, in which case the court assigned counsel.   But the Chief Justice would not listen to his exceptions, and peremptorily required him to plead guilty or not guilty.   The attorney general interposed :

" If he will demur, my lord, we will give him leave."

Col. Sidney.—" I presume your lordship will direct me, for I am an ignorant man in matters of this

* Meadley's Memoirs.   State Trials.

kind. I may be easily surprised in it. I never was at a trial in my life, of any body, and never read a law book."

Jeffries.—"Because no prisoner in your circumstances is to have counsel but in special cases to be assigned in matters of law, the court is bound by their oaths, and duty of their places, that they shall not see any wrong done to you; but the business we are to tell you now is, you are to plead guilty or not guilty, or demur, which is a concession, in point of law."

How the infamous judge kept his pledge of seeing no wrong done the prisoner, we shall presently see.

Meanwhile Sidney, still refusing to plead not guilty, or demur, urged his exceptions to the indictment, and instanced the case of Sir Henry Vane, in which such a course had been allowed. But the Chief Justice was peremptory, and again urged him to take his trial upon the indictment, thus waiving all objection to its sufficiency. Sidney then presenting a piece of parchment, which proved to be a special plea, drawn up by Sergeant Rotheram, who, with Pollexfen and one or two others, had been assigned by order of the Earl of Sunderland to assist him in preparing for his trial, desired the Chief Justice to accept it. Jeffries inquired what it was, adding that if a special plea, and the attorney-general demurred to it, the prisoner waived the fact and would have judgment of death without a trial! This was false, and the judge knew it. Had the plea been put in and found to be good, it would have had the effect of relieving the prisoner from answering an indictment containing several distinct offences, relating to different statutes, and purposely blended together; doubtless, with the veiw of entrapping him and obtaining an unfair advantage. If the plea had been overruled and the indictment held good, still the prisoner might have been admitted to plead not guilty, and put upon his trial. Any one versed in law knowledge knew such to be the fact, and yet Mr. Justice Wythins did not hesitate to endorse the lie of the Chief Justice, and when Col. Sidney informed the court that the parchment was a plea, Wythins exclaimed, " Will you stand by it? Consider yourself and your life. If you put in that plea, and the attorney demurs, *if your plea be not good, your life is gone !*"

Sidney was staggered by these remarks. He believed his plea to be good, but he had more confidence in the merits of his case, and hesitated to incur the risk of being cut off from his defence. He asked the court for a day to consider, but the Chief Justice roughly refused it, not choosing to give him the benefit of advising with his counsel, but wishing to entrap him through his own ignorance of the law. He then asked that his paper might be received, not as a plea, but as an exception to the indictment. The Chief Justice, whose brutal passions were now fast kindling into rage, replied :   " It shall not be read, unless you put it in as a plea."

Williams, one of his legal advisers, here whispered to him to put in his plea, but the attorney-general now

11

alarmed at the turn matters were taking, called upon the court to reprove Williams for daring to inform the prisoner of his rights; whereupon Williams was publicly reprimanded from the bench!

Sidney, however, refused to risk the consequences which Jeffries and Wythins had falsely assured him would follow a failure of his plea, and he merely offered it again as an exception to the bill. The clerk was thereupon directed to ask him the customary question: "Art thou guilty, or not guilty." Sidney still declining to answer, Jeffries threatened him with instant judgment in case he did not plead. Driven thus to the inevitable necessity, as he truly declared, by the violence and fraud of the Chief Justice, Sidney reluctantly plead not guilty, and thus "lost the advantage which was never to be recovered, unless the judges could have been changed."*

The accused then desired a copy of the indictment. Jeffries replied that it could not be granted by law.

The prisoner then asked if the court "would please to give him counsel."

Lord Chief Justice.—"We can't do it.† If you assign us any particular point of law, *if the Court think it such a point as may be worth the debating,*

---

* Apology.

† These severe and unjust rules of the common law were abolished after the Revolution. By the statutes, 7 W. 3. c. 3, and 7 Ann c. 21, the prisoner is entitled to a copy of the indictment ten days before the trial, with a list of the jury and of the witnesses on the part of the prosecution: Also, to have two counsel assigned him by whom he may have a full defence.

you shall have counsel, but if you ask for counsel for no other reason than because you ask it, we must not grant it. The court is bound to see that nothing be done against you but what is according to the rules of law. *I would be very loth to draw the guilt of any man's blood upon me.*"

So spake the corrupt and depraved judge who had already taken the first step toward the accomplishment of this judicial murder, and who was subsequently steeped to the lips in the blood of innocence.

The indictment was read over again, and in Latin, a particular favor, as Jeffries afterwards informed the prisoner, and a favor, too, which had been denied Sir Henry Vane on his trial. This insignificant *favor* of the chief justice was more dangerous to the prisoner than could have been a refusal of the request. It enabled Jeffries, under the pretence of having granted a *favor*, to deny the most important rights. Accordingly, when Sidney requested to be informed under what statute of treason he was to be tried, in order to enable him to prepare his defence, the Chief Justice gruffly replied, that the attorney-general would tell him what statute he went upon when he came to trial, and that he might give in evidence any act of Parliament which comprehended treason. Sidney was then notified that his trial would take place that day fortnight, after which, in custody of the lieutenant, he was carried back to the tower.

On the 21st of November, two weeks after the scene just described, Col. Sidney was brought to the bar of the king's bench for trial. The attorney-general, Sir Robert Sawyer, the solicitor-general, Heneage Finch, and several other eminent lawyers, appeared as counsel for the Crown. Against this formidable array of legal talent, the prisoner stood friendless and alone. He stood where, but a few years before, Vane had stood; where, but a few months before, Russell had stood, a martyr with them to the liberties of his country, and with them about to seal with his blood his devotion to the principles he professed. From the first, it was easy to be seen that the accused, like Vane, had been singled out, with cool premeditation, as a victim and a sacrifice. The snare had been set carefully and deliberately, and the wretched farce, the mockery of a trial, was all that stood between him and the remorseless vengeance of the government. The bench before which he was to be tried was filled with judges such as have been described; such as had been " blemishes to the bar;" the like of which never before or since have disgraced Westminster Hall—worse than the creatures of Couthon and St. Just, or the most sanguinary judges of the revolutionay tribunal. But, lest a ray of hope might remain for the prisoner in the honesty of an English jury, the most systematic and careful measures had been successfully carried into effect to *pack a jury*, drawn from among the creatures and hirelings of the Court, and men of ruined character and fortune, who were either his personal enemies, or were dependant entirely upon the royal favor.

Sidney says in his "Apology," that he thought his birth, education, and life, might have deserved a jury of the principal knights and gentlemen, free-holders in Middlesex, or at all events, if not free-holders, then the most eminent men for quality and understanding, reputation and virtue, who lived in the country. But when a copy of the panel was sent to him, he found a jury summoned of men, many of whom were of the " meanest callings, ruined fortunes, lost reputations, and hardly endowed with such under-standing as is required for a jury in a 'nisi prius' court, for a business of five pounds." The jury had been *selected* by the solicitors of the Crown; the names of a few gentlemen were inserted in the panel for form's sake; but the bailiffs had never summoned these, or, if summoned, they did not attend. Of the whole number returned, only the names of three persons were known to Col. Sidney, whom, if present, he had resolved to accept. The lord Chief Justice, too, arbitrarily refused him the right of challenge for cause against such of the jurors as were in the king's service, as wanted freeholds, or as were notoriously infamous. After a few peremptory challenges of such persons as he knew were summoned to destroy him, a jury was at length empanelled and sworn. Among the jurors were three carpenters, a tailor, a cheese monger, and a horse rider.

Before entering upon the trial, Col. Sidney again moved for a copy of the indictment, and cited for that purpose the statute of 46 Edw. II., which enacted that all persons, in all cases, should have a copy of such records as were against them. The prisoner fortified his application with the precedents of the Earl of Strafford, Lord Stafford, and the popish lords in the tower, all of whom had availed themselves of this privilege; but Jeffries again denied the application on the authority of the cases of Vane and Russell, holding that the right extended only to peers and not to commoners. Upon this part of the proceedings Sidney in his "Apology," indignantly remarks, "Although I am not a peer *I am of the wood of which they are made*, and do not find that our ancestors were less careful *of the lives of commoners than of peers*, or that one law is made for them and another for us; but are all entirely under the same law and the same rules."

And now the formal proclamation for evidence having been made, the case was opened to the jury by Mr. Dolben, one of the counsel for the Crown, who stated the substance of the indictment, to wit: that the prisoner had conspired the death of the king, and to levy war within the kingdom; and also that he had written a false, seditious libel, in which was contained these English words: "*The power originally in the people of England is delegated unto the Parliament. The king is subject to the law of God as he is a man; to the people that makes him a king, inasmuch as he is a king; the law sets a measure unto that subjection,*" etc. The attorney-general then followed in an artful and jesuitical address designed to prepossess the minds of the jury, and to prejudice them against any defence

the prisoner might make. In the course of his remarks, the attorney-general expressed himself in indignant terms upon the " seditious libel" alleged to have
been written by the prisoner, and upon the atrocious
nature of the sentiments he entertained upon government as found written in his manuscript; concluding
with the following words: "Gentlemen, if we prove
all these matters to you, I doubt not you will do
right to the king and kingdom, and show your abhor-
rence of those republican principles, which, if put in
practice, will not only destroy the king, but the best
monarchy in the world."

What mercy was the prisoner to expect from such
ruthless prosecutors, what favor from that corrupt
bench, what justice at the hands of that slavish jury!

Then the solicitor-general, Finch, the same who
twenty years before had covered himself with infamy
by his conduct in the prosecution of Vane, called
West as the first witness for the crown. This West
was the individual, who with Col. Rumsey, Keiling, and others, had been concerned in the Rye-
house Plot, which had just been discovered. Sidney
was not in the least implicated in that plot, and was
even unacquainted with the conspirators who were now
produced as witnesses, not to prove any connection of
his with the plot, but to prove *generally the existence
of a plot.*

Sidney objected to West as a witness, on the ground
that he had confessed many treasons and was not yet
pardoned.

"I don't know that," interposed the Chief Justice.

"My lord," said Sidney, "how can he be a witness then?"

"Swear him," growled Jeffries, "for I know no legal objection against him. He was a good witness in my Lord Russell's trial?"

The witness was then asked by one of the Crown lawyers what he knew "*of a general insurrection in England?*"

The prisoner here objected to the giving of any evidence except what concerned himself personally; but the court overruled his objection, and suffered West to detail his own conversations, and the conversations of others relative to the Rye-house Plot, and a projected general rising, in which Sidney was not in the slightest degree concerned. "As to the prisoner in particular," said this witness in conclusion, "I know nothing, and did never speak with him till since the discovery." In the course of the examination, while West was detailing the rumors and reports of a plot he had heard, Sidney attempted again to object to this illegal evidence. But Jeffries peremptorily silenced him with the remark: "You must not interrupt the witness. Go on, sir."

Rumsey was then called to the stand and proceeded in a similar strain. He spoke of the meeting at Shepherd's, and several meetings at West's, in which the rising was talked off, but did not pretend that Sidney was present, or had any knowledge of these meetings; or was in any way connected with the conspiracy, except that West and one Goodenough *had told the witness* that there was a Council of six, composed of the prisoner, the Duke of Monmouth, Lord Essex, Lord Howard, Lord Russell, and Mr. Hampden, who *were expected* to countenance the rising.

The infamous Keiling, who had been the first to turn evidence for the Crown and betray his associates, was then sworn. He merely testified to a conversation with Goodenough, who, the witness said, *had told him* of a design of a general insurrection, and that Col. Sidney, whom the witness admitted he did not know, was to have a considerable part in the management of it.

Col. Sidney.—My lord, I must ever put you in mind, whether it be ordinary to examine men upon indictments of treason concerning me, that I never saw nor heard of in my life.

Jeffries.—I tell you all this evidence does not affect you, and I tell the jury so.

Col. Sidney.—But it prepossesses the jury.

The Chief Justice made no reply.

Thus far not the first syllable of anything like evidence known to the common law of England, had been given against the prisoner. The hearsays, the rumors, the reports of a plot, of the very existence of which there was no proof that Sidney had even the remotest knowledge, were clearly inadmissible for any purpose ; but the tyrannical judge had suffered them to be given under the false pretence that he meant to tell the jury that this testimony did not affect the prisoner.

11*

The prosecution, now, undertook to give more definite and positive evidence, and for that purpose called the sole witness on whom they relied to prove any connection of the prisoner with the plot, Lord Howard, one of the pretended Council of six. A word in respect to this witness may be proper, before undertaking to give the substance of his testimony.

Lord Howard of Escrick is justly branded by Bishop Burnet as a monster of ingratitude. He was a man of pleasing manners, but of the most worthless and depraved character. Strangely enough, he had acquired in a high degree the good opinion of Sidney, who had befriended and aided him on many occasions. He had lent him large sums of money, which were still owing. When Howard was committed to the Tower, as the author of a treasonable libel, Sidney had remained true to him, and by means of the most active exertions had procured the withdrawal of the indictment against him. Yet, at the same time that Sidney was thus befriending this mean-spirited wretch, utterly unworthy the friendship of such a man, Howard was plotting the ruin of his benefactor. He had succeeded in introducing Sidney to the Duke of Monmouth, as we have seen, by practising a fraud on both. It was upon the representations, and at the request of Sidney alone, that Howard was admitted at the future consultations, and into the confidence of Monmouth, Essex, Russell, and Hampden, where he availed himself of the opportunity offered, to become an infamous apostate, and betray the friends who had trusted him. Sidney states, and doubtless with truth, that Howard not only attempted to defraud him out of the money he had lent him, but also had come to his house after his arrest, in the name of a friend, and endeavored to get his plate and other valuables into his own hands. After Russell's and Sidney's arrest, this craven wretch went about with eyes and hands uplifted to heaven solemnly swearing, what doubtless was then the truth, that he *knew of no plot, and believed nothing of it.* Just before Russell's trial, however, he was arrested in his own house, where he was found concealed in a chimney, and when taken into custody, commenced weeping like a child. Finding that his safety and his life were to be secured only by his giving evidence for the Crown, or, as he did not hesitate to express it himself, by "the drudgery of swearing," he without scruple volunteered his testimony, and proved traitor to those who had befriended and trusted him. Such was the ingrate whose testimony had convicted Russell of treason; whose single, unsupported, and contradictory oath sent Sidney to the scaffold.

The Lord Howard was called to the stand, and the attorney-general desired him to tell what he knew respecting the connection of the prisoner with this affair of a general insurrection. Howard then commenced his story with the preliminary flourish that in entering upon the evidence he was about to give, he could not but observe "what a natural uniformity there is in truth." He referred to the testimony of

the other witnesses, and spoke vaguely of an " enterprise that had long been in hand, and was then fallen
flat," the reviving of which the Duke of Monmouth,
the prisoner at the bar, and himself, were the first to
consult upon. What the " enterprise" was, the witness did not pretend to state. The " consultation"
spoken of was probably at the time he had succeeded
by his duplicity in getting Monmouth to dine with
Sidney. The witness further testified that Monmouth
undertook to engage Russell, and that Sidney promised to bring Essex and Hampden into the cabal.
That the six subsequently met at Hampden's house,
where, in a conversation commenced by Hampden
some mention was made of a sum of money to be
raised for an " enterprise" (what it was the witness
does not state) ; and the Duke of Monmouth mentioned twenty-five or thirty thousand pounds. The witness then went on to say that he was present at
one other meeting at the house of Russell. At this
meeting Howard said there was some discourse by
Mr. Hampden, which was thought to be *untimely
and unseasonable*, and that was (we give his own
words), " that having now united ourselves with *such
an undertaking as this was*, it could not but be expected
that it would be a question put to many of us—to
what end all this was ? Where it was we intended
to terminate ? Into what we intended to resolve ?"
Hampden then communicated his opinion that the
object ought to be, " to put the properties and liberties of the people in such hands as they should not be

easily invaded by any that were trusted with the supreme authority," and to "resolve all into the authority of Parliament." The witness stated that this was finally consented to, though it had "a little harshness to some that were there," doubtless, alluding to the Duke of Monmouth, whose object was the throne, while that of Sidney as well as of Essex, Russell and Hampden was a free, if not a republican, government. The witness testified further, that a proposition was made in respect to sending an emissary to Scotland, to some leading men there, in order to ascertain the minds of the people of that country; whereupon Sidney proposed one Aaron Smith as a proper person for such a mission. This, he said, was all that occurred to him as having passed at the meetings, and these were the only meetings at which he was. In answer to some further questions put to him by the attorney-general, he said that once in London he had seen Sidney take out several guineas, he supposed about sixty, which, he said, were for Smith, and afterwards Sidney had told him that Smith had departed for Scotland. This was the substance of Lord Howard's testimony. At its close, the Chief Justice inquired of the prisoner if he would ask any questions. Sidney replied that he had no questions to ask. Hereupon the attorney-general, catching his cue from Jeffries, responded, for the particular benefit of the jury: "*Silence—you know the proverb.*"

Foster and Atterbury were then sworn, who testified briefly and vaguely to the fact of some Scotch gentlemen coming up to London, among whom was Sir John Cockran, to whom it was pretended Smith had carried a letter, written, as Howard *believed*, by Lord Russell.

So closed this most weak, inconclusive, and extraordinary testimony, which the prosecution had so diligently prepared to sustain this branch of the case. Although nothing in reality was proved to support the indictment for the crime of conspiracy against, and imagining the death of, the king, and of levying war against him in his realm, even admitting the testimony of the perjured Howard to be true, yet the prosecutors insisted, confident that the judge would so charge the jury, that they had abundantly *proved* the overt act of treason by one witness. In order, however, to convict of the crime of treason, it was necessary, as has been mentioned, that two concurring witnesses should testify to some overt act. Thus far the Crown had produced only one, Lord Howard. In order to supply the defect of proof, they now proposed to introduce the manuscripts of Sidney, seized by Sir Philip Lloyd in his closet, at the time of his arrest, which the prosecution insisted was *equivalent to another witness*.

Sir Philip Lloyd was sworn, who testified that he had seized, under the warrant of the king and council, certain papers of Col. Sidney, at the time of his arrest. Shepherd, Cary, and Cooke, three witnesses produced by the Crown, were then sworn, who proved by *comparison of hands,* that the papers found were the writings of the prisoner.* Notwithstanding the objection of the prisoner against the illegality of the evidence, the papers were admitted, and a portion of them read to the jury. In order to show upon what evidence Sidney was convicted of the crime of high treason, we shall quote the following passages from these papers, which were read upon his trial, alleged, doubtless with truth, to have been written by him ; and which the lord Chief Justice charged the jury were to be considered equivalent to the production of another witness to prove an overt act of treason :—

" For this reason Bracton saith, that the king hath three superiors, to wit, *Deum, legem, et parliament,*† that is, the power originally in the people of England is delegated unto the Parliament. He is subject unto *the law of God,* as he is a man ; *to the people* that makes him king, inasmuch as he is a king. The law sets a measure unto that subjection, and the Parliament judges of the particular cases thereupon arising. He must be content to submit his interest unto theirs, since he is no more than any one of them in any other respect than that he is, *by the consent of all,* raised above any other."

" *If he doth not like this condition he may renounce the crown ;* but if he receive it upon that condition, as all magistrates do the power they receive, and swear to perform it, he must expect that the perform-

---

* One of them, however, had seen Sidney sign his name to the bills.
† God, law, and the parliament.

ance will be exacted, or revenge taken by those that he hath betrayed."

The clerk having finished the reading of these and similar extracts, Jeffries remarked to the jury, " The argument runs through the book fixing the power in the people." Whereupon the clerk was directed to read the titles of two other sections, which he did :—

" The general revolt of a nation from its own magistrates, can never be called a rebellion."

" The power of calling and dissolving parliaments is not in the king."

The enunciation of these two propositions—which contained within themselves an entire justification of the late revolution—seemed to fill the virtuous judges, the Crown lawyers, and the jury, with horror. The enormity of the prisoner's crime was now fully manifested. Such sentiments as these, as Jeffries subsequently remarked, were not only equivalent to another witness, but to " many witnesses." And the prosecutors having at last condescended to inform the prisoner that he was indicted under the first branch of the statute of 25th Edward III., for conspiring and compassing the death of the king, here rested the case, with all the confident assurance of men who read in the stern countenances of the court and jury the doom of their victim.

Apparently, Sidney in entering upon his defence felt the same conviction. The arbitrary and tyrannical treatment he had received, was such as to give him too plainly to understand that his death was a thing already determined. He, however, bore up manfully and resolutely, but hopelessly, against the formidable power that assailed him, like a strong swimmer vainly struggling for his life, and striving with stout heart to breast the resistless current that is steadily and surely bearing him down. Before calling any witnesses he addressed his judges, and after some pertinent and un-answerable comments upon the insufficiency of the testimony, he desired the court to relieve him from entering upon his defence, upon the ground that only one witness had been produced against him. But he was met only with the scornful answer of the Chief Justice, that if he did not choose to make any defence, the court would charge the jury upon the law pre-sently, and leave them to decide the case upon the evidence already given. Sidney then desired counsel to argue the point of there being but a single witness, but Jeffries ruled this to be a *question of fact* for the jury, who alone were to determine whether the evidence was sufficient or not! Baffled on all sides by the subtlety, the almost infernal craft of the judge, Sidney still manfully stood his ground, and undertook himself to argue before that prejudiced tribunal, that the papers found in his possession were no evidence of treason, or of any crime. He urged that they were never published, and perhaps never would have been ; that from the color of the ink they appeared to have been written twenty years ago ; that the matter of the book was not treasonable, and was connected with no plot, past, present, or to come, but that the treatise

itself, as appeared upon its face, was in answer to an
infamous book of Sir Robert Filmer on the " Divine
Right of Kings," wherein that author laid down the
doctrine of absolute power on the part of the monarch,
and passive obedience on the part of the subject ; and
that by the law of England he had a right to controvert such speculative opinions, or at least to write his
own thoughts in respect to them in his closet.   Here
the argument of Sidney began to grow too troublesome to the Chief Justice.   He abruptly interrupted
him (as he constantly did in such parts of his discourse
as he saw might influence the jury) and sternly re-
minded him that it was not his business to "spend
your time and the court's time in that which serves to
no other purpose than to gratify a *luxuriant way of
talking you have* ;" and thereupon he repeated, that
when he came to direct the jury, he should instruct
them that the law required two witnesses, but that
whether there was such proof or not was to be solely
determined by the jury, as a question of fact.   His
learned associates, Wythins and Holloway, chimed in
their notes of approval.   Col. Sidney calmly answered :
" Truly, my lord, I do as little intend to mis-spend my
own time, and your time, as ever any man that came
before you."

Whereupon Jeffries brutally rejoined ; " Take your
own method, Mr. Sidney ; but I say if you are a man
of low spirits and weak body, 'tis a duty incumbent
on the court to exhort you not to spend your time upon
things that are not material."

Overruled thus on all sides—the contents of papers written many years before, being held evidence of an existing plot to murder the king—the innocent speculations of a philosopher being construed into the plottings of the rankest treason, and his objections to these absurd constructions of law being held entirely immaterial, Sidney still pressed his last point, that the discourses were never published, observing that he thought it " a right of mankind, and exercised by all studious men, to write what they pleased in their own closets for their own memory, without ever being called in question for it." But Jeffries did not so understand the law. " Pray, don't go away with that right of mankind," he remarked, " I have been told, curse not the king, not in thy thoughts, not in thy bedchamber, the birds of the air will carry it ; I took it to be the duty of mankind to observe *that*."

Such was one of the judges, who but little more than a century and a half ago, administered the law in Westminster Hall on the bench of a tribunal whose decisions have the weight of authority in our own country, and which are daily quoted in our own court as the highest evidences of the common law !

Put thus to the necessity of rebutting what the court was pleased to consider the facts proved against him, Col. Sidney called several witnesses for the purpose of impeaching the statements of Lord Howard. Among these were Howard's two kinsmen, Mr. Philip and Mr. Edward Howard, the Earl of Anglesey, Lord Clare, Lord Paget and Bishop Burnett. It is unneces-

sary in this place to go into the particulars of the
testimony given by these witnesses. They all concurred in the fact that Lord Howard, before his arrest,
had continually disavowed the existence of any plot,
and treated it with ridicule, and that even in the
midst of the most familiar and intimate conversations
with his friends, asserted the same facts, and even fortified his statements with an oath. Bishop Burnet,
for example, testified that Howard protested to him
with hands and eyes uplifted to heaven, that he knew
nothing of any plot, and believed nothing of it, and
looked upon it as a ridiculous thing. His cousin,
Edward Howard, with whom he had always been on
the closest terms of intimacy, testified that he had
stated to him confidentially, in a private conversation,
the same thing, assuring him that the whole plot was
a sham, to his knowledge, devised by *Jesuits* and
Papists. The apparent sincerity of the communication on that occasion, was so totally irreconcileable
with the truth of Lord Howard's present statements,
that his cousin assured the jury he would not believe
Lord Howard under oath.

Here the Chief Justice, who feared the effect of his
testimony onthe minds ot the jury, interfered: " This
must not be suffered."

The attorney-general angrily remarked to the witness, " You ought to be bound to your good behavior
for that."

And Jeffries promptly told the jury they were bound

by their oaths to go according to the evidence, and were not " *to go by men's conjectures.*"

In addition to this evidence, the infamous character of Howard was proved by other confessions and acts. A witness, Blake, testified that after the discovery of the pretended plot, Howard had told him he could not have his pardon "till the drudgery of swearing was over." Howard himself admitted on the trial that he owed Sidney money on a mortgage. Grace Tracy and Elizabeth Penwick, two of Sidney's servants, testified that Howard came to the house after Sidney's arrest, and after calling upon God to witness that he knew nothing of a plot, and was sure Col. Sidney knew nothing of one, desired *to obtain possession of Sidney's plate,* and ordered it to be sent to his own house *to be secured.* Upon this the testimony closed, and the prisoner was directed by the court to apply himself to the jury.

The brief address of Sidney to the jury, as it is found published in the " State Trials," appears to us embarrassed and restrained. He was, doubtless, sensible, though conscious of his own innocence, that his defence was desperate before that partial and bigoted tribunal. The argument of the legal questions involved, is both acute and logical, and at times he rises to a lofty and manly eloquence; yet, throughout the whole, though he never for a moment loses his calmness and self-possession, he seems to be laboring as a man who struggles against hope. One fact is singularly significant of the utter hopelessness of the position in which he found himself placed. It is, that he did not venture to justify to the jury, as he had previously done to the court, a single passage from the manuscript which had been read against him. He urged the defect in the proof of the hand-writing, and that the similitude of hands to which the witnesses had sworn was no proof; but he does not place his defence on the broad ground that the sentiments contained in the manuscript are justifiable.

"If anything is to be made of them," he says, "you must produce the whole; for 'tis impossible to make anything of a part of them. You ask me what other passages I would have read? I don't know a passage in them. I can't tell whether it be good or bad. But if there are any papers found ('tis a great doubt whether they were found in my study or whether they be not counterfeited, but though that be admitted that they were found in my house), the hand is such that it shows they have been written very many years. Then, that which seems to be an account of the sections and chapters, that is but a scrap. And what, if any body had, my lord, either in my own hand or another's found papers that are not well justified, is this treason? Does this imagine the death of the king? Does this reach the life of the king? If any man can say I ever printed a sheet in my life, I will submit to any punishment."

Speaking further of Howard's statement in respect to the meeting of the Council of six, he says :—

" This was nothing, if he was a credible witness, but a few men talking at large of what might be, or might not be—what was likely to fall out without any manner of intention or doing anything. They did not so much as inquire whether there were men in the country, arms, or ammunition. A war to be made by five or six men, not knowing one another—not trusting one another! What said Dr. Coxe in his evidence at my Lord Russell's trial, of my Lord Russell's trusting my Lord Howard? He might say the same of some others. So that, my lord, I say these papers have no manner of coherency—no dependence upon any such design. You .must go upon conjecture, and after all you find nothing, but only papers—never perfect—only scraps—written many years ago; and that could not be calculated for the raising of the people. Now pray, what imagination can be more vain than that? What man can be safe if the king's counsel can make such (whimsical, I won't say, but) groundless constructions ?"

Such was Sidney's explanation to the jury of the papers found in his possession. Doubtless, his course in assuming this cautious position was the most prudent he could have taken before such a jury, so far as the probable issue of the trial was concerned; but we cannot look over his defence without a feeling of disappointment at its comparative tameness, and the conviction that he suffered to pass by him the glorious opportunity of boldly justifying the noble sentiments contained in his discourses, and that too with-

out realizing the least benefit from his excess of prudence. Sidney's defence, though firm, manly, and
elevated, and though not disfigured by a word or
thought unworthy the man or the occasion, yet com-
pares unfavorably with the masterly and every way
glorious defence by Vane, when arraigned and condemned on a similar charge. Though Sidney possessed a larger degree of physical courage, and a
greater share of what the world calls intrepidity and
daring, yet the highest conception we can form of his
character does not clothe it with that elevated, that
almost sublime, moral heroism—that high-wrought
enthusiasm in the discharge of duty—that unshrinking, undying devotion to principle, even at the judgment tribunal, and in the face of the scaffold, which
embalms the memory of Sir Harry Vane. Vane, in
presence of his judges, fearlessly avowed and justified
every act and sentiment of his whole life ; he spoke
not for himself alone, but for his fellow men—not for
his own sake merely, as he told his judges, but for
theirs, and posterity ; and at the close of his trial,
the issue of which he had all along foreseen, he
blessed the Lord " that he had been enabled to discharge, to his own entire satisfaction, the duty he
owed to his country and to the liberty of his countrymen." But it should be remembered at the same
time, that the defence of Vane, if more striking and
noble than that of Sidney, was made under more
advantageous circumstances. Deeply skilled in the
subtle dialectics of the day; possessing a profound, an

acute, and a wonderfully versatile intellect; able at once to deal with the most abstruse questions of metaphysics, of controversial divinity, and of law, Vane was precisely the man, with his high-wrought and just conceptions of liberty and right, and his unshrinking moral firmness, to stand manfully up in justification of every word he had ever uttered in favor of the freedom of his countrymen. So he did; and for several days baffled the ingenuity of the most accomplished lawyers of the kingdom, and averted, and almost foiled the efforts of a court that wielded the whole power of the law to crush him. It does not detract from the merits of Sidney's defence, nor from that of any other victim of political persecution who ever stood at the bar of the king's bench in Westminster Hall, to say that none can be found to rival in greatness and moral sublimity this last public effort of the most illustrious statesman of the Commonwealth.

When Sidney had concluded his speech in his own defence, the solicitor-general, Sir Heneage Finch, arose to address the jury. Finch was an able and skilful advocate, versed in all the subtlety and craft of his profession. His harangue on this occasion was an ingenious tissue of calumnies, misrepresentations, and sophistry; exhibiting throughout the practised hand of the pampered and unscrupulous advocate, whose business, as king's counsel, it had been, through a long series of years, as Sidney expressed it, to drive men headlong into verdicts upon no evidence. And

surely never had a case occurred in which that feat
was more successfully accomplished. At the close of
Finch's speech the prisoner attempted to correct
some of his misrepresentations of the evidence, and
false construction of the law; but he was sternly
and peremptorily silenced by the court.

Then Jeffries stood up to charge the jury. He
spoke about an hour and a quarter, in a tone of violence, and in a spirit of gross partiality, that would
have been censurable in an advocate at the bar. In
his "Apology," Sidney, speaking of this charge of the
judge, says of it: "I can give no other account of it
than that, as he had been long observed to excel in
the laudable faculty of misleading juries, he did
exercise it with more confidence upon the bench than
ever he had done at the bar; declared treasons that
had been hitherto unknown, and that the jury was
obliged to take that to be law which he judged to be
so, and misrepresented the evidence *even more than
the Solicitor had done.*"

All this was true to the very letter. Jeffries did
not even preserve the semblance of the judge, but
throughout the entire charge assumed the tone of an
advocate for the Crown, and with a facility of perversion both of the law and evidence, which the greater
self-respect of the solicitor-general did not permit him
to use, and with a tact and ready talent, and an art
of expression almost infernal, which never failed him
when mischief was to be accomplished, he so presented
the case to the jury as rendered a conviction certain.

It will be remembered that Jeffries, in answer to an objection of the prisoner, had stated during the trial, that he should charge the jury as a matter of law, that two witnesses were necessary to convict of high treason, but that it was a question *of fact for the jury to determine* whether there was such evidence or not. He now, however, took the whole matter out of the hands of the jury, and in effect ordered them to bring in a verdict of guilty. Having first carefully charged them that they were bound to receive the law from the Court, he went on to stigmatize Sidney's manuscript as a " most traitorous and seditious libel." "If you believe," he remarks, " that that was Col. Sidney's book, *no man can doubt but it is sufficient evidence that he is guilty of compassing and imagining the death of the king.*" After pressing upon the jury, with a lawyer's peculiar and ready tact, the moral certainty that this book was the writing of the prisoner, he thus proceeds to characterize its enormities :

" Another thing which I must take notice of in this case is to remind you how this book contains all the malice and revenge and treason that mankind can be guilty of. *It fixes the sole power in the Parliament and the people,* so that he carries on the design still, for their debates at their meetings were to that purpose. And such doctrines as these suit with their debates; for there a general insurrection was designed, and that was discoursed of in this book and encouraged. They must not give it an ill name; it must not be called a *rebellion,* it being *the general act of the people.* The king, it says, is reponsible unto them; the king is but their trustee ; that he had betrayed his trust. he had misgoverned, and now he is to give it up, that they may be all kings tnemselves. Gentlemen,

I must tell you I think *I ought more than ordinarily to press this upon you*, because I know the misfortunes of the late unhappy rebellion, and the bringing the late blessed king to the scaffold, *was first begun by such kind of principles.* They cried, he had betrayed the trust that was delegated to him from the people," &c., &c.

He finally sums up his detestable comments upon the book with the remark—" So that it is not *upon two*, but it is upon GREATER EVIDENCE THAN TWENTY-TWO, if you believe this book was writ by him."

This was charged as a matter of law, which the jury were bound by their oaths to receive—that the contents of the papers were treasonable, and were equivalent to many witnesses, and that unless the jury found the papers were not written by the prisoner, they were bound by their oaths to convict him. What course was left for this poor, ignorant and enslaved jury, but to follow the directions of a tyrannical government, uttered through the lips of a corrupt and shameless judge!

As for the rest, Jeffries proceeded to examine, with much ingenuity of artifice, the prisoner's objections to the testimony, and to demonstrate to the jury, step by step, that all were untenable and absurd. The objections against Lord Howard, so far from impeaching him, he said, went rather to his credit, by proving him to be an unwilling witness! And, finally, having arrived at the comfortable conclusion, that no shadow of doubt ought to be entertained of the prisoner's guilt, the Lord Chief Justice took his seat. The sage and oracular Justice Wythins then stood up, but merely to declare the opinion of the rest of the court, that "in all the points of law we concur with my Lord Chief Justice."

The jury now retired. Jeffries followed them, as he pretended, to get a cup of sack, but for the purpose, as it is asserted, of giving them further and private instructions. In half an hour's time they returned with a verdict of GUILTY.

The trial had lasted from ten o'clock in the morning till six in the evening. During the whole of this period the prisoner had manifested the utmost steadiness and serenity of temper. He was frequently observed to smile at the conduct of his persecutors, and he listened to the verdict of the jury with calmness and indifference. Before the verdict was recorded, he desired to avail himself of the right of inquiring severally of the jurors whether each one had found him guilty, and especially whether each one had found him guilty of compassing the king's death; of levying war against the king; of any treason within the statute of 25 Edward III.;* or of any proved against him by two witnesses. But the Chief Justice overruled his request, and he was again remanded to the tower.

Three days after the trial, the Duke of Monmouth surrendered himself to the government. He was admitted into the presence of the king, his father, penitently confessed his errors, and was graciously for-

---

* The case of Sidney was not attempted by the Crown lawyers to be brought under any head of the statute of treasons other than the first, namely: "When a man doth compass or imagine the death of our lord the king, of our lady his queen, or of their eldest son and heir."

given.   The friends of Sidney began to entertain hopes that a new and more impartial trial might be obtained, and that the important testimony of Monmouth might be used with effect to acquit him.   With this view he was persuaded to present a petition to the king, which he did on the 25th of November, by the hands of Lord Halifax. The petition set forth briefly the irregularities of the trial, and the gross injustice the prisoner had sustained at the hands of the court, and prayed that the petitioner might be admitted into the presence of his majesty.   The nature of Charles, though cold and perfidious, was not cruel, and the request might have been granted, but the vengeful and blackhearted Duke of York was at that time high in favor in the councils of the king.   He seems to have taken the case of Sidney under his especial patronage, and to have committed it to the sure hands of his *protege* Jeffries. The prisoner's petition, and all his grievances, were referred back to the very judges by whom he had been tried.   Jeffries had before declared, in his furious way, that the prisoner must die, or he himself would die. And the Duke of York, by taking the petition out of the hands of the king, and placing it in those of the Chief Justice and his satellites, knew that he was signing the death-warrant of the prisoner.

On the following day, November the 26th, Col. Sidney was brought up to the bar for sentence.   The remarkable scene that ensued is but partially detailed in the printed report of the trial, which has been mainly followed in this sketch, but which it seems

was corrected, and some of the most atrocious proceedings expunged by order of the Chief Justice. The
" Apology" of Sidney, " in the day of his death," has
supplied some of these defects. Thus it appears, that
while Sidney was stating his reasons why the judgment should be arrested, Mr. Justice Wythins, who on
this occasion was drunk on the bench, gave him the
lie in open court. To this the prisoner made the mild
but dignified reply, that, " having lived above three-
score years, I have never received or deserved such
language, for that I have never asserted anything that
was false."

We pass over the colloquy that ensued between the
prisoner at the bar and his judges on the bench. Sidney presented a variety of points on his motion for a
new trial, embracing substantially the irregularities
already mentioned, in summoning the jury, and in
denying him a fair and impartial trial. The court,
however, interrupted him before he had finished stating
his points, and refused to allow him to proceed. At
every step he encountered the determined opposition
of the Chief Justice, who overruled each of his objections without a hearing, and seemed impatient to enjoy
the luxury of pronouncing the sentence. Placed thus
beyond the pale of the law, the court stated to him,
in the midst of his objections, that nothing now remained but to pronounce the judgment the law
required to be pronounced in cases of high treason.
Sidney, turning in despair from that corrupt tribunal,
exclaimed:

"I must appeal to God and the world. I am not heard!"

"Appeal to whom you will," answered Jeffries, and proceeded with mock solemnity to pass the customary sentence of the law for high treason. As he concluded, Sidney, raising his hands to Heaven, exclaimed :

"Then, O God! I beseech thee to sanctify these sufferings unto me, and impute not my blood to the country, nor to the great city through which I am to be drawn ; let no inquisition be made for it, but if any, and the shedding of blood that is innocent must be avenged, let the weight of it fall upon those that maliciously persecute me for righteousness sake."

To this solemn and striking invocation Jeffries brutally replied :

"I pray God work in you a temper fit to go to the other world, for I see you are not fit for this."

Conceiving these words were meant to intimate that he spoke in a disordered state of mind, Sidney held out his hand and proudly answered :

"My lord, feel my pulse and see if I am disordered. I bless God I never was in better temper than I am now."*

During the interval between his sentence and exe-

---

* Alluding to this occurrence in his "Apology," he says : "And I do profess that, so far as I do know and did then feel myself, I was never in a more quiet temper; glory and thanks be unto God forever, who has filled me with comforts, and so upholds me, that having, as I hope, through Christ, vanquished sin, he doth preserve me from the fear of death."

cution, powerful intercession was made in his behalf, and it was thought that a commutation of his sentence might be obtained. Sidney himself was prevailed upon to present a second brief petition to the king, praying that his sentence might be remitted by suffering him to go beyond seas on giving security never to return to England. The petition, however, was denied; and the prisoner, who now expected nothing from the mercy of his persecutors, calmly and courageously prepared to meet his fate. He drew up his " Apology in the day of his death," containing a faithful history of his trial, and a noble vindication of his principles and actions. This paper he deposited with a faithful servant, Joseph Ducasse, a Frenchman, whom he had brought with him into England, and who, unlike his rich and powerful relatives, never deserted him. He also drew up a briefer statement, containing the substance of his " Apology," for the purpose of delivering it to the sheriff on the scaffold, in lieu of any speech to the multitude that might be expected of him. A copy of it he deposited for safe keeping with a friend, fearful that the officer might suppress this vindication of his memory. It closes with an impressive and solemn invocation to Heaven to avert from the nation the evils that threatened it, and to forgive the practices that had brought him to the scaffold. Nor was the noble cause for which he suffered forgotten or disavowed with his latest breath : " Grant that I may die glorifying thee for all thy mercies, and that at the last thou hast permitted me to be singled out as a witness of thy truth, and even, by the confession of my opposers, for that OLD CAUSE in which I was from my youth engaged, and for which thou hast often and wonderfully declared thyself."

Henceforth Sidney resumed his stoicism of character, and manifested the utmost indifference to the unjust fate that his enemies had prepared for him. The warrant for his execution was at last signed, but in compliment to his illustrious family, it is said, the most barbarous portions of the sentence for high treason were remitted, and he was ordered simply to be beheaded. When the sheriffs brought it to him, he examined it with calmness and unconcern. He told them he would not expostulate with them on his own account, for the world was now nothing to him; but he desired them, for their own sakes, to consider how guilty they had been in returning a jury packed by the solicitors for the Crown. One of the officers, doubtless conscience-stricken at this reproach, wept when he heard these words.

On the 7th day of December, 1683, Sidney was executed on Tower Hill. We have a brief account of the transaction in the original paper of the sheriff, preserved in the state paper office. From it we infer that the victim met death with all his constitutional intrepidity and insensibility to fear; with the stoicism of a Cato, and yet with the confidence and hope of one who had made his peace with God. Unlike Vane, he undertook to make no harangue, nor did he enter into any justification of his actions on the scaffold. There was no parade, no display, no effort, as there was no shrinking or fear on the part of the victim. He uttered but a word or two to his executioners, but they were strikingly impressive and full of meaning, and such as were calculated to live long in the memories of those who heard him.

The sheriffs asked him at the tower if he had any friends to accompany him on the scaffold; he said none but two servants of his brother.

They conducted him on foot up to the scaffold. He said nothing in all his passage.

As he came up to the scaffold, he said, " I have made my peace with God, and have nothing to say to men ; but here is a paper of what I have to say."

On being asked by the sheriff if he should read it, he answered in the negative, and told him if he refused to take the paper he would tear it. To a question of the officer if the writing was in his own hand, he replied, " Yes."

Sidney then took off his hat, coat, and doublet, gave the customary fee to the executioner, and said, " I am ready to die ; I will give you no farther trouble." Observing the executioner grumble, as though he had given him too little, he directed one of his servants to give him a guinea or two more, which he did. The victim then knelt down for a few moments in silence, apparently engaged in devotion. He then calmly laid his head on the block. The executioner, as was customary in such cases, asked him if he should rise again. " NOT TILL THE GENERAL RESUR-

RECTION. Strike on," was the laconic and sublime reply—the last words that ever passed his lips. The sheriff reports that " execution was done at one blow, only some skin with a knife the executioner took off, and so took up his head and showed it round the scaffold, which was hung with mourning, and the floor also covered with black, and a black coffin."

His body, by order of the secretary of state, was delivered to his brother's servants who accompanied him to the scaffold, and was the next day privately buried with his ancestors at Penshurst. His remains were subsequently removed into a small stone coffin, and placed in front of the family vault, with a brief inscription engraved on a brass plate, containing only his name, his age, and the date of his death.*

The condemnation of Sidney has been universally and justly regarded as one of the most atrocious and tyrannical acts of the reign of Charles II.† The trials of Vane and the regicides, and of Russell and Hampden, if they really equalled, did not exceed it, in cold-blooded and almost fiendish malignity. The illegality and injustice of the proceedings are, if possible, more monstrous than their atrocity. Sidney may be regarded as guiltless of any political crime. Taking the whole of the testimony of Howard, together with the hearsay of the other witnesses, to be absolutely true, there is no legal evidence of any con-

* Meadley's Memoirs.

† Hume himself speaks of it as " one of the greatest blemishes of the present reign."

spiracy for an insurrection in which he was to act a part ; and even if there were, the conspiracy is of precisely the same nature with that which, five years later, drove out the tyrant James II., and called William and Mary to the throne. The unsuccessful conspiracy becomes a treason ; the successful one a benign and necessary revolution ; the crime of the proscribed Sidney, is the glory of the patriot states- men who wrested the crown from James and placed it on the brows of the Prince of Orange.

The revolution of 1688, which so fully vindicated the principles of popular resistance to arbitrary power professed by Sidney, placed the constitution and liberties of England under the guardianship of men who did not fear to do full justice to his memory, and to brand, as they deserved, the infamous proceed- ings in his trial and execution. One of the earli- est acts of William and Mary was the annulling of Sidney's attainder on the petition of his brothers, Philip, Earl of Leicester, and Henry, Viscount Sid- ney. The act itself recites that he was condemned "*without sufficient legal evidence of any treason committed by him*," and that " by a partial and un- just construction of the statute, declaring what was his treason, was most *unjustly* and *wrongfully* con- victed and attainted, and afterwards executed for high treason." The act, besides reversing the attainder, orders that " all records and proceedings relating to the said attainder be wholly cancelled, and taken off the file, or otherwise defaced or obliterated, *to the in-*

tent that the same may not be visible in after ages."
It is stated by Lord Brougham, in a speech delivered
by him in the House of Commons, in June, 1824,
and in which he denounced "those execrable attain-
ders of Russell and Sidney, that the committee of the
House of Lords did not scruple to use the word *murder* as applicable to these executions," and that on the
journals of that house stands the appointment of the
committee " to inquire of the advisers and prosecutors
of the *murder* of Lord Russell and Col. Sidney."
Such was the first act of public justice done to the
memory of this illustrious man. From that day to
this, it has been difficult to find an apologist of the
bloody deed, either on the score of its justice, its
legality, or its political necessity. The most eminent
jurists, the ablest and most enlightened statesmen,
have united in censuring the act, and in execrating
the vile instruments of a viler government, by whom
it was done.* In so doing, they have but given expression to the general judgment of mankind. No
where, perhaps, has that judgment been more truly or
forcibly pronounced, than on the page of that fragment
of history† left by the noblest of British statesmen,
Charles James Fox. After speaking of the execution
of Russell as a "most flagrant violation of law and

---

* The learned Sir John Hawles remarks, " He was merely talked to
death under the notion of a Commonwealth's man, and found guilty by
a jury who were not much more proper judges in the case than they
would have been if what he had written had been done by him in
Syriac or Arabic."

† History of the Stuarts, p. 47

justice," Mr. Fox observes : " The proceedings in Sidney's case were still more detestable.   The production
of papers containing speculative opinions upon government and liberty, written long before, and, perhaps,
never even intended to be published, together with
the use made of those papers, in considering them as
a substitute for the second witness to the overt act,
exhibited such a compound of wickedness and nonsense, as is hardly to be paralleled in the history of
juridical tyranny.   But the validity of pretences was
little attended to at that time in the case of a person
whom the court had devoted to destruction; and upon
evidence such as has been stated, was this great and
excellent man condemned to die."

Even the historian Hume, the ready apologist of
monarchy in its exercise of arbitrary power, where
apology is possible, does not undertake to justify or
to extenuate this act.   But in that spirit of adulation
towards the Stuarts which marks his writings, he
attempts to throw the blame entirely upon *the jury,*
to exonerate the government, and particularly to justify the criminal inaction of the king.   Hume admits
that the evidence against Sidney was not legal, and
adds, that the jury who condemned him were, *for
that reason,* very blameable ; " but," he remarks, " that
the king should interpose to pardon a man who was undoubtedly guilty, who had ever been a most Inveterate enemy to the royal family, and who lately had
even abused the king's clemency, might be an act of

heroic generosity, but can never be regarded as *a necessary and indispensable duty.*"

Mr. Hume could not have read very attentively the trial of Sidney, and especially the charge of the judge, or he never would have held the jury wholly responsible for the verdict. Under the circumstances of the case, perhaps the jury were not so very blameable ; certainly they could not have rendered any other verdict without disregarding totally the directions of the court. It will be remembered that Jeffries very carefully laid down the proposition, that while the jury were the judges of *the fact*, they were bound to take *the law* from the court. He then charged them, as matter of law, that the writing produced was a " sufficient evidence" of treason. " It is not," he says, " upon *two*, but it is upon greater evidence than *twenty-two, if you believe this book was writ by him.*" The only question of fact, therefore, left to the jury to pass upon, was, whether the manuscript had been written by the prisoner or not; everything else having been taken out of their hands by the court. We do not see how the jury, under their oaths, could find this fact differently from what they did. It is true Sidney had objected to the evidence offered to prove the writing by *comparison of hands*, and the objection, though technical, was a valid one ; but the court overruled it, and charged the jury that the evidence was competent. Besides, it must be admitted that there was something more than mere comparison of handwriting ; for the first witness swore that he had seen the prisoner write the endorsements upon several bills of exchange. A modern writer, eminent as authority upon the law of evidence,* speaking of this case, remarks, that though it may be objected to the testimony of the last two witnesses that the endorsements mentioned by them were not sufficiently proved to have been written by the prisoner, that objection will not apply to the other witness, whose evidence was certainly admissible. The ignorant and deluded jury, therefore, whom alone Mr. Hume considers blameable, were, in reality, excusable, if not justifiable. The only fact left for them to find, they found affirmatively, upon competent, perhaps sufficient evidence; at all events, no jury in a civil case upon the same state of facts, and under the charge of the court, could have failed to pronounce that the writing was the prisoner's. The bench, and not the jury-box, was the effective instrument which accomplished the nefarious designs of the government. Jeffries insisted upon the maxim, " *scribere est agere*"—" to write is to act," and laid it down as a principle of law applicable to this case. Upon this point he directed the verdict of the jury. The perversion of law was monstrous and glaring. The principle had not the remotest application to Sidney's case, and has been so laid down by the ablest writers on criminal law since that time.† Sidney was literally murdered under color of law, and scarcely the

---

* Phillips—Law of Evidence, vol. i. p. 485.

† Foster's Cr. L. 198. 4 Black. Com. 80.

forms of a judicial proceeding were preserved on his trial.

But though the guilt of the jury, if, indeed, they may be pronounced guilty at all, was as nothing in comparison with the guilt of the corrupt bench before which he was tried, yet the infamy and wickedness of the bench itself did not exceed, if it equalled, that of the government which ordered and directed the prosecution. Jeffries, himself, was the mere tool and hireling of the court. He was influenced and directed upon the trial by the king and his counsellors, particularly the Duke of York. He had been appointed by the king, who well knew his detestable character, to perform just such services as these. For similar services he was afterwards rewarded by a ring from the hands of his royal master, as a peculiar mark of favor. This act of his was looked upon with singular complacency by the careless, witty, and debonair monarch, and was regarded with savage and vindictive exultation by his brother James. The memory of Charles Stuart can never be cleansed from the stain that has been left upon it by the innocent blood of Algernon Sidney. Posterity will hold him as an accomplice, if not a principal, in the crime, as he was in that other crime, the death of Vane, whom he directed his chancellor to put "honestly out of the way," even at the trifling expense of violating the faith which he had solemnly pledged. And yet such is the monarch, whose conduct in refusing to interpose his pardon upon a conviction which his creatures had

so infamously procured, is not only palliated but justified by a historian so eminent, and in some respects
so impartial, as Mr. Hume.   The indignant comment
upon this passage, by the illustrious statesman whose
words we have just quoted, may be properly added :
" As well might we palliate the murders of Tiberius,
who seldom put to death his victims without a previous decree of the senate.   The moral of all this
seems to be, that whenever a prince can, by intimi-
dation, corruption, illegal evidence, or other such
means, obtain a verdict against a subject whom he
dislikes, he may cause him to be executed without
any breach of indispensable duty—nay, that it is an
act of heroic generosity if he spares him."

CHAPTER IX.

The writings of Sidney—Introductory remarks—Extracts—Common notions of liberty are derived from nature—Men are by nature free—Choice of forms of government originally left to the people—The social contract considered—Such as enter into society in some degree diminish their liberty—The natural equality of man—Virtue only gives a preference of one man to another—There is no hereditary right of dominion—Men join together and frame greater or less societies, and give them such forms and laws as they please—They who have the right of choosing a king, have the right of making a king—As to the forms of government—Those best which comprise the three simple elements—Democracy considered—Sidney in favor of a popular or mixed government—Civil governments admit of changes in their superstructure—Man's natural love of liberty is tempered by reason—Seditions, tumults, and wars considered—In what cases justified—When necessary to overthrow a tyranny, or depose a wicked magistrate—The right of insurrection traced to the social contract—The contracts between the magistrates and the nations which created them, were real, solemn, and obligatory—Same subject continued—The general revolt of a nation cannot be called a rebellion—Duties of magistrates as representatives of the people—No people that is not free can substitute delegates—The representative system—Legislative power not to be trusted in the hands of any who are not bound to obey the laws they make—Reflections on the writings and political opinions of Sidney—The sincerity of his motives—His religious sentiments—His private character—Conclusion.

In bringing to a close the narrative of the public career of Algernon Sidney, little remains to be added respecting a character whose best commentary is to be found in the actions of a life of entire and rigid consistency, and whose finest illustration is in his published correspondence and other writings. His polical opinions, his sentiments respecting government, human rights and public liberty, have already in the progress of this work been freely discussed. They will be more fully understood by the extracts from his once celebrated *Discourses concerning Government*, contained in the present chapter. These extracts have been made rather with the view of illustrating Sidney's opinions than of presenting a connected chain of his argument, or of doing full justice to the subject matter of the discourses. The plan of our work necessarily forbids the idea of attempting to do more than to glean here and there from these writings a few general truths and maxims, and to present such brief passages only as will serve to convey to the mind of the reader, in Sidney's own language, his views of popular liberty, and of the origin and ground of government.

A few remarks in relation to the nature and object of the work, may be properly made here. The book is an answer to Sir Robert Filmer's *Patriarcha*, and is designed to refute that absurd theory of government which, under the name of the *patriarchal system*, was so resolutely asserted under the Stuart dynasty, and was never finally abandoned in England, until the last of that hapless family was driven from the throne by the Revolution of 1688. The ideas upon which the work of Sidney was based, were first promulgated in the reign of James I., and were strenuously insisted upon by the high churchmen and obsequious courtier of that day. It was maintained that a hereditary monarchy, as opposed to a limited or popular government, was instituted by the Supreme Being; that the authority of the hereditary prince was absolute, his person was sacred, and his throne hedged round by a higher power than constitutions or the will of the nation. Passive obedience to the will of the sovereign, and non-resistance on the part of the people, were the doctrines inculcated by this theory. The king could do no wrong; or as James I. expressed it—" to contest the power of kings is to dispute the power of God."* The most celebrated philosoper of his age, Thomas Hobbes, pushed this theory still further, and maintained that the will of the monarch was the standard of right and wrong, and that every subject ought to be ready to profess any form of religion which the reigning dynasty chose to ordain—a theory, Hume himself does not hesitate to pronounce the offspring of a philosopher, whose politics are fitted only to promote tyranny, and whose ethics to encourage licentiousness.

It was also maintained by the patriarchal system,

---

* It may be said, indeed, with truth, that the doctrine was not even then finally abandoned. More than a century afterwards, England, under the administration of Pitt, practically asserted it when she joined the coalition to put down popular government in France. It was the system of Filmer—the *jus divinum*—as opposed to the French declaration o. rights, which turned Europe into one vast encampment and battle ground for a quarter of a century.

that the laws which limited the king's prerogative were merely temporary concessions, which might, at any moment, be revoked, for a king could make no contract with his subjects which was binding upon him. Primogeniture was regarded as a divine institution, and the lineal heir of the legitimate prince was entitled to the throne of right, though centuries of adverse possession intervened.

These doctrines were exactly suited to the times of the Stuarts. James I. claimed to be the heir of Egbert and William the Conqueror, and consequently, by the law of primogeniture, held the throne by a better title than Elizabeth or Henry VII. had done. It became the fashion among the statesmen and ecclesiastics of that day, who wished to flatter the monarch, to promulgate and defend these ideas ; and they continued steadily to advance down to the period of the breaking out of the Revolution. That event, however, checked for a time the further progress of these absurd political dogmas. The prompt and energetic resistance of the Parliament, the revolt of the nation, and the execution of the king, were terrible commentaries on the patriarchal system. The active and vigorous intellect of the age then launched out into the boldest and freest speculation. Milton brought all the strength of his great mind to the defence of freedom of intellect, freedom of the press, and popular sovereignty : Harrington employed his ingenious pen in sketching his plans of an ideal and perfect republic ; while the more practical and profound genius of Vane sought out the true foundation of free government—a written constitution, and equal popular representation.

The restoration of the monarchy brought with it the reign of despotic ideas, the philosophy of Hobbes, and the patriarchal theory of government. Sir Robert Filmer laying hold of these ideas of the two last reigns, moulded them anew into a political system, which he published to the world, and which found singular favor with the enthusiastic royalists. It was in answer to this work of Filmer that Sidney's *discourses upon government* were written. It is remarkable as being one of the earliest if not the first complete and systematic treatise, by any English writer, on the origin and ground of government, which maintains the true principles of civil and religious liberty —traces the origin of all just power to the people— vindicates the right of the nation to frame its own laws and institutions, and defends the doctrine of the " social compact" in opposition to that of hereditary tyranny ordained by a higher law than the popular will

At first glance it is almost a matter of amazement that a theory so absurd and inconsistent as the *patriarchal system*, should have seriously occupied a mind like Sidney's in its refutation. But our wonder ceases when we find the dogmas of Filmer universally disseminated throughout the kingdom. They were avowed in the Parliament, proclaimed from the bench, taught in the church and universities. Doctrines like Sidney's were looked upon by some with horror as re-

volutionary or treasonable; by others with an aversion
and contempt, such as the highest-toned conservative
of our day entertains for the doctrines of Fourier.
Long after the *discourses concerning government*
were written, and but a few years before they were
first published to the world, the public mind of
England yet succumbed to the monstrous tenets of the
patriarchal system. The pulpits of the established
church resounded with homilies against the sin of
revolution, and with lessons inculcating the principles
of non-resistance. Jeffries, from the bench in Westminster Hall declared that by the common law and
statutes of England the principles of Sidney were
treasonable; and on the very day of Russell's death,
the university of Oxford by a solemn public act adopted the doctrines of Filmer, and ordered the political
works of Buchanan, Milton, and Baxter to be burned.*
It was but a few years after this, when the violence
and tyranny of James II. created a revolution in the
public mind which drove that monarch from his kingdom, and practically overturned the whole pernicious
theory of government which the high tories and
churchmen of that day had advocated. The practical
working of the system under the last of the house of
Stuart was too much for the warmest disciple of
Filmer to endure. Even the loyalty of the Church of
England was shaken, and from preaching passive
obedience, it set the example of resistance to the royal
prerogative. The Parliament, on the abdication of

* Macaulay, Hist. Eng. vol. I. p. 97.

James, embodied in a solemn act Sidney's fundamental idea of popular sovereignty, by declaring that James II. had endeavored "to subvert the constitution of the kingdom by breaking the ORIGINAL CONTRACT between king and people." Despite the doctrine of legitimacy the throne was declared vacant. The Parliament, too, reversed the law laid down by Jeffries in the king's bench, by annulling the attainder of Sidney, and declaring that he was most unjustly and wrongfully convicted and executed for high treason.

It was then* that the political writings of Sidney were published to the world, and from that day they have been read, studied, and admired by the most enlightened statesmen and civilians.

In his preface to the first edition, Toland remarks that Sidney left a large and a lesser treatise written against the principles contained in Filmer's book. It was a portion of the smaller treatise that had been produced in evidence against him on the trial. It was there said that the smaller treatise neither was, and probably never would have been finished. The published *discourses on government* comprise only the larger treatise.

With these explanatory remarks we present to the reader such passages from the work as will serve to illustrate the opinions of Sidney and the political

* The work first appeared in 1698. It was published by Toland, who also collected and published Milton's prose works and Harrington's *Oceana*, &c.

system he advocated. It opens with the following appropriate introduction :—

"Having lately seen a book entitled " Patriarcha," written by Sir Robert Filmer, concerning the universal and undistinguished right of all kings, I thought a time of leisure might be well employed in examining his doctrine, and the questions arising from it, which seem so far to concern all mankind, that, besides the influence upon our future life, they may be said to comprehend all that in this world deserves to be cared for. If he say true, there is but one government in the world that can have anything of justice in it; and those who have hitherto been esteemed the best and wisest of mankind, for having constituted commonwealths or kingdoms, and taken much pains so to proportion the powers of several magistracies, that they might all concur in procuring the public good ; or so to divide the powers between the magistrates and people, that a well regulated harmony might be preserved in the whole, were the most unjust and foolish of men. They were not builders, but overthrows, of government. Their business was to set up aristocratical, democratical, or mixed governments, in opposition to that monarchy, which, by the immutable laws of God and nature is imposed upon mankind, or presumptuously to put shackles upon the monarch, who, by the same laws, is to be absolute and uncontrolled."

*   *   *   *   *   *

" According to Sir Robert Filmer," Sidney continues, " men are not to inquire what conduces to their own good. God and nature have put us into a way from which we are not to swerve. We are not to live to him, nor to ourselves, but to the master that he hath set over us. One government is established over all, and no limits can be set to the power of the person that manages it. This is the prerogative, or as another author of the same stamp calls it, ' *the royal charter granted to kings by God.*' "

*   *   *   *   *   *

' I have been sometimes apt to wonder how things of this nature could enter into the head of any man ; or if no wickedness or folly be so great but some may fall into it, I could not well conceive why they should publish it to the world. But these thoughts ceased when I considered that a people, from all ages in love with liberty, and desirous to maintain their own privileges, could never be brought to resign them, unless they were made to believe that in conscience they ought to do it ; which could not be unless they were also persuaded that there was a law set to all mankind, which none might transgress, and which put the examination of all those matters out of their power. This is our author's work. By this it will appear whose throne he seeks to advance, and whose servant he is, whilst he pretends to serve the king."

The common notions of liberty are not from school divines, but from nature.—EXTRACT, CHAP. I., SEC. 1.

In this section, Sidney refutes the doctrine of Filmer, that the notions men entertain of liberty are derived from the schoolmen and from the teachings of the Puritan divines. After some general remarks on this point, he thus vindicates the natural right of a people to govern themselves :—

" Did the people make the king, or the king make the people ? Is the king for the people, or the people for the king ? Did God create the Hebrews that Saul might reign over them ? or did they, from an opinion of procuring their own good, ask a king that might judge them and fight their battles ? If God's interposition, which shall be hereafter explained, do alter the case, did the Romans make Romulus, Numa, Tullus, Hostilius, and Tarquinius Priscus, kings, or did they make or beget the Romans ? If they were made kings by the Romans, 'tis certain they that made them sought their own good in so doing ; and if they were made by, and for the city and people, I desire to know if it was not better that when their successors departed from the end of their institution, by endeavoring to destroy it, or all that was good in it, they should be censured and rejected, than be permitted to ruin that people for whose good they were created. Was it more just that Caligula or Nero should be suffered to destroy the poor remains of the Roman nobility and people, with the nations subject to that empire, than that the race of such monsters should be extinguished, and a great part of mankind, especially the best, against whom they were most fierce, preserved by their deaths.

" I presume our author thought these questions might be easily decided, and that no more was required to show the forementioned assertions were not all desperate, than to examine the ground of them ; but he seeks to divert us from this inquiry, by proposing the dreadful consequences of subjecting kings to the censures of their people, whereas no consequence can destroy any truth ; and the worst of this is, that if it were received, some princes might be restrained from doing evil, or punished if they will not be restrained. We are, therefore, only to consider whether the people, senate, or any magistracy, made by and for the people, have, or can have, such a right; for if they have, whatsoever the consequences may be, it must stand ; and as the one tends to the good of mankind, in restraining the lusts of wicked kings, the other exposes them, without remedy, to the fury of the most savage of all beasts. I am not ashamed in this to concur with Buchanan, Calvin, or Bellarmine, and, without envy, leave Filmer and his associates the glory of maintaining the contrary."

✳　　✳　　✳　　✳　　✳　　✳

" The productions of Laud, Manwaring, Sibthorp, Hobbes, Filmer, and Heylin, seem to have been reserved as an additional curse to complete the shame and misery of our age and country. Those who had wit and learning, with something of ingenuity and modesty, though they believed that nations might possibly make an ill use of their power, and were very desirous to maintain the cause of kings, as far as they could put any good color upon it ; yet never denied that some had suffered justly (which could not be, if there were no power of judging them), nor ever asserted anything that might arm them with an irresistible power of doing mischief—animate them to persist in the most flagitious courses, with assurance of perpetual impunity, or engage nations in an inevitable necessity of suffering all manner of outrages. But Filmer, Heylin, and, their associates, scorning to be restrained by such considerations, boldly lay the axe to the root of the tree, and rightly enough affirm, ' that the whole fabric of that which they call popular sedition, would fall to the ground if the principle of natural liberty were removed. And, on the other hand, it must be acknowledged that the whole fabric of tyranny will be much weakened, if we prove that nations have a right to make their own laws, constitute their own magistrates, and that such as are so constituted owe an account of their actions to those by whom and for whom they were appointed."

God leaves to man the choice of forms in government, and those who constitute one form may abrogate it.—CHAP. I., SEC. 5.

" But Sir Robert ' desires to make observations on Bellarmine's words, before he examines or refutes them.' And, indeed, it were not possible to make such stuff of his doctrine as he does, if he had examined, or did understand it. First, he very wittily concludes, ' that if, by the law of God, the power be immediately in the people, God is the author of democracy.' And why not as well as of a tyranny ? Is there anything in it repugnant to the being of God ? Is there more reason to impute to God Caligula's monarchy than the democracy of Athens ? or is it more for the glory of God to assert his presence with the Ottoman or French monarchs, than with the popular governments of the Switzers and Grisons ? Is pride, malice, luxury, and violence so suitable to his being, that they who exercise them are to be reputed his ministers ? And is modesty, humility, equality, and justice so contrary to his nature, that they who live in them should be thought his enemies ! Is there any absurdity in saying that since God in goodness and mercy to mankind hath, with an equal hand,

given to all the benefit of liberty, with some measure of understanding how to employ it, it is lawful for any nation, as occasion
shall require, to give the exercise of that power to one or more
men, under certain limitations and conditions, or to retain it to
themselves if they think it good for them ? If this may be done,
we are at an end of all controversies concerning one form of government established by God, to which all mankind must submit;
and we may safely conclude that, having given to all men, in
some degree, a capacity of judging what is good for themselves,
he hath granted to all likewise a liberty of inventing such forms as
please them best, without favoring one more than another.

The conclusion here arrived at is precisely that
which the statesmen who achieved our own independence laid down in the " Declaration" as an elementary political truth, namely, that governments are
instituted among men *deriving their just powers*
from the consent of the governed. The same simple
and direct proposition was subsequently put forth as
the basis of the French declaration of rights, and
also in that able manifesto of the national assembly,
drawn up by Condorcet, and published to the world,
vindicating the revolution and the right of a people
to " alter or abolish" a government that had become
oppressive. This right, which is an obvious consequence of the doctrine already asserted, Sidney also
discusses and boldly avows.

" The next point is subtle, and he thinks thereby to have brought
Bellarmine, and those who agree with his principles, to a nonplus.
He doubts who shall judge of the lawful cause of changing the
government, and says—' It is a pestilent conclusion to place that
power in the multitude.' But why should this be esteemed pestilent, or to whom ? If the allowance of such a power in the

Senate was pestilent to Nero, it was beneficial to mankind; and the denial of it, which would have given to Nero an opportunity of continuing in his villanies, would have been pestilent to the best men, whom he endeavored to destroy, and to all others that received benefit from them. But this question depends upon another; for if governments are constituted for the pleasure, greatness, or profit of one man, he must not be interrupted; for the opposing of his will, is to overthrow the institution. On the other side, if the good of the governed be sought, care must be taken that the end be accomplished, though it be with the prejudice of the governor. If the power be originally in the multitude, and one or more men to whom the exercise of it, or part of it, was committed, had no more than their brethren, till it was conferred on him or them, it cannot be believed that rational creatures would advance one or a few of their equals above themselves, unless in consideration of their own good; and then I find no inconvenience in leaving to them a right of judging, whether this be duly performed or not. We say in general, '*he that institutes may abrogate*,'* most especially when the institution is not only by, but for, himself. *If the multitude therefore do institute the multitude may abrogate; and they themselves, or those who succeed in the same right, can only be fit judges of the performance of the ends of the institution.* Our author may perhaps say, the public peace may be hereby disturbed; but he ought to know there can be no peace where there is no justice; nor any justice, if the government instituted for the good of a nation, be turned to its ruin. But in plain English, the inconvenience with which such as he endeavor to affright us, is no more than that he or they, to whom the power is given, may be restrained or chastised if they betray their trust."

Such as enter into society, must, in some degree, diminish their liberty.—CHAP. I., SECT. 9.

"Reason leads them to this; no one man or family is able to

* Cujus est instituere, ejus est abrogare.

provide that which is requisite for their convenience or security, whilst every one has an equal right to everything, and none acknowledges a superior to determine the controversies that, upon such occasions, must continually arise, and will, probably, be so many and great, that mankind cannot bear them. Therefore, though I do not believe that Bellarmine said a commonwealth could not exercise its power, for he could not be ignorant that Rome and Athens did exercise theirs, and that all the regular kingdoms in the world are commonwealths; yet there is nothing of absurdity in saying, that man cannot continue in the perpetual and entire fruition of the liberty that God hath given him. The liberty of one is thwarted by that of another; and whilst they are all equal, *none will yield to any otherwise than by a general consent. This is the ground of all just governments;* for violence or fraud can create no right, and the same consent gives the form to them all, how much soever they differ from each other. Some small numbers of men, living within the precincts of one city have, as it were, cast into a common stock, the right which they had of governing themselves and children, and by common consent joining in one body, exercised such power over every single person as seemed beneficial to the whole; and this men call perfect 'democracy.' Others chose rather to be governed by a select number of such as excelled most in wisdom and virtue; and this according to the signification of the word was called 'aristocracy.' Or, when one man excelled all others, the government was put into his hands under the name of 'monarchy.' But the wisest, best, and far the greatest part of mankind, rejecting these simple species, did form governments mixed or composed of the three, as shall be proved hereafter, which commonly received their respective denomination from the great part that prevailed, and did deserve praise or blame as they were well or ill proportioned.''

*   *   *   *   *   *

" If men are naturally free, such as have wisdom and understanding will always frame good governments; but if they are born under the necessity of a perpetual slavery, no wisdom can be of

13*

use to them; but all must forever depend on the will of their lords, how cruel, mad, proud, or wicked soever they be."

In the succeeding sections of this chapter, Sidney examines that portion of the argument of Filmer wherein he attempts to base his theory of the divine institution of monarchy upon a pretended paternal right of the monarch, derived from the same source, and having the same sanctions, as the necessary and natural authority which a father exercises over his children. He thoroughly exposes this fallacy both by argument and by copious illustrations drawn from history. He shows that there was no shadow of such paternal kingdom among the Hebrews, nor was it found among any of the enlightened nations of antiquity. The Greeks and Romans chose those to be kings who excelled in the virtues most beneficial to civil societies. The absurdity of the doctrine that a right of dominion by the law of nature is hereditary is shown, and the principle advocated that the people is the source of all political authority. The following passage occurs in the last section of this chapter under the head " *All just magisterial power is from the people.*"

"Upon the same grounds we may conclude that no privilege is peculiarly annexed to any form of government; but that all magistrates are equally the ministers of God, who perform the work for which they were instituted; *and that the people which institutes them, may proportion, regulate, and terminate their power as to time, measure, and number of persons, as seems most convenient to themselves, which can be no other than their own good.* For it cannot be imagined that a multitude of people should send for Numa, or any other person to whom they owed nothing, to reign over them, that he might live in glory and pleasure, or for any other reason than that it might be good for them and their posterity. This shows the work of all magistrates to be always and every. where the same, even the doing of justice, and procuring the wel. fare of those that create them."

The second chapter of the *Discourses on Government* opens with some remarks on the natural equality of man. Having proved men by nature *free*, the author next undertakes to prove them *equal;* not indeed equal in physical strength, or in their mental or moral faculties, but endowed with an equality of rights. The distinctions of society, he contends, are artificial. Virtue, not birth, should exalt one man above another, and an hereditary prerogative of domi. nion, is at once opposed to reason, revelation, and common sense.

That it is natural for nations to govern, as to choose governors; and that virtue only gives a natural preference of one man above another, or reason why one should be chosen rather than another.—CHAP. II., SEC. 1.

"That which I maintain," Sidney remarks in the opening of this section, "is the cause of mankind; which ought not to suffer, though champions of corrupt principles have weakly defended, or maliciously betrayed it; and therefore, not at all relying on their authority, I intend to reject whatever they say that agrees not with reason, scripture, or the approved examples of the best polished nations."

* * * * * *

"We have already seen that the patriarchal power resembles not the regal in principle or practice; that the beginning and con.

tinuance of regal power was contrary to, and inconsistent with the patriarchal; that the first fathers of mankind left all their children independent of each other, and in equal liberty of provid ing for themselves; that every man continued in this liberty, till the number so increased that they became troublesome and danger ous to each other; and finding no other remedy to the disorders growing or like to grow among them, joined many families into one civil body, that they might the better provide for the conve- nience, safety, and defence of themselves and their children. This was a col'ation of every man's private right into a public stock; and no one having any other right than what was common to all, except it were that of fathers over their children, they were all equally free when their fathers were dead; and nothing could induce them to join, and lessen that natural liberty by joining, in societies, but the hopes of a public advantage. Such as were wise and valiant, procured it by setting up regular governments, and placing the best men in the administration; whilst the weakest and basest fell under the power of the most boisterous and violent of their neighbors. Those of the first sort had their root in wis- dom and justice, and are called lawful kingdoms or common- wealths, and the rules by which they are governed are known by the name of laws. These governments have ever been the nurses of virtue; the nations living under them have flourished in peace and happiness, or made wars with glory and advantage. Whereas the other sort, springing from violence and wrong, have ever gone under the odious title of tyrannies, and by fomenting vices, like to those from which they grew, have brought shame and misery upon those who were subject to them. This appears so plainly in Scrip- ture, that the assertors of liberty want no other patron than God himself; and his word so fully justifies what we contend for, that it were not necessary to make use of human authority, if our ad- versaries did not oblige us to examine such as are cited by them."

      *   *   *   *   *   *

"That equality which is just among equals, is just only among equals. But such as are base, ignorant, vicious, slothful, or cowardly, are not equal in natural or acquired virtues to the generous, wise, valiant, and industrious; nor equally useful to the societies in which they live. They cannot, therefore, have an equal part in the government of them; they cannot equally provide for the common good; and it is not a personal, but a public benefit, that is sought in their constitution and continuance. There may be an hundred thousand men in any army who are all equally free; but they only are naturally most fit to be commanders or leaders, who most excel in the virtues required for the right performance of those offices; and that not because it is good for them to be raised above their brethren, but because it is good for their brethren to be guided by them, as it is ever good to be governed by the wisest and the best. If the nature of man be reason, *detur digniori*, in matters of this kind is the voice of nature; and it were not only a deviation from reason, but a most desperate and mischievous madness, for a company going to the Indies to give the guidance of their ship to the son of the best pilot in the world, if he want the skill required in that employment, or to one who was maliciously set to destroy them; and he only can have a right, grounded upon the dictates of nature, to be advanced to the helm, who best knows how to govern it, and has given the best testimonies of his integrity and intentions to employ his skill for the good of those that are embarked. *But as the work of a magistrate, especially if he be the supreme, is the highest, noblest, and most difficult that can be committed to the charge of a man, a more excellent virtue is required in the person who is to be advanced to it, than any other; and he that is most excellent in that virtue is reasonably and naturally to be preferred before any other.*

Aristotle, having this in view, seems to think that those who believed it not to be natural for one man to be lord of all the citizens, since a city consists of equals, had not observed that inequality of endowments, virtues, and abilities, in men which renders some more fit than others for the performance of their duties, and the work intended. But it will not be found, as I suppose, that he did ever dream of a *natural superiority* that any man could ever have in a civil society, unless it be such a superiority in virtue as most conduces to the public good."

Sidney then proceeds to examine the argument of his adversary derived from the writings of Plato and Aristotle, and shows conclusively, by quotations from these writers, that their authority is against the doctrine which Filmer advocates, of a natural inequality of men by birth, and a hereditary right of dominion. While, however, refuting the positions of Filmer from the pages of the very authors quoted by him, Sidney does not undertake to defend all the speculative political opinions of these authors. On this point he adds :—

"'Tis not my work to justify these opinions of Plato, and his scholar Aristotle. They were men, and though wise and learned, subject to error. If they erred in these points, it hurts not me, nor the cause I maintain, since I make no other use of their books than to show the impudence and prevarication of those who gather small scraps out of good books to justify their assertions concerning such kings as are known amongst us; which being examined are found to be wholly against them, and if they were followed would destroy their persons and power."

Freemen join together, and frame greater or lesser societies, and give such forms to them as best please themselves.—CHAP. II., SEC. 5.

"But since he (Filmer) raises a question, 'whether the supreme power be so in the people that there is but one and the same power in all the people of the world, so that no power can be granted unless all men upon the earth meet and agree to choose a governor,' I think it deserves to be answered, and I might do it by prop ing a question to him: whether, in his opinion, the empire of the world doth by the laws of God and nature belong to one man, and who that man is? Or how it came to be so divided, as we have ever known it to have been, without such an injury to the universal monarch as can never be repaired? But intending to proceed more candidly and not to trouble myself with Bellarmine or Laurez, I say, that they who place the power in a multitude, understand a multitude composed of freemen, who think it for their convenience to join together and to establish such laws and rules as they oblige themselves to observe: which multitude, whether it be great or small, has the same right, because ten men are as free as ten millions of men; and though it may be more prudent in some cases to join with the greater than the smaller number, because there is more strength, it is not so always: but, however, every man must therein be his own judge, since, if he mistake, the hurt is only to himself; and the ten may as justly resolve to live together, frame a civil society, and oblige themselves to laws, as the greatest number of men that ever met together in the world"

* * * * * *

"By this means every number of men, agreeing together, and framing a society, became a complete body, having all power in themselves over themselves, subject to no other human law than their own. All those that compose the society being equally free to enter into it or not, no man could have any prerogative above others, unless it were granted by the consent of the whole; and nothing obliging them to enter into this society, but the consideration of their own good, that good, or the opinion of it, must have been the rule, motive, and end of all that they did ordain. It is lawful therefore for any such bodies to set up one or a few men to govern them, or to retain the power in themselves; and he or they who are set up, having no other power but what is conferred upon them by that multitude, whether great or small, are truly by them made what they are; and by the law of their own creation, are to exercise those powers according to the proportion, and to the ends for which they were given. These rights, in several nations and ages, have been variously executed in the establishment of monarchies, aristocracies, democracies, or mixed governments according to the variety of circumstances; and the governments have been good or evil according to the rectitude or pravity of their institutions, and the virtue and wisdom, or the folly and vices of those to whom the power was committed; but the end which was ever proposed, being the good of the public, they only performed their duty who procured it according to the laws of the society which were equally valid as to their own magistrates, whether they were few or many."

They who have a right of choosing a king have the right of making a king.—CHAP II., SEC. 6.

"Though the right of magistrates essentially depends upon the consent of those they govern, it is hardly worth our pains to examine, 'whether the silent acceptation of a governor by part of the people be an argument of their concurring in the election of him; or by the same reason the tacit consent of the whole commonwealth may be maintained;' for, when the question is concerning right, fraudulent surmises are of no value; much less will it from thence follow, 'that a prince commanding by succession, conquest or usurpation, may be said to be elected by the people;' for evident marks of dissent are often given. Some declare their hatred; others murmur more privately; many oppose the governor or government, and succeed according to the measure of their strength, virtue, or fortune. Man would resist but cannot; and it were ridiculous to say, that the inhabitants of Greece, the kingdom of Naples, or duchy of Tuscany, do tacitly assent to the government of the Great Turk, King of Spain, or Duke of Florence, when nothing is more certain than that those miserable nations abhor the tyrannies they are under; and if they were not mastered by a power that is much too great for them, they would soon free themselves. And those who are under such governments do no more assent to them, though they may be silent, than a man approves of being robbed, when, without saying a word he delivers his purse to a thief that he knows to be too strong for him.

"It is not therefore the bare sufferance of a government when a disgust is declared, nor a silent submission where the power of opposing is wanting, that can imply an assent or election, and create a right; but an explicit act of approbation when men have ability and courage to resist or deny."

Having given the foregoing brief extracts to illustrate Sidney's views on the origin of government and the source of political power—the institution of society—the freedom of man in a state of nature—the concessions of personal liberty he makes when he enters into the social compact for the mutual benefit and advantage of all—the natural equality of rights as well as freedom of men, including their right to choose their own magistrates from among those whose virtues and talents best qualify them to administer the affairs of a free state—we pass on to present one or two extracts illustrative of the author's opinion as to what constitutes the best government—his partiality for popular institutions—and his views of the necessity and right of altering or changing a frame of government to suit the exigencies of the times. In the following passage, it will be seen, he takes a distinction between a *pure democracy*, i. e.., where the people collectively in popular assembly enact the laws—and a mixed popular or representative government.

The best governments of the world have been composed of monarchy, aristocracy, and democracy.—CHAP. II., SEC. 16.

"Our author's cavils concerning, I know not what, vulgar opinions, that democracies were introduced to curb tyranny, deserve no answer; for our question is, whether one form of government be prescribed to us by God and nature, or we are left, according to our own understanding, to constitute such as seem best to ourselves. As for democracy, he may say what pleases him of it; and I believe it can suit only with the convenience of a small town accompanied with such circumstances as are seldom found. But this by no way obliges men to run into the other extreme, inasmuch as the variety of forms between mere democracy and absolute monarchy, is almost infinite; and if I should undertake to say there never was a good government in the world that did not consist of three simple species of monarchy, aristocracy, and democracy, I think I might make it good."

Sidney here illustrates his proposition by comparing the government of the Hebrews, of Sparta, Athens, Rome, the Italian Republics, Germany, Poland, etc., and adds :—

"Some nations, not liking the name of king, have given such a power as kings enjoyed in other places, to one or more magistrates; either limited to a certain time, or left to be perpetual, as best pleased themselves. Others, approving the name, made the dignity purely elective. Some have, in their elections, principally regarded one family as long as it lasted; others considered nothing but the fitness of the person, and reserved to themselves a liberty of taking where they pleased. Some have permitted the crown to be hereditary as to its ordinary course, but restrained the power, and instituted officers to inspect the proceedings of kings, and to take care that the laws were not violated. Some have continued long, and it may be always, in the same form; others have changed it. Some being incensed against their kings, as the Romans, exasperated by the villanies of Tarquin, and the Tuscans by the cruelties of Mezentius, abolished the name of king; others, as at Athens, Sicyon, Argos, Corinth, Thebes, and the Latins, did not stay for such extremities, but set up other governments when they thought it best for themselves, and by this conduct prevented the evils that usually fall upon other nations when their kings degenerate into tyrants, and a nation is brought to enter into a war by which all may be lost and nothing can be gained which was not their own before.

"Our author, in pursuance of his aversion of all that is good, disapproves this, as if it were not as just for a people to lay aside their kings when they receive nothing but evil, and can rationally hope for no benefit by them, as for others to set them up in expectation of good from them."

Sidney's preference for a mixed government, comprising the three simple elementary forms, but with a popular executive, chosen by the nation, is clearly expressed. These views, however, do not in the least conflict with the consistency of his prior course in support of the Commonwealth, or his stern republican principles. The best forms of republican government, our own included, are thus constituted. In our own institutions, for example, though the democratic element largely preponderates, yet it is found united with the other two—the monarchic in the person of the executive, and the conservative or aristocratic* in the senate. Sidney's views upon the impracticability of a pure democracy as the government of a large nation, are strictly philosophical. It would do for the cabin of the Mayflower, but was not found to answer, after a few years, for the little colony of Massachusetts. Elsewhere the author says :—

"As to popular government in the strictest sense (that is pure democracy where the people in themselves, and by themselves, perform all that belongs to government), I know of no such

* Sidney uses this word also in its pure sense—*aristos*, the best.

thing, and if it be in the world have nothing to say for it. In asserting the liberty generally, as I suppose granted by God to all mankind, I neither deny that so many as think fit to enter into a society, may give so much of their power as they please to one or more men for a time, or perpetually to them and their heirs, according to such rules as they prescribe; nor approve the disorders that must arise if they keep it entirely in their own hands. And looking upon the several governments which, under different forms and names have been regularly constituted by nations, as so many undeniable testimonies that they thought it good for themselves and their posterity so to do, I infer that as there is no man who would not rather choose to be governed by such as are just, industrious, valiant, and wise, than by those that are wicked, slothful, cowardly, and foolish; and to live in society with such as are qualified like those of the first sort, rather than with those who will always be ready to commit all manner of villanies, or want experience, strength, or courage to join in repelling the injuries that are offered by others; so there are none who do not according to the measure of understanding they have, endeavor to set up those who seem to be best qualified, and to prevent the introduction of those vices which render the faith of the magistrate suspected, or make him unable to perform his duty in providing for the execution of justice and the public defence of the state against foreign and domestic enemies. For as no man who is not absolutely mad will commit the care of a flock to a villain that has neither skill, diligence, nor courage to defend them, or, perhaps, is maliciously set to destroy them, rather than to a stout, faithful, and wise shepherd, it is less to be imagined that any would commit the same error in relation to that society which comprehends himself, with his children, friends, and all that is dear to him."— *From Chap. II., Sec.* 19.

Alluding again to this same branch of his subject in another part of the work, he says :—

" However, more ignorance cannot be expressed than by giving

the name of democracy to those governments that are composed
of the three simple species, as we have proved that all the good
ones have ever been ; for in a strict sense it can only suit with
those where the people retain to themselves the administration of
the supreme power; and more largely, when the popular part, as
in Athens, greatly overbalances the other two, and that the denomination is taken from the prevailing part. But our author, if I
mistake not, is the first that ever took the ancient governments of
Israel, Sparta, and Rome, or those of England, France, Germany,
and Spain to be democracies, only because every one of them had
senates and assemblies of the people, who, in their persons, or by
their deputies, did join with their chief magistrates in the exercise
of the supreme power. That of Israel to the time of Saul is
called by Josephus an aristocracy. The same name is given to
that of Sparta, by all the Greek authors, and the great contest in
the Peloponesian war was between the two kinds of government.
The cities that were governed aristocratically, or desired to be so,
followed the Lacedemonians; and such as delighted in democracy,
taking part with the Athenians. In like manner, Rome, England,
and France were said to be under monarchies; not that their
kings might do what they pleased, but because one man had a pre-
eminence above any other."—*From Chap. II., Sec.* 30.

*Mixed and popular governments preserve peace, and manage
wars, better than absolute monarchies.*—CHAP. II., SEC. 21.

" Being no way concerned in the defence of democracy, and
having proved that Xenophon, Thucydides, and others of the
ancients, in speaking against the over great power of the common
people, intended to add reputation to the aristocratical party to
which they were addicted, and not to set up absolute monarchy,
which never fell under discourse among them, but as an object of
scorn and hatred even in itself, and only to be endured by base
and barbarous people, I may leave our knight, like Don Quixote,
fighting against the phantasms of his own brain, and saying what
he pleases against such governments as never were, unless in such

a place as San Marino, near Sinigaglia, in Italy, where a hundred clowns govern a barbarous rock that no man invades, and relates nothing to our question. If his doctrine be true, the monarchy he extols is not only to be preferred before unruly democracy and mixed governments, but is the only one that without a gross violation of the laws of God and nature, can be established over any nation. But having, as I hope, sufficiently proved that God did neither institute nor appoint any such to be instituted, nor approve those that were; that nature does not incline us to it, and that the best as well as the wisest men have always abhorred it; that it has been agreeable only to the most stupid and base nations; and if others have submitted to it, they have done so only as to the greatest evils brought upon them by violence, corruption, or fraud—I may now proceed to show that the progress of it has been in all respects suitable to its beginning

"To this end it will not be amiss to examine our author's words: 'Thus,' says he, 'do they paint to the life this beast with many heads. Let me give the cypher of their form of government. As it is begot by sedition, so it is nourished by crimes: it can never stand without wars, either with an enemy abroad, or with friends at home.' And in order to this I will not criticise upon the terms, though 'cypher of a form, and 'war with friends' may justly be called nonsense. But coming to his assertion that popular or mixed governments have their birth in sedition, and are afterwards vexed with civil or foreign wars, I take liberty to say, that whereas there is no form appointed by God or nature, those governments only can be called just, which are established by the consent of nations. These nations may at the first set up popular or mixed governments, and *without the guilt of sedition, introduce them afterwards, if that which was first established prove unprofitable or hurtful to them ; and those that have done so, have enjoyed more justice in times of peace, and managed wars, when occasion required, with more virtue and better success than any absolute monarchies have done.*"

After laying down the above general proposition,

Sidney proceeds to prove its truth, by a copious and accurate reference to the history of nations, ancient and modern, showing by contrast the advantage constantly on the side of popular governments. In the foregoing passage, it will be observed, that Sidney asserts the right of popular insurrection, or, in his own words, the right of a people "without the guilt of sedition, to introduce popular or mixed governments." This doctrine is constantly recognised throughout the work, and we shall hereafter cite some passages in which it is more forcibly and directly asserted. We now quote from another section, wherein, from the same general principle of popular sovereignty, he adduces the absolute and uncontrollable right of a nation to revise or alter its constitution and fundamental laws.

Good governments admit of changes in the superstructures, whilst the foundations remain unchangeable.—CHAP. II., SEC. 17.

" Though I mention these things,* it is not with a design of blaming them, for some of them deserve it not. And it ought to be considered that the wisdom of man is imperfect, and unable to foresee the effects that may proceed from an infinite variety of accidents, which, according to emergencies, *necessarily require new constitutions to prevent or cure the mischiefs arising from them, or to advance a good that at the first was not thought on.* And as the noblest work on which the wit of man can be exercised, were, (if it could be done,) to constitute a government that should last forever, *the next to that is to suit laws to present exigencies, and so much as in the power of man to foresee.* He that should resolve to

* He refers to a number of historical examples of changes in government commented on in a previous part of the section.

persist obstinately in the way he first entered upon, or to blame those who go out of that in which their fathers had walked, when they find it necessary, does, as far as in him lies, render the worst of errors perpetual. Changes, therefore, are unavoidable, and the wit of man can go no farther than to institute such, as in relation to the forces, manners, nature, religion, or interests of a people, and their neighbors, are suitable and adequate to what is seen, or apprehended to be seen. He who would oblige all nations, at all times, to take the same course, would prove as foolish as a physician who should apply the same medicine to all distempers, or an architect that would build the same kind of house for all persons, without considering their estates, dignities, the number of their children, or servants, the time or climate in which they live and many other circumstances; or, which is, if possible more sottish, a general who should obstinately resolve always to make war in the same way, and to draw up his army in the same form without examining the nature, number, and strength of his own and his enemies forces, or the advantages and disadvantages of the ground. But as there may be some universal rules in physic, architecture, and military discipline, from which men ought never to depart, so there are some in politics also which ought always to be observed; and wise legislatures adhering to them only, will be ready to change all others as occasion may require to the public good."

* * * * * *

" That no change of magistracy as to the name, number, or form, doth testify irregularity, or bring any manner of prejudice, *as long as it is done by those who have a right of doing it ;* and he or they who are created continue within the power of the law to accomplish the end of their institution, many forms being in themselves equally good, and may be used, as well one as another, according to times and other circumstances."—*From Chap. II.*, Sec. 13

* * * * * *

" It is a rare thing for a city at first to be rightly constituted. Men can hardly at once foresee all that may happen in many ages, and the changes that accompany them ought to be provided for."— *Ibid.*

* * * * * *

"All human constitutions are subject to corruption, and must perish unless they are timely renewed and reduced to their first principles."—*Ibid.*

* * * * * *

"This being the state of the matter on both sides, we may easily collect, that all governments are subject to corruption and decay ; but with this difference, that absolute monarchy is by principle led unto, or rooted in it; whereas mixed or popular governments are only in a possibility of falling into it. As the first cannot subsist unless the prevailing part of the people be corrupted, the other must certainly perish unless they be preserved in a great measure free from vices. I doubt whether any better reason can be given why there have been, and are, more monarchies than popular governments in the world, than that nations are more easily drawn into corruption than defended from it; and I think that monarchy can be said to be natural in no other sense than that our depraved nature is most inclined to that which is worst."— *From Chap. II., Sec.* 19.

In the next section Sidney endeavors to prove that " *man's natural love of liberty is tempered by reason, which originally is his nature.*" The virtuous, he says, are willing to be restrained *by the law,* and the vicious to submit *to the will of a man,* in order to gain impunity in offending. Wretches have, in all times, endeavored to put the power into the hands of a king who might protect them in their villainies, and advance them to exorbitant riches or undeserved honors ; while the best men, desiring no other riches or preferments than what their merits might deserve, were content with a due liberty under the protection

of a just law. In illustration of this truth, he pointed
with a finger of scorn to the worthless favorites, the
corrupt courtiers, and sycophant statesmen who sur.
rounded the reigning monarch.

" If this be not sufficient, they may be pleased a little to reflect
upon the affairs of our own country, and seriously consider
whether Hyde, Clifford, Falmouth, Arlington, and Danby, could
have pretended to the chief places, if the disposal of them had been
in a well-regulated Parliament? Whether they did most resemble
Brutus, Publicola, and the rest of the Valerii, the Fabii, Quintii,
Cornelii, &c., or Narcissus, Pullas, Icetus, Laco, Brunius, and the
like? Whether all men, good or bad, do not favor that state of
things which favors them; and such as they are? whether Cleave.
land, Portsmouth, and others of the same trade, have attained to
the riches and honors they enjoy by services to the Commonwealth? And what places Chiffinch, Fox, and Jenkins could pro.
bably have attained, if our affairs had been regulated as good men
desire? Whether the old arts of begging, stealing, or bawding,
or the new ones of informing and trepanning, thrive best under
one man who may be weak or vicious, and is always subject to
be circumvented by flatterers, or under the severe scrutiny of a
senate or people? In a word, whether they who live by such
arts, and know no other, do not always endeavor to advance the
government under which they enjoy, or may hope to attain the
highest honors, and abhor that in which they are exposed to all
manner of scorn and punishment? Which being determined, it
will easily appear why the worst men have ever been for absolute
monarchy and the best against it; and which of the two in so
doing, can be said to desire an unrestrained liberty of doing that
which is evil."

Having thus presented, in his own language, some
of the views of Sidney as to the absolute right of a
people originally to institute any system of govern.

ment which they chose, and subsequently to reform and alter the constitution and laws of the state through the customary forms of legislation, we shall conclude our extracts from this chapter by selecting some passages wherein he discusses the doctrine of sedition and rebellion, and justifies a general insurrection, as a last resort, to overthrow a tyranny, or depose a magistrate who usurped the public liberties and defies the laws.

"It may seem strange," he says, "to some that I mention seditions, tumults, or wars, but I can find no reason to retract the term. God intending that men should live justly with one another does certainly intend that he or they who do no wrong, should suffer none; and the law which forbids injuries were of no use if no penalties might be inflicted on those who will not obey it.

"The ways of preventing or punishing injuries are judicial or extrajudicial. Judicial proceedings are of force against those who submit or may be brought to trial, but are of no effect against those who resist, and are of such power that they cannot be constrained. It were absurd to cite a man to appear before a tribunal who can awe the judges, or has armies to defend him; and impious to think that he who has added treachery to his other crimes, and usurped a power above the law, should be protected by the enormity of his wickedness. Legal proceedings, therefore, are to be used when the delinquent submits to the law, and all are just when he will not be kept in order by the legal.

"If the laws of God and man are therefore of no effect, when the magistracy is left at liberty to break them; and if the lusts of those who are too strong for the tribunals of justice cannot be otherwise restrained than by sedition, tumults, and war, THESE SEDITIONS, TUMULTS, AND WARS, ARE JUSTIFIED BY THE LAWS OF GOD AND MAN.

"I will not take upon me to enumerate all the cases in which this may be done, but content myself with three which have most frequently given occasion for proceedings of this kind.

"The first is, when one or more men take upon them the power and name of a magistracy to which they are not justly called.

"The second, when one or more being justly called, continue in their magistracy longer than the laws by which they are called do prescribe.

"And the third, when he or they, who are rightly called, do assume a power, though within the time prescribed, that the law does not give; or turn that which the law does give to an end different and contrary to that which is intended by it."

The author then proceeds to consider each one of these cases separately, and at some length. We give the following passages from that part of the argument applicable to the third head.

"If I mention some of these cases, every man's experience will suggest others of the like nature; and whoever condemns all seditions, tumults, and wars, raised against such princes, must say that none are wicked or seek the ruin of their people; which is absurd. Caligula wished the people had but one neck, that he might cut it off at a blow. Nero set the city on fire: and we have known such as have been worse than either of them. They must either be suffered to continue in the free exercise of their rage, that is, to do all the mischief they design, or must be restrained by a legal, judicial, or extrajudicial way; and they who disallow the extrajudicial do as little like the judicial. They will not hear of bringing a supreme magistrate before a tribunal when it may be done. 'They will,' says our author, 'depose their kings.' Why should they not be deposed if they become enemies of their people, and set up an interest in their own persons inconsistent with the public good for the promoting of which they were erected? If they were created by the public consent for the public good, shall they not be removed when they prove to be of public damage? If they set up themselves may they not be thrown down ? Shall it be lawful for them to usurp a power over the liberty of others, and shall it not be lawful for an injured people to resume their own ? If injustice exalt itself, must it be forever established ?"

*　　*　　*　　*　　*　　*

" There must therefore be a right of proceeding judicially or extrajudicially against all persons who transgress the laws, or else those laws and the societies that should subsist by them cannot stand; and the ends for which governments are constituted, together with the governments themselves, must be overthrown. *Extrajudicial proceedings by sedition, tumult, or war, must take place when the persons concerned are of such a power that they cannot be brought under the judicial.* They who deny this, deny all help against an usurping tyrant, or the perfidiousness of a lawfully created magistrate who adds the crimes of ingratitude and treachery to usurpation. These, of all men, are the most dangerous enemies to supreme magistrates; for as no man desires indemnity for such crimes as are never committed, he that would exempt all from punishment, supposes they will be guilty of the worst; and by concluding that the people will depose them if they have the power, acknowledge that they pursue an interest annexed to their persons, contrary to that of their people, which they would not bear if they could deliver themselves from it. Thus showing all those governments to be tyrannical, lays such a burden upon those who administer them as must necessarily weigh them down to destruction.

" If it be said that the word *sedition* implies that which is evil, I answer that it ought not then to be applied to those who seek nothing but that which is just; and though the ways of delivering an oppressed people from the violence of a wicked magistrate, who has armed a crew of lewd villains, and fatted them with the blood and confiscations of such as were most ready to oppose him, be extraordinary, *the inward righteousness of the act doth fully justify the authors:* 'He that has virtue and power to save a people, can never want a right of doing it.'"

In the last section of this chapter Sidney continues the argument on this branch of the subject, and traces the right of insurrection to the original compact between king and people.

The contracts made between magistrates and the nations which created them were real, solemn, and obligatory.—CHAP. II., SEC. 32.

"Our author having with big words and little sense inveighed against popular and mixed governments, proceeds as if he had proved they could not, or ought not, to be. 'If it be,' says he, 'unnatural for the multitude to choose their governors, or to govern, or to partake in the government, what can be thought of that damnable conclusion which is made by too many, that the multitude may correct or depose their princes if need be ? Surely the unnaturalness and injustice of this position cannot sufficiently be expressed. For, admit that a king makes a contract or paction with his people originally in his ancestors, or personally at his coronation (for both these pactions some dream of, but cannot offer any proof of either), yet by no law of any nature can a contract be thought broken, except, first, a lawful trial be had by the ordinary judge of the breakers thereof, or else every man may be both party and judge in his own case, which is absurd once to be thought : for then it will lie in the hands of the headless multitude, when they please to cast off the yoke of government that God hath laid upon them, and to judge and punish them by whom they should be judged and punished themselves.

"To this I first answer briefly, that if it be natural for the multitude to choose their governors, or to govern, or to participate in the government as best pleases themselves, or that there never was a government in the world that was not so set up by them in pursuance of the power naturally inherent in themselves, what can be thought of that damnable conclusion which has been made by fools or knaves, that the multitude may not, if need be, correct or depose their own magistrates? Surely the unnaturalness or injustice of such a position cannot be sufficiently expressed. If that were admitted, all the most solemn pacts and contracts made between nations and their magistrates, originally or personally, and confirmed by laws or oaths, would be of no value. He that would break the most sacred bonds that can be amongst men, should, by perjury and wickedness become judge of his own case, and by the worst of crimes procure impunity for all. It would be in his power by folly, wickedness, and madness, to destroy the multitude which he was created and sworn to preserve, though wise, virtuous, and just, and headed by the wisest and justest of men, or to lay a yoke on those who, by the laws of God and nature, ought to be free."

*· * * * * *

"Besides, if every people may govern, or constitute and choose one or more governors, they may divide the power between sev-eral men, or ranks of men, allotting to every one so much as they please, or retaining so much as they think fit. This has been practised in all the governments which, under several forms, have flourished in Palestine, Greece, Italy, Germany, France, and England, and the rest of the world. The laws of every place show what the power of the respective magistrate is, and by declaring how much is allowed to him, declare what is denied ; for he has not that which he has not, and is to be accounted a magistrate while he exercises that which he has."

In the third and last chapter of the "Discourses," Sidney continues the argument respecting the origin and ground of government—examines the reciprocal duties and obligations of magistrates and people— insists that the law makers are themselves amenable to the laws, and traces the legislative authority and all political power originally to the social compact. The following extract is from the first section of this chapter, the object of which is to show that magis-

trates can have no just power other than what is given
by the constitution and laws :—

" He that neither is, nor has any title to be a king, can come to
be so only by force or by consent. If *by force*, he does not confer
a benefit upon the people, but injures them in the most outrageous
manner. If it be possible, therefore, or reasonable to imagine,
that one man did ever subdue a multitude, he can no otherwise resemble a father than the worst of all enemies, who does the greatest mischiefs, resembles the best of all friends who confers the
most inestimable benefits, and consequently does as justly deserve
the utmost effects of hatred as the other does of love, respect, and
service. If *by consent*, he who is raised from amongst the people,
and placed above his brethren, receives great honors and advantages, but confers none. The obligations of gratitude are on his
side, and whatsoever he does in acknowledgment to his benefac-
tors for their love to him, is no more than his duty, and he can
demand no more from them than what they think fit to add to the
favors already received. If more be pretended, it must be by virtue of that contract, and can no otherwise be proved than by producing it to be examined that the true sense, meaning, and intention of it may be known.

" This contract must be in form and substance according to a
general rule given to all mankind, or such as is left to the will of
every nation. If a general one be pretended, it ought to be
shown that by inquiring into the contents, we may understand the
the force and extent of it. If this cannot be done, it may justly
pass for a fiction ; no conclusion can be drawn from it, and we
may be sure that what contracts never have been made between
nations and their kings, have been framed according to the will
of those nations, and, consequently, how many soever they are,
and whatsoever the sense of any or all of them may be, they can
oblige no man except those, or, at the most, the descendants of
those who made them. Whoever, therefore, would persuade us
that one or more nations are, by virtue of those contracts, bound
to bear all the insolences of tyrants, is obliged to show that by

those contracts they did for ever indefinitely bind themselves so to do, how great soever they might be.

"I may justly go a step farther and affirm that if any such thing should appear in the world, the folly and turpitude of the thing would be a sufficient evidence of the madness of those that made it, and utterly destroy the contents of it. But no such having been as yet produced, nor any reason given to persuade a wise man that there has ever been any such, at least among civilized nations (for whom only we are concerned), it may be concluded there never was any, or, if there were, they do not at all relate to our subject, and, consequently, that *nations still continue in their native liberty, and are no otherwise obliged to endure the insolence of tyrants than they, or each of them, may esteem them tolerable.*"

The views of Sidney above expressed as to the position and responsibility of a magistrate in a free state, raised to honors and office by the voice of the people, are admirable and just. That part of the argument which denies that any original contract between king and people, whether real or imaginary, can justify absolute dominion and hereditary tyranny, no one, we think, in our day, will be apt to controvert. His conclusion is bold, clear, and irresistible, that nations have a natural right to assert their liberty, and to throw off the yoke of a tyrant whenever they deem it proper. Elsewhere in this chapter he expresses himself more fully upon this branch of his subject.

The general revolt of a nation cannot be called a rebellion.—
CHAP. III., SEC. 36.

"As impostors seldom make lies to pass in the world without putting false names upon things, such as our author endeavors to

14*

persuade the people that they ought not to defend their liberties, by giving the name of rebellion to the most just and honorable actions that have been performed for the preservation of them, and to aggravate the matter fear not to tell us that rebellion is like the sin of witchcraft. But those who seek after truth will easily find that *there can be no such thing in the world as the rebellion of a nation against its own magistrates, and that rebellion is not always an evil.* That this may appear, it will not be amiss to consider the word as well as the thing understood by it, as it is used in an evil sense.

" The word is taken from the Latin *rebellare*, which signifies no more than to renew a war. When a town or province had been subdued by the Romans, and brought under their dominion, if they violated their faith after the settlement of peace, and invaded their masters who had spared them, they were said *to rebel.* But it had been more absurd to apply that word to the people that rose against the decemviri, kings, or other magistrates, than to the Parthians, or any of those nations who had no dependence upon them; for all the circumstances that would make a rebellion were wanting, the word implying a superiority in them against whom it is as well as the breach of an established peace. But though every private man, singly taken, be subject to the commands of the magistrate, *the whole body of the people is not so, for he is by and for the people, and the people is neither by nor for him.* The obedience due to him from private men, is grounded upon, and measured by, the general law; and that law, regarding the welfare of the people, cannot set up the interests of one or a few men against the public. The whole body, therefore, of a nation, cannot be tied to any other obedience *than is consistent with the common good according to their own judgment;* and having never been subdued, nor brought to terms of peace with their magistrates, they cannot be said to revolt or rebel against them, to whom they owe no more than seems good to themselves, *and who are nothing of or by themselves more than other men.*"

The reciprocal obligations that exist between the

governor and the governed, and the rights and duties of the magistrate as the representative of the people, are fully discussed by the author in this last chapter of his work. He asserts the principle that a magistrate can justly lay claim to no other power than what is conferred upon him by the people, his constituents, who elect him, and that by accepting his official trust, certain duties and obligations devolve upon him, prescribed by law, which, under no pretence, is to be disregarded. If the magistrate does presume to set the constitution and laws at defiance, he is to be restrained or deposed, by impeachment or otherwise, through the customary judicial or legislative forms; but if these are insufficient, either by reason of a defect in the constitution, or of the usurped power of the magistrate, than that the last remedy, the *ultima ratio, revolution* is justifiable. And that however difficult and dangerous this remedy may be, through any defect of the original constitution, yet, that when oppression renders it necessary, it must be tried. We take leave of this part of the subject without presenting any further extracts to illustrate Sidney's views in regard to it. An additional passage or two, from which some idea may be derived of the author's views regarding popular representation, and the powers, duties, and obligations of delegates of the people, will close our selections from these writings.

No people that is not free can substitute delegates.—CHAP. III., SEC. 44.

" How full soever the power of any person or people may be,

he or they are obliged to give only so much to their delegates as seems convenient to themselves or conducing to the ends they desire to attain; but the delegate can have none except what is conferred upon him by his principal. If, therefore, the knights, citizens, and burgesses sent by the people of England to serve in parliament have a power, it must be more perfectly and fully in those that send them. But (as was proved in the last section) proclamations and other significations of the king's pleasure, are not laws to us. They are to be regulated by the law, not the law by them. They are to be considered only so far as they are con - formable to the laws, from which they receive all the strength that is in them, and can confer none upon it. We know no laws but our own statutes, and those immemorial customs established by the consent of the nation which may be, and often are, changed by us. The legislative power, therefore, that is exercised by the parliament, cannot be conferred by the writ of summons, *but must be essentially and radically in the people, from whom their delegates and representatives have all that they have.* But, says our author, ' they must only choose, and trust those whom they choose, to do what they list, and that is as much liberty as many of us deserve for our irregular elections of burgesses.' This is ingeniously concluded. I take what servant I please, and when I have taken him I must suffer him to do what he pleases. But from whence should this necessity arise? Why may not I take one to be my groom, another to be my cook, and keep them both to the offices for which I took them? What law does herein restrain my right? And if I am free in my private capacity to regulate my particular affairs according to my own discretion, and to allot to each servant his proper work, why have not I, with my associates, the freemen of England, the like liberty of directing and limiting the powers of the servants we employ in our public affairs? Our author gives us reasons proportionable to his judgment: ' This were liberty with a mischief, and that of choosing only is as much as many of us deserve.' I have already proved that as far as our histories reach, we have had no princes or magistrates but such as we have made, and they have had no other power but what we have conferred upon them. They cannot be the judges of our merit who have no power but what we gave them, through an opinion they did or might deserve it; they may distribute in parcels to particulars that with which they are entrusted in the gross, but it is impossible that the public should depend absolutely upon those who are nothing above other men, except what they are made to be for and by the public."

These views of popular representation, and the duties and obligations of the representative, are liberal and philosophical. The representative is not merely chosen and clothed with all the power he possesses by the people, but he is actually the servant of the people, their delegate, bound to respect their wishes and even obey their instructions, as a servant respects the wishes and obeys the instructions of the man who employs him. In the next chapter, Sidney farther discusses the obligations of the representative of the people, and his duty to obey the laws he makes :—

The legislative power is always arbitrary, and not to be trusted in the hands of any who are not bound to obey the laws they make.—CHAP. III., SEC. 45.

"If it be objected that I am a defender of arbitrary powers, I confess I cannot comprehend how any society can be established or subsist without them, for the establishment of government is an arbitrary act, wholly depending on the will of men. The particular forms and constitution, the whole series of the magistracy, together with the measure of power given to every one, and the rules by which they are to execute their charge are so also. Magna Charta, which comprehends our ancient laws, and all the subsequent statutes, were not sent from heaven, but made according to the will of men. If no men could have a power of making laws, none could ever have been made; for all that are or have been in the world, except those given by God to the Israelites, were made by them—that is, they have exercised an arbitrary power in making that to be law which was not, or annulling that which was. The various laws and governments, which are or have been in several ages and places, are the product of various opinions in those who had the power of making them. This must necessarily be, unless a general rule be set to all; for the judgments of men will vary if they are left to their liberty; and the variety that is found among them shows they are subject to no rule but that of their own reason, by which they see what is fit to be embraced or avoided according to the several circumstances under which they live. The authority that judges of these circumstances is arbitrary, and the legislators show themselves to be more or less wise and good as they do rightly or not rightly exercise this power. The difference, therefore, between good and ill governments is not that those of one sort have an arbitrary power which the other have not—for they all have it; but that those which are well constituted, place this power so as it may be beneficial to the people, and set such rules as are hardly to be transgressed, while those of the other sort fail in one or both these points."

*　　*　　*　　*　　*　　*

"I think I may justly say that an arbitrary power was never well placed in any men and their successors who were not obliged to obey the laws they should make. This was well understood by our Saxon ancestors. They made laws in their assemblies and councils of the nation; but all those who proposed or assented to those laws, as soon as the assemblies were dissolved, were comprehended under the power of them, as well as other men. They could do nothing to the prejudice of the nation that would not be as hurtful to those who were present, and their posterity, as to those who, by many accidents, might be absent. The Normans entered into, and continued in the same path. Our parliaments at this day are in the same condition. They may make prejudicial wars, ignominious treaties, and unjust laws; yet, when the session is ended, they must bear the burden as well as others, and when they die the teeth of their children will be set on edge with the sour grapes they have eaten. But it is hard to delude or corrupt so many. Men do not, in matters of the highest importance, yield to slight temptations. No man serves the devil for nothing; small wages will not content those who expose themselves to perpetual infamy, and the hatred of a nation for betraying their country. Our kings had not wherewithal to corrupt many till these last twenty years; and the treachery of a few was not enough to pass a law. The union of many was not easily wrought, and there was nothing to tempt them to endeavor it, for they could make little advantage during the session, and were to be lost in the mass of the people, and prejudiced by their own laws as soon as it was ended. They could not in a short time reconcile their various interests or passions so as to combine together against the public; and the former kings never went about it. We are beholden to Hyde, Clifford, and Danby, for all that has been done of that kind. They found a parliament full of lewd young men, chosen by a furious people, in spite of the Puritans, whose severity had distasted them. The weakest of all ministers had wit enough to understand that such as these might be easily deluded, corrupted, or bribed. Some were fond of their seats in parliament, and delighted to domineer over their neighbors by continuing in them; others preferred the cajoleries of the court before the honor of performing their duty to the country that employed them. Some sought to relieve their ruined fortunes, and were most forward to give the king a vast revenue, that from thence they might receive pensions; others were glad of a temporary protection against their creditors. Many knew not what they did when they annulled the triennial act, voted the militia to be in the king, give him the excise, customs, chimney money, made the act for corporations by which the greatest part of the nation was brought under the power of the worst men in it, drunk or sober, passed the five mile act, and that for uniformity in the church. This emboldened the court to think of making parliaments to be the instruments of our slavery, which had in all ages past been the firmest pillars of our liberty. There might have been, perhaps, a possibility of preventing this pernicious mischief in the constitution of our government. But our brave ancestors could never think their posterity would degenerate into such baseness as to sell themselves and their country. But how great soever the danger may be, it is less than to put all into the hands of one man and his ministers. The hazard of being ruined by those who must perish with us, is not so much to be feared as by one who may enrich and strengthen himself by our destruction. It is better to depend upon those who are under a possibility of being again corrupted, than upon one who applies himself to corrupt them, because he cannot otherwise accomplish his designs. It were to be wished that our security were more certain; but this being, under God, the best anchor we can have, it deserves to be preserved with all care, till one of a more unquestionable strength be framed by the consent of the nation."

The limits marked out for this work, will not permit us to make any further selections from these writings of Sidney. The foregoing are deemed sufficient to acquaint the reader generally with his views of government and the nature of his political opinions. They show conclusively the firm and settled conviction of an enlightened and powerful intellect, which, after mature reflection, had embraced the doctrines of popular liberty, as the elementary truths of political science, and having once embraced them, cherished them with the same faith that lighted the path of Gallileo to his dungeon, and sustained him against the ignorance, the incredulity, the intolerance of his age. The political theories of Sidney in his day in England met with the same reception as did the magnificent discoveries of Gallileo in Europe. The heresy of the philosopher was rewarded with a dungeon; the treason of the stateman with the scaffold. And yet in a few years the speculations of Sidney were no longer visionary theories; in a few years men wondered in amazement that a system like Gallileo's should have ever encountered opposition. Such is the history of the progress of truth.

Sidney's opposition to the government of Charles II. has sometimes been attributed to his deep-rooted animosity to the Stuart family. This is a mistake, and in its origin was doubtless a calumny. No man ever acted more directly from a sincere and honest conviction, or more tenaciously adhered to principle. He was from principle and conviction a friend of liberal institutions, and an enemy of absolute monarchy. His contemporary, Bishop Burnet, who well knew his opinions, declares that he was "stiff to all republican principles," and attributes his opposition to Cromwell solely to his hatred to " everything that looked like a monarchy." In short, Sidney's opinions were formed, and his course of action guided not by foolish prejudice, or selfish animosities, but by the honest convictions of conscience, and the clear dictates of right and duty.

While the political opinions of Sidney have been misunderstood, his religious sentiments and the nature of his religious professions, have been much misrepresented. Entirely free from that wild, religious enthusiasm which was so deeply impressed upon characters like those of Harrison and Hugh Peters, and many of the Puritans, yet it cannot be denied that Sidney was a sincere Christian.   Hume, with an almost inexcusable ignorance, classes him with Harrington, Neville, and Challoner, the deists, who denied the truth of revelation, and whose sole object in co-operating with the Independents was political liberty.   That Hume is not less mistaken in this, than in many other statements respecting the English republicans, is evident from the remark of Bishop Burnet, who knew Sidney well, and who says of him : He seemed to be a Christian, but in a particular form of his own ; he thought it was to be like a divine philosophy of the mind."   Burnet adds that he was opposed to external forms of public worship and to "everything that looked like a church;" but the worthy bishop doubtless uses the term *church* in what he conceives to be its true acceptation, and not as applicable to the chapels and conventicles of the dissenters.   In this sense the remark might be equally true of Vane, in whose "preaching and praying" Burnet found such a "peculiar darkness."   And yet Vane was known to be thoroughly imbued with the doctrines of Calvin.   The religious opinions of Sidney, like Vane's, doubtless conformed in the main, to the theology of Geneva, but like Vane he was an Independent, opposed to the hierarchy of the Church of England, and unalterably opposed to the establishment by law of any particular creed or form of worship.   In other words, he desired to establish that primary doctrine of free government UNIVERSAL TOLERATION, securing to every man full freedom of conscience and freedom of intellect, and keeping the Church, as an institution, entirely separate and distinct from the state. These views were shared by all the leading republicans—by those who professed, as well as those who manifested little regard, for the truths of religion—by Cromwell, Bradshaw, and St. John, as well as by Marten, Challoner and Harrington. They prove that the Independents, as statesmen, were in advance of their age in just conceptions of the principles of free government, and in comprehending the political rights of mankind. The charge of scepticism is also refuted by the words and writings which Sidney left behind him. His discourses contain frequent illustrations from the Scriptures, both the Old and New Testaments. These were written many years before his death. That his belief remained unshaken down to the hour of his execution, is apparent from his conduct and confessions. In his last hours he sent for several dissenting ministers, to whom he expressed deep penitence for whatever sins he had committed, and a firm confidence and hope in the mercies of God. His last public declaration, left to the world in the day of his death, contains his solemn recognition of the truths of Christianity: "I lived in this belief and am about to die for it. I know that my Redeemer lives; and as he has, in a great measure, upheld me in the day of my calamity, I hope that he will still uphold me by his spirit in this last moment, and giving me grace to glorify him in my death, receive me into the glory prepared for those that fear him, when my body shall be dissolved."

The private character of this illustrious man, was as exemplary as his public was upright and independent. It has been truly said of him, that a more honorable or a higher moral character did not exist ; that he had all the elevation and dignity of mind of a man who was untainted with the profligate vices of the age in which he lived ; that he was a man of the strictest veracity, and incapable of uttering a falsehood to save his life. It is not meant by this that Sidney's was a *perfect* character ; that he was exempt from the common frailties of humanity, or that his philosophy elevated him above those passions and weaknesses to which even the wisest and best of mankind are subject. Such was by no means the case. Like all other men, he had his imperfections and his faults. He was hasty, irascible, and imperious in temper, tenacious of his opinions, even to obstinacy, and impatient of contradiction. Bishop Burnet mentions his " rough and boisterous temper," but he also speaks of his sincerity and his frankness of disposition. In his manners he was not unfrequently austere and cold, and he sometimes gave way to despondency of mind ; but he was possessed of a most insinuating address, and of extraordinary colloquial power—or as Jeffries sneeringly characterized it—" a luxuriant way of talking," which never failed to please and fascinate whenever he chose to employ it. His minor faults of temper and disposition, are lost in the contemplation of those nobler attributes and manly virtues which gave such lustre to his character. While it certainly should not be the aim of the biographer, who seeks to delineate correctly the character of his subject, to conceal or attempt to extenuate its blemishes or faults, it is yet his province to dwell with most satisfaction, and to present most prominently those attributes which dignify and those virtues which ennoble it. The end of biography is finely expressed by Dr. Channing to be " to give immortality to virtue, and to call forth present admiration towards those who have shed splendor on past ages."

In a spirit of sympathy with the subject, which, perhaps, needs no apology, I have thus attempted to trace the career and sketch the character of Algernon Sidney. Errors may well be passed over in silence and his faults forgotten, where so much remains to be admired and venerated. One of the noblest martyrs of that liberty which the progress of civilization and the developments of time seem to point out as the heritage of the Anglo-Saxon race. His were virtues which deserve immortality, and his a name which will go down with honor to remote generations of men. The man dies, the principles he cherished are immortal. That cause for which Sidney suffered, proscribed in his day, has been gloriously vindicated in ours. The doctrines of resistance to oppression— of popular sovereignty—of the inalienable right of mankind to intellectual and moral, to civil and religious freedom—of which he was the champion in life,

and in death the martyr, have become the foundation
and corner stone of those democratic institutions
which since his day have sprung up in the New
World.   No nobler cenotaph than the free institutions
of America can be reared to the memory of the dust
which sleeps in its ancestral vault at Penshurst.   No
more glorious epitaph can be written for the patriot
martyr than that which so eloquently speaks in the
silent workings of those institutions.   Surely while
they endure, and while the doctrines which Sidney
taught shall continue to be regarded as the elementary
truths of our political creed, it may with truth be said
that the noble blood shed in their defence on Tower,
Hill has not been spilled in vain.

THE END.

Lightning Source UK Ltd.
Milton Keynes UK
UKHW020658241218
334505UK00008B/473/P